Afro-Caribbean Immigrants and the Politics of Incorporation
Ethnicity, Exception, or Exit

This book considers the political behavior of Afro-Caribbean immigrants in New York City to answer a familiar but nagging question
about American democracy: Does racism still complicate or limit the
political integration patterns of racial minorities in the United States?
With the arrival of unprecedented numbers of immigrants from Asia,
Latin America, and the Caribbean over the last several decades, there is
reason once again to consider this question. For the first time in its history, the country is confronting the challenge of incorporating a steady,
substantial stream of non-white, non-European voluntary immigrants
into the political system. Will racism make this process as difficult for
these newcomers as it did for African Americans? The book concludes
that discrimination does interfere with the immigrants' adjustment to
American political life. But their strategic options and political choices
in the face of this challenge are unexpected ones, not anticipated by standard accounts in the political science literature. The book thus offers
a fresh theoretical perspective on how foreign-born racial minorities
adapt to the American political system.

Reuel R. Rogers is an assistant professor of political science at Northwestern University. His general field of study is American politics, with
interests in race, ethnicity, urban politics, immigration, political behavior, and African-American politics. He completed this book during a
year-long fellowship at the Radcliffe Institute for Advanced Study at
Harvard University.

Afro-Caribbean Immigrants and the Politics of Incorporation

Ethnicity, Exception, or Exit

REUEL R. ROGERS

Northwestern University

CAMBRIDGE
UNIVERSITY PRESS

CAMBRIDGE UNIVERSITY PRESS
Cambridge, New York, Melbourne, Madrid, Cape Town, Singapore, São Paulo

Cambridge University Press
40 West 20th Street, New York, NY 10011-4211, USA

www.cambridge.org
Information on this title: www.cambridge.org/9780521859226

First published 2006

Printed in the United States of America

A catalog record for this publication is available from the British Library.

Library of Congress Cataloging in Publication Data

Rogers, Reuel Reuben, 1969–
Afro-Caribbean immigrants and the politics of incorporation : ethnicity, exception,
or exit / Reuel R. Rogers.
p.   cm.
Includes bibliographical references and index.
ISBN 0-521-85922-0 (hardback) – ISBN 0-521-67640-1 (pbk.)
1. Caribbean Americans – New York (State) – New York – Politics and government.
2. Caribbean Americans – New York (State) – New York – Ethnic identity.
3. Blacks – New York (State) – New York – Politics and government.   4. Blacks –
New York (State) – New York – Race identity.   5. Immigrants – New York (State) –
New York – Political activity.   6. Political participation – New York (State) – New York.
7. Ethnicity – Political aspects – New York (State) – New York.   8. Racism – Political
aspects – New York (State) – New York.   9. New York (N.Y.) – Race relations – Political
aspects.   10. New York (N.Y.) – Politics and government – 1951–   .   I. Title.
F128.9.C27R64   2006
323.196′07471 – dc22   2005023295

ISBN-13   978-0-521-85922-6 hardback
ISBN-10   0-521-85922-0 hardback

ISBN-13   978-0-521-67640-3 paperback
ISBN-10   0-521-67640-1 paperback

For my parents

Contents

Tables

Illustrations

Figures

Charts

CORRECTIONS FOR FIRST PRINTING OF
"AFRO-CARIBBEAN IMMIGRANTS AND THE POLITICS OF INCORPORATION,"
BY REUEL R. ROGERS.

Page 7, lines 7 and 9 from the top should read:

"African Americans face greater psychological and political barriers to success than most immigrant groups. . . . [N]o group (except native Americans, whose story is quite different) has experienced the depth of enmity and height of obstacles that blacks have. . . . [T]he external barriers and the internal ambivalences faced by African Americans are of a different order of magnitude than they have been for any immigrant group over a long period of time." (Hochschild 1993, 167, quoted in Chong and Kim 2004, 6-7)[4]

Page 31, line 7 from the top should read:

"It is a reasonable first approximation to place all minorities into the general category of subordinate groups and to contrast their [disadvantaged] structural position and [even their] subjective [perspective with] those of whites. But [buried] within the common [situation] of minority populations are important differences" of history, experience, numbers, and so on (Chong and Kim 2004, 5).

Acknowledgments

Though my name alone appears on the cover of this book, I could not have written it without the support of family, friends, colleagues, and several organizations. From the first field interview to the very last typescript sentence, I had considerable assistance in bringing it all together in the pages that follow. I am very happy to credit the great many sources of support, guidance, inspiration, and constructive criticism that helped me complete this book.

First, I thank Michael Danielson, Jennifer Hochschild, and Tali Mendelberg, who all read early versions of the entire manuscript, offered incisive suggestions for improving it, and inspired me with their example, encouragement, and enthusiasm for this project. My sincere thanks as well to Cathy Cohen, Nancy Foner, Michael Jones-Correa, Jane Junn, Philip Kasinitz, Ann Chih Lin, John Mollenkopf, Andrea Simpson, Rogers Smith, Mary Waters, and Janelle Wong, all of whom read versions of many of these chapters and provided insightful feedback and encouragement.

I also am especially grateful to Mary Waters, Philip Kasinitz, and John Mollenkopf, for the inspiring example of their own work on immigrant life in New York City. I owe a special debt to John, his sometime collaborator John Logan, Kyle Crowder, Suzanne Model, and Karthick Ramakrishnan for their generous data support. Their expertise is reflected in several of the tables and figures on census and voting statistics. I also am thankful for the excellent research assistance of Dale Vieregge, Catherine Paden, and Jonathan Webber, who was especially helpful in the final stretch. Wenquan Zhang deserves special mention for his first-rate work on the census maps. As the book neared completion, I benefited from the expert guidance of my editor at Cambridge University Press,

Lewis Bateman; his assistant, Ciara McLaughlin; my production editor, Janis Bolster; and my copy editor, Susan Thornton. The comments of the anonymous readers also were quite helpful.

I presented early versions of several of these chapters at meetings of the American Political Science Association, the Midwest Political Science Association, and the Social Science Research Council International Migration Program. I also shared drafts of chapters at workshops at the Woodrow Wilson International Center for Scholars; the Radcliffe Institute for Advanced Study at Harvard University; the Maxwell School of Citizenship and Public Affairs at Syracuse University; the Frederick Douglass Institute for African and African American Studies at the University of Rochester; the Center for the Study of Race, Inequality, and Poverty at Yale University; Florida International University; and the Research Institute for the Study of Man. I wish to thank the many bright minds I encountered at these various meetings. Their tough questions and illuminating observations helped strengthen my work.

Several institutions and organizations furnished support in the form of space, time, and resources for me to research, think, and write. They include the Social Science Research Council, the Ford Foundation, the Center for Domestic and Comparative Policy Studies at Princeton University, and the Radcliffe Institute for Advanced Study at Harvard University. The Department of Political Science at Northwestern University also granted me resources and leave time to finish the book. Several of my colleagues in the department took the time to review draft chapters and offer encouragement. I am especially grateful to Dennis Chong, who kindly read the entire manuscript and offered useful suggestions for improving it. I thank him for his friendship, professional advice, and intellectual support.

Though writing a book might seem like a mostly solitary enterprise, I had the company and support of several good friends while finishing this one. My fond thanks and appreciation go to my dear friend and colleague Hawley-Fogg Davis for her great humor and encouragement and our always scintillating conversations about the curiosities of race and life in general. I am also grateful for the warm support and good cheer I have enjoyed over the years from my friends Laura Lee Berry, Geoffrey Giddings, and Patrik-Ian Polk. I owe a special debt of gratitude to Shawn McGuffey for showing such sensitivity and concern for me and interest in my work. I thank him for holding my hand, having my back, and sending good chi when the going got tough.

During my time in the field, I was fortunate to have the assistance of many people in New York's Caribbean community. Though they are too many to acknowledge individually, I wish to thank them collectively for helping me find my bearings in the field and get this project off the ground. The staff at the Caribbean Research Center at Medgar Evers College deserve special mention for putting me in touch with the right people. I also wish to thank Norma Blaize, who transcribed the field interviews with meticulous care. My largest debt of gratitude is to the Caribbean immigrants who generously shared their time, experiences, and ideas during the interviews. Their insights helped make this book what it is.

Finally, I could not have completed this work without the support of my family. I thank my brothers for their loving support. I found great comfort in their company when I took breaks from my research and reassurance in the knowledge they were always in my corner. My deepest thanks are to my mother and father. I could never quantify just how much their unwavering love and quiet confidence have helped me in my career and in the completion of this book. But they should know their support has meant everything to me.

Strangers at the Gate

Immigrant Political Incorporation in a New Century

The United States has been a nation of immigrants for much of its history. Although it has not always extended the ready welcome implied by the famous Emma Lazarus poem, it has nonetheless long been the leading host country for the world's migrants. At the turn of the last century, this country absorbed unprecedented numbers of newcomers. Today, at the dawn of a new millennium, the United States is experiencing yet another great wave of immigration. More than 25 million immigrants have entered the country since the 1960s (Jones-Correa 2002). The current immigration flow is, in fact, historically unprecedented, both for its numerical proportions and for its demographic composition.

First, the number of newcomers to the United States in the last four decades has exceeded the high-water mark achieved during the last great wave of migration to this country from 1880 to 1920. With this latest influx of immigrants, there are now over 35 million foreign-born people living in the United States, that is, more than 10 percent of the total population. The proportions are even more substantial in cities around the country. Thirteen of the nation's cities house more than half of the immigrant population. For instance, roughly one of every three New Yorkers is a person of foreign birth (Logan 2003). Immigrants constitute even greater shares of the population in Los Angeles and Miami (ibid.). Their proportions are expected to continue inching upward, as the current immigration trends show no signs of abating.

Even more striking than the numbers, however, is the demographic composition of this latest wave of newcomers. The current immigration stream is the first ever to the United States that has not been dominated by immigrants from Europe. Immigration to the United States until World

War II consisted largely of European newcomers – the German, Irish, Italian, and Polish immigrants who eventually would become the white ethnics of America's melting-pot myth. But major congressional reforms in 1965 radically altered the complexion of the immigration inflow.[1] Today's huddled immigrant masses are mostly non-whites from Asia, Latin America, and the Caribbean. These three regions account for more than 85 percent of all immigration to the United States since 1965 (Passel and Edmonston 1994).

Asian, Caribbean, and Latin American immigrants have expanded and diversified the ranks of the nation's minority population. Taken together, the three major minority groups – Asians, Latinos, and blacks – now account for almost a third of all people living in the United States (U.S. Census Report 2001). Even the most glancing review of today's headlines reveals a great deal of popular focus on the growth of the non-white population, especially the foreign born. Again, the numbers at the city level bring this demographic shift into even sharper focus. Minorities actually now outnumber whites in most of the country's largest cities, such as New York and Los Angeles. What is more, the term "minority" no longer refers just to African Americans, Puerto Ricans, or Mexicans. Flat-footed minority categories like black, Latino, and Asian have been stretched to encompass a diverse mix of new foreign-born groups. In sum, what it means to be an immigrant and a minority in the United States has changed dramatically over the last few decades.

As these unprecedented immigration trends and demographic shifts have taken shape, the inevitable questions about what it all means for the United States likewise have emerged. Anxieties about how this latest wave of newcomers will change American life dominate the news headlines. Will they precipitate economic losses for those who are already here, pose terrorist threats, place new burdens on government resources, or unsettle the cultural norms and values of the country (e.g., Kelly 2005; Kirkpatrick 2005; Marosi 2004)? Other headlines and ongoing debates focus on how these immigrants will fit into American politics and society (Huntington 2004). How will they adapt to American culture, change our conceptions of race, participate in politics, or become dutiful citizens and patriots in

---

[1] The Hart-Cellar Immigration Reform Act of 1965 abolished the restrictive national quota system that had governed American immigration policy since 1924. Designed to reflect the racial and ethnic composition of nineteenth-century America, the old quota system favored immigration from Europe, while sharply restricting the number of newcomers from regions such as Asia and the Caribbean. The Hart-Cellar law replaced that flagrantly racist system with cumulative limits for the Western and Eastern Hemisphere.

their new country? An endless number of questions and anxieties have surfaced in the wake of this latest immigrant stream.

One of the most important of these questions is how the new, non-white immigrants will adapt to the American democratic experiment. More precisely, how will these newcomers be incorporated into the political system? Political incorporation is a vital process for any democracy. Democracies rest on the bedrock principle of equal consideration – if not outright representation – of the preferences and interests of every citizen (Verba, Schlozman, and Brady 1993). When new groups achieve incorporation – when they secure citizenship and become active in the political process – they lend legitimacy to representative democracy. Their presence and participation mean they have a reasonable prospect of seeing their preferences and needs met by government. When new groups fall short of incorporation, however, their interests cannot be considered by government and democracy is thus undermined.

The question is whether today's newcomers will achieve this basic standard of political inclusion in American democracy. How will they mobilize and achieve political influence in the cities where they now constitute a significant presence? This is not a new question. As a nation of immigrants, the United States has confronted almost perennially the challenge of absorbing and integrating newcomers. There is a long record, and perhaps even some settled assumptions, about how the foreign born are incorporated into American political life (e.g., Huntington 2004). Yet this current wave of newcomers give scholars occasion to revisit the question with a set of new cases that provide an empirical basis for generating fresh theoretical insights about the dynamics of political incorporation at the turn of a new century. First, the new immigrants allow us to test – and perhaps update – conventional accounts of how the process unfolds. Second and even more critically, the fact that these newcomers are mostly non-white minorities is an invitation to explore how America's deepest dilemma, the problem of race, affects political incorporation.

I. RACE AND POLITICAL INCORPORATION

Today American cities are confronting for the first time ever the challenge of incorporating large numbers of non-European, non-white voluntary immigrants into the political system. Racial discrimination historically has made incorporation a difficult and sometimes uncertain enterprise for minority groups in the United States. For centuries, minority populations

were formally barred from participation in the political process and had
no serious or meaningful prospect of achieving incorporation. They were
essentially excluded from participation in the American democratic experiment. But since the civil rights reforms of the 1960s, full political rights
and the other formal benefits of citizenship have been available to all
minority groups.

In fact, the 1965 change in immigration rules that helped trigger the current wave of non-European newcomers to the United States was enacted in
part because civil rights leaders and interest groups insisted such reform
was a necessary step for ending racial discrimination (Tichenor 2002;
Yu 2001). Forty years later few would suggest discrimination has ended,
but the question is how much it has diminished. Is racism still a significant obstacle in the path of non-white groups seeking political inclusion in
this country? Studying how the growing numbers of foreign-born minority groups are faring in their adjustment to American political life is an
opportunity to answer this question. It is also a chance to gauge the success of the civil rights revolution begun in the 1960s and to determine
whether the promise of democratic inclusion held out by its reforms actually has been achieved.

The literature on the experiences of the new, non-white immigrant
arrivals is small but growing rapidly. There is only a modest body of
research on how these newcomers are adapting to the political process.
Even fewer studies have explored how the racial minority status of these
immigrants affects their political adjustment to this country, despite the
fact so much has been made of their predominantly non-European and
non-white origins. There is, in short, no settled theoretical framework for
analyzing the unfolding dynamics of contemporary immigrant political
incorporation (Jones-Correa 2002).

Nevertheless, there are normative guideposts in the wider political science literature and the winding course of American history to help us
understand the experiences of these newcomers. First, there is an older,
classic literature on immigrant incorporation that includes studies like
Robert Dahl's seminal work *Who Governs?* (1961). Based largely on the
experiences of early European immigrants, this body of research arguably
provides predictive cues for charting and understanding the incorporation patterns of today's newcomers. By this light, the current immigrants, like their European predecessors, will overcome initial prejudice,
secure economic mobility, and achieve political incorporation in a gradual, steady march into the American mainstream – without significant
disruption to the political system. A number of scholars have taken their

cues from this classic literature and have arrived at just this conclusion (e.g., Portes and Rumbaut 1996; Skerry 1993; Portes and Stepick 1993; Chavez 1991).

Yet other researchers believe the fact that today's newcomers are mostly non-European, non-white minorities vitiates any easy comparisons with early European immigrants. America's record of incorporating non-whites into the political system has been deeply problematic. To be sure, some early European immigrant groups initially were viewed as non-white, inferior "races" by so-called old-stock white Americans and suffered the stigma of those racial labels; yet, they were all gradually accepted as white and incorporated into the political system (e.g., Jacobson 1998; Ignatiev 1996; Roediger 1991).[2] Not so for non-European, non-white groups. African Americans are the paradigmatic case in this regard. Political incorporation for them has been a slow, tortuous, and arguably incomplete process, complicated by the rigors of American racism (Dawson 1994a; Reed 1988; Pinderhughes 1987). Accordingly, some scholars believe the road awaiting today's non-white arrivals will be more like the difficult one navigated by African Americans and less like the path traced by early European immigrants.

Most of these researchers acknowledge racism has been receding from American life over the last several decades. They also concede the racial obstacles these non-white newcomers encounter perhaps will not be as formidable or severe as those faced by African Americans. Yet they believe serious discriminatory barriers remain and are bound to influence how new minority groups adapt to the political system. These obstacles, they argue, will complicate and impede the political incorporation process for the new, non-white immigrants just as they have for African Americans (e.g., Kim 2001; Hero 1998; 1992; Takaki 1989; Browning, Marshall, and Tabb 1984).[3] They contend these newcomers will follow the same path as their native-born black counterparts. In short, this argument casts African Americans as a kind of "model minority" group for other non-whites in American society. Their experiences with discrimination and

---

[2] The fact many of today's so-called whites would have been marked as members of alien, inferior races at the turn of the last century underscores the now de rigueur observation that racial categories are socially constructed. They may shift and expand to include – as well as exclude – particular groups over time. But even as the definition of who counts as "white" has broadened to encompass a variety of European groups, blacks have retained their distinction as non-white and remained saddled with the disadvantages this ascriptive category entails.

[3] For an analogous historical argument, see Ngai 2003; Takaki 1982; 1989.

their strategic responses to it form a behavioral mold most other minority groups are likely to follow.

There are thus two major perspectives for understanding how today's newcomers are likely to adapt to the American political process. Each one suggests a different empirical model of political incorporation. One, the pluralist view, is informed by European immigrant history; the other, the minority group view, derives from the experiences of African Americans. Each of these models also carries distinct normative and practical implications about how American democracy works and how these new-comers will affect political life. The pluralist model suggests the system is relatively open, liberal, and egalitarian for all groups, notwithstand-ing the anomaly of the African-American experience. Newcomers thus can be expected to secure a firm foothold and a share of influence in the give-and-take of political life in the cities where they live.

The minority group view, however, suggests racial inequalities pose a dilemma for America democracy and render it less inclusive for non-white groups. Full political inclusion for racial minorities is thus anything but certain. Implicit in this minority group perspective is the presumption non-whites will find political common cause and strategy in their shared racial predicament. It places most non-whites on one side of the racial divide and whites on the other. The pluralist view, in contrast, sees no such chasm in American political life and casts blacks as a vexing anomaly – a grim, unfortunate exception to the usually egalitarian workings of liberal democracy.

These two perspectives represent competing sides of an emerging debate about how the new foreign-born arrivals will be incorporated into American politics. Most scholars agree the political incorporation pat-terns of whites and blacks have differed sharply. The question is where the new non-European, non-white immigrants will fit. Predicting and chart-ing the political incorporation process for these newcomers is not a matter of drawing simple historical parallels between them and early European immigrants or African Americans. After all, what counts as a point of similarity between the current immigrants and one population – say, the voluntary immigrant experience of European ethnics or the racial minor-ity status of African Americans – is actually a point of difference with the other.

For instance, although many of today's newcomers share non-white status with African Americans, they, like earlier generations of European white ethnics, are voluntary immigrants to the United States. African Americans can claim no such voluntary immigrant experience. Rather, theirs is a singularly bitter history of coerced importation, enslavement, and discrimination.

African Americans face greater psychological and political barriers to success than most immigrant groups...[N]o group (except Native Americans, whose story is quite different) has experienced the depth of enmity and height of obstacles that blacks have...[T]he external barriers and the internal ambivalences are of a different order of magnitude than they have been for any immigrant group over a long period of time. (Hochschild 1995, 167)[4]

Likewise qualifications might be stipulated for comparisons drawn between today's newcomers and previous immigrants from Europe. In short, the parallels between contemporary immigrants and their European predecessors or African Americans only go so far.

What is more, American political institutions, practices, and attitudes about race have undergone significant transformations over the last several decades. Add to those changes the possibility that this new wave of non-white immigrants actually might destabilize and scramble the American racial system, and easy comparisons with the past become all the more untenable. In light of these analytic and historical complications, the question of whether either of these perspectives applies to contemporary immigrants is very much open to debate.

II. AFRO-CARIBBEAN IMMIGRANTS

This book wades into the debate by evaluating the two models alongside each other. It also considers less well-known alternatives such as transnationalism that are not well developed in the political science literature but warrant serious attention.[5] The goal is not only to ascertain how well these

---

[4] Claims about the unique severity of African-American racial suffering sometimes invite disagreement or calls for qualification. After all, other groups have faced racial barriers and felt the sting of discrimination. Here, then, is my caveat: The historical record clearly shows some immigrant groups suffered serious discrimination after their arrival on American shores – some for a generation or two, others for much longer. But African Americans' history of enslavement and their continued suffering from racial discrimination over successive generations set them apart from all voluntary immigrants to this country. Acknowledgment of the severity and persistence of their racial hardship is hardly a denial of the prejudice other groups have faced. Conversely, the historical reality of discrimination against these other groups ought not lead to the mistaken conclusion that they and African Americans have all borne equivalent racial disadvantages.

[5] Most of the research on transnationalism has been developed in sociology and anthropology. Transnationalism emphasizes immigrants' continuing attachments to their home countries. This view stands in contrast to the assimilationist logic of pluralism, which holds that such ties diminish over time.

models explicate the experiences of recent non-white arrivals, but also to shed light on how race affects their political incorporation patterns. To do so, the book turns to the contemporary case of Afro-Caribbean immigrants in New York City, the largest group of foreign-born blacks in the United States.[6] These Caribbean newcomers are among the city's largest and fastest-growing immigrant groups (Logan and Deane 2003). But their analytic importance goes well beyond their numbers. These foreign-born blacks furnish a uniquely instructive case for studying contemporary political incorporation patterns. Among recent non-white newcomers to the United States, they are the only group that allows for a natural case study of the impact of race on the political incorporation process, without bracketing the question of black exceptionalism.

Most of the emerging research on today's non-white immigrants has focused on Latino and Asian newcomers: that is, groups that are not black (e.g., Wong 2006; Ramakrishnan 2001; Jones-Correa 1998; Hero 1992).[7] Yet most researchers agree Latinos and Asians, though they encounter prejudice, do not face anything like the harsh, systematic forms of discrimination blacks have tended to encounter in this country. For example, there is considerable evidence Latinos and Asians confront fewer racial obstacles in the housing market than blacks, leading one pair of scholars (Massey and Denton 1989) to conclude "it is black race, not non-white race per se that matters" in the United States. It is also difficult to know whether the bias these immigrants confront is due to their racial minority or foreign-born status. Racism may thus prove to be a far less significant factor in the political adaptation patterns of these two groups than it has been for African Americans. In short, Asian and Latino immigrants do not allow for a straightforward, rigorous test of the impact of racism on the political incorporation process.

Afro-Caribbeans, on the other hand, do. As black immigrants, they share a common racial classification with African Americans. By phenotype, in fact, the two groups are indistinguishable and thus ostensibly vulnerable to the same forms of racial discrimination. They wear the "racial stigmata of subordination" in their physical appearance (Mills 1998, 84). Afro-Caribbeans and African Americans also have some obvious history in common: the deplorable legacy of enslavement and racial domination

---

[6] I use the term "Afro-Caribbean" to refer to black immigrants from the English-speaking Caribbean and to distinguish them from their counterparts from the French- and Spanish-speaking Caribbean.

[7] A small proportion of Latinos identify as black.

by whites. Of all the recent non-white immigrants, then, Afro-Caribbeans are the ones most likely to encounter and experience the same strain of American racism as African Americans.

Despite these racial commonalities, however, there are significant differences between the two groups. Unlike their native-born black counterparts, Afro-Caribbeans are voluntary immigrants who claim a distinctive ethnic identity and hail from countries with very different racial dynamics than the United States'. They migrate from a region of the world where the population is predominantly black. They are accustomed to living as part of the majority and seeing people who look like them in control of political and economic power. The countries of the Caribbean are also largely unfamiliar with the historical experience of Jim Crow and more contemporary American patterns of racial segregation.[8] Racial classificatory schemes in the Caribbean also historically have been less rigid and more fluid than the fixed, dichotomous black-and-white categorizations that prevail in the United States (e.g., James and Harris 1993; Patterson 1987; 1972). Finally, there is some evidence whites in this country occasionally make distinctions between Afro-Caribbeans and African Americans, treating the immigrants more favorably than their native-born counterparts (e.g., Waters 1999; Kasinitz 1992). With their immigrant background, distinctive ethnic heritage, and particular home country experiences, then, Afro-Caribbeans are perhaps more like early European immigrants.

These foreign-born blacks thus have a great deal in common with both African Americans and European ethnics. It is precisely this mix of racial, ethnic, and immigrant attributes that makes these foreign-born blacks an especially powerful case for testing the relative validity of the two dominant models of political incorporation. Even more significantly, their experiences provide an unusually clear window for observing and understanding the impact of racial discrimination on the political incorporation process. The question is whether racism still shapes the political adaptation patterns of minorities, especially blacks. It may be that racial hurdles still impede the path to incorporation for these groups. Or these barriers may loom larger and have a greater effect on blacks than on other

---

[8] Mary Waters (1999) has observed, "the combination of fluid boundaries and demographic majorities of blacks [in the Caribbean has] meant that while racism was endemic it was not defining [as it has been in the United States]." This is not to say the countries of the Caribbean have been completely free of white or European domination since the abolition of slavery. Europeans left their oppressive mark on these countries through years of colonial rule. Today American-style racism makes its way to the Caribbean through media, tourism, economic involvement, and occasional military deployments.

minorities. Or it may be that the impact of discrimination has diminished altogether – as a result of either the recent steps toward racial equality or the gradual collapse of the country's bipolar racial system under the weight of an unprecedented mix of new minority groups that defy easy categorization.

If any of these empirical alternatives holds true, its effects should be plainly evident in the experiences of a group of black immigrants such as Afro-Caribbeans. Will they follow the path of political incorporation marked out by their native-born black counterparts and complicated by racism, in keeping with the minority group view? Or will their voluntary immigrant status and ethnic heritage enable them to replicate the far easier route to incorporation traced by earlier European immigrants, as the pluralist model predicts? An analysis of Afro-Caribbeans' political incorporation patterns promises to shed light on these questions.

The book also uses the Afro-Caribbean case to consider the political significance of internal divisions within the black population. Over the last two decades, political scientists have begun to pay increasing attention to social differences among blacks, breaking with a long-standing and unfortunate tendency of treating the population as if it were monolithic. Most of this research has focused on the political implications of class and gender divisions (e.g., Gay and Tate 1998; Hochschild 1995; Dawson 1994a; Tate 1993). Comparatively little attention has been directed to other cleavages such as ethnicity, region, and generation. The rapid growth of the Afro-Caribbean population in New York and other cities over the last few decades is an invitation to shift the analytic lens to ethnic divisions: that is, to consider the political significance of the differences between native- and foreign-born blacks.

The growing literature on Afro-Caribbean immigrants has been dominated by sociologists, economists, and historians. Their research has yielded important insights on how ethnicity influences social and economic differences between Caribbean- and American-born blacks (e.g., Waters 1999; Vickerman 1999; Model 1995; Kasinitz 1992). Some of these studies actually have contributed to long-standing popular debates about whether non-white immigrant groups, such as Afro-Caribbeans, are "model minorities" by comparison with African Americans (e.g., Sowell 1978). There long has been considerable media interest in the relative socioeconomic performance of the two groups (e.g., Fears 2003). In fact, popular and policymaking interest in the differences between Afro-Caribbean immigrants and their native-born counterparts has reignited once again, but this time with a new twist.

Policymakers, pundits, and public intellectuals lately have been wondering which blacks ought to be the principal beneficiaries of affirmative action in university admissions and whether Afro-Caribbean immigrants and their children are benefiting disproportionately – and perhaps unfairly – from existing policies (e.g., Rimer and Arenson 2004).[9] Studying the political incorporation patterns of Afro-Caribbeans and the extent to which they encounter racial discrimination ought to provide useful insights that could be applied to this ongoing debate. But political scientists have been conspicuously absent from this and other public policy discussions involving Caribbean immigrants. Consequently, there has been much less attention to the political experiences of these black ethnics than to their social or economic mobility trends.[10]

This book attempts to help fill this gap. It explores whether Afro-Caribbeans' distinctive ethnic background and immigrant status make for differences in how they and their native-born counterparts perceive and participate in the political process. An alternative framing of the question is to ask whether the intraracial commonalities between the two groups ultimately outweigh their interethnic differences and unify them around similar political attitudes and choices. To answer this question, this book offers a comparison of the interests, identifications, and ideological outlooks of the two groups, as well as an analysis of their political relations.

The book's focus on the interethnic differences and similarities of Afro-Caribbeans and African Americans reveals some of the complexity of black political life in New York City. But the implications of the analysis go well beyond the New York case. The complexity uncovered by the study provides a view of some of the political consequences of the growing social diversity within the black population. Further, it allows for a reconsideration of some long-standing theoretical assumptions about how racial discrimination influences the attitudes and behavior of minority groups pursuing political incorporation. Most of what political scientists know about this question has been informed by studies of native-born blacks. The book explores whether the experiences of Afro-Caribbeans – a group of foreign-born blacks – confirm or challenge those assumptions.

Here, then, are the main research questions addressed in this study: First, do the dominant models of political incorporation apply to today's non-white newcomers, particularly black immigrants from the

---

[9] See Chapter 2 for a discussion and analysis of these "model minority" debates.
[10] Kasinitz (1992) and James (1998) are exceptions. But neither of these studies is situated in the political science literature.

Caribbean? Second, how does racial discrimination affect the political incorporation process for these foreign-born blacks? Finally, do Afro-Caribbeans' immigrant status and ethnic background make for significant differences in how they and their native-born black counterparts pursue incorporation? More precisely, does it lead to any notable differences in how they and African Americans perceive and adapt to the political system?

To answer these questions, the book examines various dimensions of Afro-Caribbeans' ongoing bid for political incorporation in New York City. The study is based primarily on two sets of in-depth interviews conducted in New York – one with fifty-nine first-generation Afro-Caribbean immigrants and the other with fifteen Afro-Caribbean elites (see Appendix A for details on the methods used for this study, and Appendix B for the interview schedules). The interviews featured questions on participation, ideology, policy attitudes, group identification, experiences with discrimination, and a number of other issues, all designed to illuminate how the process of incorporation is unfolding for individual immigrants and their families. I supplement the interview results with other empirical materials, including census statistics, voting data, and case studies of key historical episodes and trends in the political experiences of Afro-Caribbean New Yorkers. The additional empirical materials serve two purposes: First, they help to draw a fuller picture of how Afro-Caribbean immigrants are adapting to American life and politics. Second, I use these other materials to assay the validity of the insights drawn from the interviews.

III. THE POLITICAL INCORPORATION OF AFRO-CARIBBEAN IMMIGRANTS

The book concludes neither the pluralist, nor the minority group model is entirely applicable to Afro-Caribbeans. Over the course of six chapters, I catalog and analyze the group's experiences and find many of them are neither anticipated nor well explained by these two dominant frameworks. To be sure, both perspectives provide a number of valid insights, but each is mistaken in some of its fundamental normative assumptions and empirical predictions about the dynamics of political incorporation: specifically its institutional workings and how immigrants perceive and navigate the process.

Even the most recent pluralist accounts of how immigrants are incorporated into American politics tend to underestimate the impact of racial inequality and discrimination. Although the minority group perspective gives due consideration to these racial obstacles, its emphasis on race can gloss over important background differences between African Americans and foreign-born non-white groups, such as Afro-Caribbeans, that also influence their political incorporation patterns. In particular, the fact these new minority groups are immigrants with ties to other countries informs their adjustment to the American political system in ways not anticipated by either the minority or the pluralist perspective.

The book demonstrates Afro-Caribbean immigrants do not make the steady, inevitable adjustment to American politics predicted by the pluralist model. Their path is complicated by institutional resistance in the political arena, racism, and their own home country ties. Yet their response to the challenges posed by racism does not follow the model established by African Americans, as the minority group perspective would predict. As voluntary immigrants, Afro-Caribbeans have strategic and cognitive options for adjusting to life in America that are not available to their native-born black counterparts. As I show in the chapters to come, these options make for important differences in how these foreign-born blacks navigate the incorporation process.

Home country or transnational ties, in particular, have a powerful hold on Afro-Caribbean immigrants. Other researchers have highlighted the emotional grip home country attachments have on immigrants even after they have settled in the United States (Karpathakis 1999; Jones-Correa 1998). Yet the book shows that an emphasis on the emotional pull of home country attachments is too narrow. These ties have considerable cognitive influence on Afro-Caribbeans' political thinking, behavior, and view of themselves. In sum, they inform how the immigrants adapt to the challenging process of political incorporation in the United States.

IV. OVERVIEW OF THE BOOK

I present the empirical findings in five chapters. Chapter 2 takes stock of Afro-Caribbean socioeconomic trends to see how well they are faring in their adjustment to American life. These socioeconomic details matter because they could very well influence the immigrants' pattern of political incorporation. The popular perception is that Afro-Caribbeans are doing much better than their African-American counterparts. Chapter 2 marshals data that call this thinking into question. I conclude the immigrants have a slight socioeconomic edge over African Americans on some indicators, but are virtually just as disadvantaged as their native-born black counterparts relative to whites.

I begin my consideration of the political incorporation patterns of these black immigrants in Chapter 3, which offers an analysis of their early patterns of political participation. Afro-Caribbeans have been much slower to naturalize and become involved in formal politics than the pluralist perspective would predict. The chapter concludes the normal institutional workings of urban politics do not encourage immigrant participation. In particular, political parties are not the immigrant mobilizers Dahl and other early pluralists made them out to be. Rather, the parties act as gate-keepers, ignoring new groups, such as Afro-Caribbean immigrants, and relegating them to the political margins.

Still, there are other routes to political involvement than the conventional party system. In fact, the minority group perspective suggests racial exclusion compels most non-white groups to join together to mobilize for radical reform outside regular party channels. Chapter 4, however, finds the most likely pair of coalition partners for this kind of movement – Afro-Caribbean immigrants and African Americans – have not been able to build or sustain a race-based alliance. The chapter argues the two groups of blacks share a number of common interests that could easily serve as the basis for a coalition. Yet, I find interethnic conflicts between the two groups over descriptive representation have often deflected attention from their intraracial common interests. I conclude African-American politicians therefore have been lukewarm about or resistant to the prospect of Afro-Caribbean mobilization.

Chapter 5 argues the immigrants themselves have shown little interest in political participation. I examine Afro-Caribbeans' ties to their home countries and conclude their strong home country attachments have dampened their interest in political involvement in New York City. But I also find when home country ties are expressed through civic activity they actually may promote political engagement in American politics. In focusing on the lingering political effects of home country ties, the chapter challenges the assimilationist logic of the standard pluralist view on how immigrants adjust to American life. Home country or transnational attachments have far more sustained importance to immigrants than the accounts of the early pluralists would suggest.

In fact, these ties have a powerful influence on Afro-Caribbeans' view of themselves and their political thinking and behavior. Chapter 6 finds home country attachments largely explain why these foreign-born blacks do no not conceive of their racial identity in the same manner as their native-born counterparts. They do not attach the same political meanings to being black that African Americans do. The immigrants' home country ties and experiences give them an alternate frame of reference for defining themselves and making sense of the political world.

Chapter 7 argues this alternate frame of reference or cognitive lens explains why the immigrants have not followed the same model of political incorporation as their native-born counterparts. Counter to the predictions of the minority group view, Afro-Caribbeans, in their bid for political inclusion, have not made the same demands for redistribution and systemic reform we saw among African Americans in their own earlier attempts to achieve political power.

The immigrants draw on their home country experiences to make many political evaluations, whereas their native-born counterparts often interpret political life through the lens of their long history of racial subordination in this country. These contrasting cognitive frames make for subtle, but nonetheless important differences in how the two groups see the political world. Still, I ultimately conclude racism complicates the political incorporation process for Afro-Caribbean immigrants no less than it has for African Americans.

Before I delve into the political experiences of these foreign-born blacks, I use Chapter 1 to outline the theoretical framework of the book. The chapter offers an analysis of the dominant models of political incorporation that have been applied to contemporary non-white immigrants. I highlight the strengths and limitations of these perspectives and show how they might be amended to illuminate and explain better the experiences of these newcomers.

I

Beyond Black and White

Theories of Political Incorporation

> I am the poor white, fooled and pushed apart,
> I am the Negro bearing slavery's scars...
> I am the immigrant clutching the hope I seek...
> Langston Hughes

How are Afro-Caribbeans and the millions of other recent immigrants from Asia and Latin America adapting to the American political system? How is the political incorporation process unfolding for these newcomers in the cities where they have settled? These groups are part of a long historical succession of outsiders who have attempted to become insiders and gain a foothold in American democracy – from European immigrants in the early twentieth century to African Americans only a few decades ago. Although the research on today's newcomers is just emerging, there is an established political science literature on the earlier generations of outsiders, European immigrants and African Americans. This body of research potentially provides a road map for charting how the new wave of newcomers might adapt to American political life.

Before I delve into the experiences of Afro-Caribbean immigrants, I use this chapter to explore this literature and establish the theoretical scaffolding for the study. First, I offer a definition of political incorporation that extends beyond the usual focus on outcomes to consider the dynamics of the process. I then review the details of the dominant models of incorporation – specifically, the pluralist and minority group approaches – to set the stage for the analysis in the following chapters. I parse the existing literature with a view toward identifying the relative strengths and weaknesses of each perspective. I conclude that both models fail to give due weight to the analytic significance of the immigrant status and home country ties of foreign-born minority groups. My own theoretical amendment is that immigrants' home country ties and experiences serve as a kind of cognitive frame or lens through which these newcomers make sense of American political life and the challenges of incorporation.

I. APPROACHES TO STUDYING POLITICAL INCORPORATION

The research on political participation and urban politics together provide a basic definition for political incorporation (e.g., Browning, Marshall, and Tabb 2003; 1997; Verba, Schlozman, and Brady 1995; Dahl 1961). It is the process through which new groups begin to participate in politics and eventually achieve representation and influence in government. Implicit in this definition is a broad continuum of possible political outcomes. On one end are voting and other basic forms of political participation, which constitute the lowest level of incorporation.[1] At the other end is actual political representation.

There are two forms of representation: descriptive and substantive. Descriptive representation occurs when members of a group secure elective or appointive positions in government. Substantive representation means that the group has actual influence on the policymaking process. This strongest form of incorporation signifies something more than simple officeholding; it indicates a group has attained a role in a governing coalition and thus can influence policymaking to satisfy their particular interests.

Political incorporation, however, is not simply an outcome, measured in voting rates, representation, and policy benefits. It is also a kind of socialization process during which groups adapt to the routines of American political life. Too many studies of political incorporation focus solely on outcomes, while leaving this process, especially from the perspective of the groups themselves, unexamined.[2] During the incorporation process, groups obviously may or may not become engaged in politics and pursue representation. But whether they do or not is hardly the end-all and be-all of incorporation.

---

[1] Among new immigrants, the incorporation process formally begins with naturalization, although some individuals engage in various forms of conventional and unconventional political activity even before becoming United States citizens.
[2] Jones Correa (1998) and Lin (n.d.) are notable exceptions.

Incorporation is also a question of how groups adjust or acculturate to the norms of American politics, which in turn shape their prospects for participation and representation. During the incorporation process, newcomers learn the rules of the game: how to identify and define themselves, how to frame their policy interests, where to draw alliances, where to position themselves within the party system, and where their ideological allegiances lie. Incorporation is, in short, a political learning process for new groups to American democracy.

Institutions and elites are the dominant sources of cues for understanding the norms and rules of American politics, but the lessons immigrants learn also may be drawn from their social networks: neighbors, coworkers, civic groups, and so on. Learning these rules, playing by them, or even challenging them is what it means to become a politically active American. This learning trajectory is at the heart of the political incorporation process and influences the outcomes researchers typically emphasize. How new groups pursue representation or secure policy benefits and whether they even pursue such goals depend on how this political learning process unfolds.

Hence, this study focuses closely on the political incorporation process from the perspective of Afro-Caribbean immigrants, although it also considers outcome measures. The following discussion of the dominant models of political incorporation zeroes in on their respective accounts of how the process unfolds. It details and analyzes the models' predictions on how groups define themselves, which claims they make in their bids for incorporation, and generally how they become active citizens of American democracy.

II. THE PLURALIST STANDARD AND THE
AFRICAN-AMERICAN EXCEPTION

Dahl put forward the seminal account of the political incorporation process in his 1961 case study of New Haven politics. Hailed as the locus classicus of pluralist scholarship, the work is based largely on the experiences of successive waves of European immigrants to the city. Although Dahl's interpretation has been subject to endless criticisms, challenges, and even amendments by the author himself, it nonetheless retains considerable currency. His account of how outsider groups, such as new immigrants, become active in American politics set the standard for the pluralist model of political incorporation.

The Pluralist Model

Dahl (1961) argued new actors take their first step toward political incorporation when they begin to view themselves as part of a cohesive group. He reasoned immigrants from the same country often identify with each other as foreigners in a strange, new nation facing similar challenges. These shared feelings bind them together and become the basis for a common ethnic group identity. This identity then serves as fuel for political mobilization. Incorporation among the European immigrants Dahl studied, for example, began with the emergence of ethnic politics. In his view, immigrants tend to mobilize around their new shared sense of ethnic identity to elect coethnics to local political office and encourage others in their group to become involved in politics through voting, grassroots party activity, and so on. Ethnic group politics is thus a vehicle for immigrants to win political representation, policy influence, and secure footing in the democratic process. It propels these new actors into the political system, transforming them from immigrant outsiders into ethnic insiders.

Local political parties play a vital role in this process. Dahl argued party organizations and their elected officials court immigrants as ethnic constituencies and thus draw them into the political system. In New Haven, "[t]hey made it easy for immigrants to become citizens, encouraged ethnics to register [to vote], and put them on the party rolls" (34). They also fielded ethnic candidates for political office to give the immigrants symbolic recognition and a chance at descriptive political representation. Following Dahl's logic, local parties engaging in such practices promote ethnic group politics. Party organizations supply immigrants with the learning cues for engaging in this group-based form of political engagement that has long been standard fare in most American cities. They, in turn, bind the allegiance of newcomers to their particular party organization and the political system as a whole. Dahl reasons that immigrants feel a sense of wider social acceptance and develop a stake in the political system when they are courted by parties and see their coethnics elected to political office.[3] In sum, parties use ethnic politics to appeal to immigrant outsiders, socialize them to the norms of urban political life, and draw them into the political process.

---

[3] Implicit in Dahl's claim is a standard assimilationist assumption that immigrants yearn for acceptance in the United States. See Chapter 5 for a challenge to this conventional view.

Dahl also contended ethnic group politics has a deradicalizing effect on immigrants. Even as it binds the allegiance of these newcomers to the political system, it also subdues their more radical ideological impulses. It does so by deflecting their attention from their lower-class concerns and the frustrations of adjusting to life in a new country, focusing them instead on their ethnic group loyalties.[4] Recall early European immigrants were predominantly poor and desperate for economic mobility and security. Their poverty made them ripe for radical political appeals emphasizing redistribution and other major reforms to American government. But the ethnic group politics promoted to the immigrants by early political parties had no substantive ideological content. Indeed, Dahl (52–59) argued ethnic group politics tends to center on allocational policy interests and calls for symbolic recognition, while retreating from more radical or redistributive demands.[5] Ethnic group politics is thus largely non-reformist and poses little or no threat to the political status quo.

The non-reformist or conservative nature of ethnic group politics has a stabilizing effect on the political system. Integrating new groups into the political process always has the potential to disrupt entrenched regimes, stable coalitions, and established patterns of political precedence. But according to Dahl, ethnic group politics eliminates the threat of disruption. The process of political incorporation for European immigrants was at the same time a process of deradicalization. Returning to the political learning process framework I sketched at the outset of the chapter, incorporation is not simply a matter of new groups' becoming active voters and winning representation. It is also a process through which they develop their ideological bearings within the landscape of American politics. To put it simply, it is a process of ideological orientation. Ethnic politics encourages this orientation process. It pulls new groups toward the ideological center of American politics and thus defuses any potential they may harbor for making radical demands and disrupting the political system.[6]

---

[4] Of course, Dahl overlooks the possibility that ethnic or racial group identity actually could be the basis for radical political action or challenges to the political system. It certainly has in the case of African Americans, as I discuss later in the chapter.

[5] Allocational policies address public employment and the housekeeping functions of government; they have little or no impact on prevailing systemic arrangements. Redistributive policies are intended to redress inequality and often entail systemic reform. Also see Peterson 1981 and Wolfinger 1965.

[6] For a similar argument from an institutionalist perspective, see Shefter 1986.

Finally, Dahl contended ethnic group politics is ultimately a transitional phase in the incorporation process. As groups achieve upward economic mobility and political integration, their ethnic loyalties gradually melt away.[7] According to Dahl, as immigrants move up the socioeconomic ladder, their voting behavior, once highly informed by ethnic attachments, is instead increasingly dictated by their pocketbook concerns. Upwardly mobile immigrants begin to vote less in line with their ethnic group and more in accord with the interests of their new middle-class cohort. Ethnic group identity thus loses whatever political significance it once had. It becomes for the middle class a kind of nostalgic fancy or symbolic adornment to be trotted out at cultural celebrations, religious observances, and the like.[8] As Dahl (1961, 35) puts it, "To these people, ethnic politics is often embarrassing or meaningless."

Accompanying upward economic mobility, political integration, and the decline in ethnic identity are other indicators of inclusion in the wider society: residential integration, higher rates of intermarriage, occupational mobility, and so on. These are all signs of what sociologists call assimilation and acculturation (e.g., Alba and Nee 2003; Lieberson 1980). These dynamics tend to unfold over the course of two or three generations in a single group. But signs of incorporation ought to be evident in the trajectory of individual group members even in the first generation as they climb the socioeconomic ladder. Dahl believed all groups ultimately would follow this path to full political incorporation in a continuing and relatively seamless saga of urban ethnic and racial succession. (See Figure 1.1 for a schematic model of this process.)

A number of scholars (e.g., Erie 1988; Parenti 1967; Wolfinger 1965) have offered important amendments and criticisms to Dahl's model. For instance, he glosses over the prejudices and discrimination faced by the immigrant generation and the ways such challenges might affect their prospects for incorporation. Still, his pluralist framework has remained mostly intact as a description of the political incorporation process. At the very least, it seems to account adequately for the experiences of European immigrants, who in keeping with Dahl's model became the white ethnics of America's melting pot ideology.

---

[7] Here Dahl reproduces the "melting pot" logic of early assimilationist thinkers. For example, see Park 1950.

[8] Echoing Dahl's prediction, Waters (1990) has argued expressions of ethnicity among the descendants of earlier European immigrants are largely symbolic and voluntary. Also see Alba 1990.

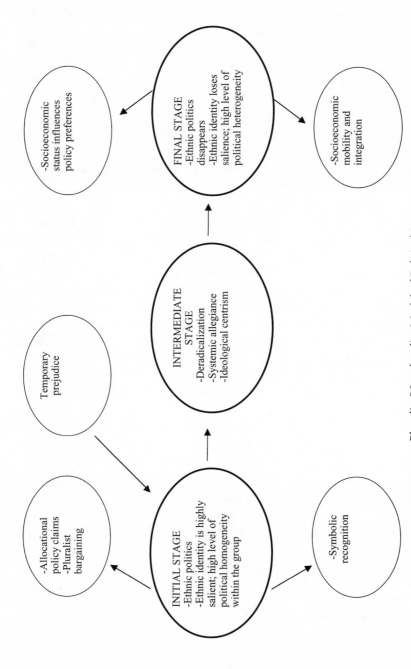

FIGURE 1.1. Pluralist/Neopluralist Model of Political Incorporation

Socioeconomic status influences policy preferences

FINAL STAGE
-Ethnic politics disappears
-Ethnic identity loses salience; high level of political heterogeneity

Socioeconomic mobility and integration

Temporary prejudice

INTERMEDIATE STAGE
-Deradicalization
-Systemic allegiance
-Ideological centrism

-Allocational policy claims
-Pluralist bargaining

INITIAL STAGE
-Ethnic politics
-Ethnic identity is highly salient; high level of political homogeneity within the group

-Symbolic recognition

The African-American Exception

It does not, however, apply as readily to African Americans. Their experiences pose a striking contravention to the pluralist model. For example, African Americans at the time of Dahl's study still had not achieved political incorporation after several generations of settlement in New Haven. Dahl himself was hard pressed to account for the anomalous political trajectory of blacks in the city. He bracketed the group's experiences as an unhappy exception to a model that seemed to work well for everyone else. Still, he predicted African Americans eventually would achieve incorporation, as their white counterparts had, and join in the long continuous line of ethnic group advance in American cities, albeit belatedly. He reasoned racism had only stalled blacks' march toward eventual political incorporation. His prediction, however, was more hope than confident hypothesis.

The inconsistencies between the predictions of his model and the experiences of African Americans were plainly exposed in the harsh light of the civil rights movement and the racial upheaval of the 1960s. No other group in American history had faced racial barriers to mobility as imposing and entrenched as those confronted by African Americans. Nor had any other group been compelled to press for incorporation by means of such a radical, large-scale episode of grassroots mobilization. It took the legislative and constitutional reforms of the civil rights era, in fact, to eliminate many of the racial hurdles African Americans faced and to jump start their formal bid for political incorporation.

A fundamental weakness of the pluralist model lay in its failure to take these racial obstacles and inequalities into serious account. Several scholars over the last few decades, however, have addressed this troubling lacuna in the pluralist literature, with works that explain the peculiar incorporative trajectory of African Americans (e.g., Dawson 1994a; Gurin et al. 1989; Reed 1988; Pinderhughes 1987; Walton 1985). Taken together, their studies advance an alternative model for understanding African-American political incorporation, one that stands in sharp contrast to the pluralist interpretation put forward by Dahl and other scholars.

The political incorporation process for African Americans, as for European immigrants, begins with the mobilization of group identity. The similarities, however, practically end there. First, African Americans rely much more heavily on collective political action than European immigrants ever did. They also tend to be more inclined to combine unconventional and conventional forms of political participation. They have turned to demonstrations and protests, as well the ballot box, to press for political incorporation. When disenfranchisement prevented African Americans from even casting ballots, they were forced to rely on these more unconventional or extra-systemic tactics to make political demands. European immigrants, in contrast, had far less experience with such strategies. The civil rights movement is an obvious example of this one critical political difference between African Americans and European immigrants. But there are others.

Whereas ethnic group politics among whites is typically non-reformist, racial group politics among African Americans tends to have a pronounced reformist, sometimes even radical, agenda. African-American politics often combines the usual calls for symbolic recognition and allocational policy benefits with demands for redistribution. Mindful of their unequal racial status, African Americans have tended to reject the standard pluralistic, non-reformist politics practiced by white ethnics. As Reed (1988, 154) observes, "The black regime typically comes to power in a spirit of reform, surrounded by images of redress for long-standing [racial] inequities and breaking through the walls of entrenched privilege." In short, African Americans demand reform and redistribution to redress racial inequalities and clear the way for their full integration into American society.

I would sum up African Americans' group-based bids for incorporation following Reed and others, but using the political learning process framework I laid out at the beginning of this chapter. These native-born blacks learn the rules of the game and then proceed to challenge these rules with calls for reform and redistribution to eradicate the racial inequalities that block their mobility and constrain their opportunities for full inclusion. This account of African-American group politics contrasts almost diametrically with Dahl's description of the non-redistributive, non-reformist ethnic group politics of European immigrants. When these immigrant outsiders became ethnic insiders and politically active Americans, they rarely made aggressive or consistent demands for systemic reform or redistribution. When African Americans have joined the political fray in cities, however, they often have called for significant antidiscriminatory reforms and an end to the conditions that have kept them at the bottom of the socioeconomic ladder.

Racial group politics also has had very different ideological consequences for African Americans than the ethnic group politics of European immigrants. Whereas ethnic group politics tended to deradicalize European newcomers and bind their support to the political system, racial group politics among African Americans often has had a radicalizing effect on group members. Most public opinion research indicates politically active African Americans largely occupy the Left on the American ideological spectrum (e.g., Dawson 2001; 1994a).[9] Nor does African-American politics necessarily inspire or reinforce allegiance to the political system. As Pinderhughes (1987, 40) has observed, African-American political attitudes and beliefs often reject the legitimacy of American political institutions and authority symbols; such rejection in turn produces the demand for systemic reform.

It is no wonder, then, African Americans and whites often seem to inhabit separate and distinct political universes. Most whites cluster toward the center of the American ideological spectrum. African Americans, in contrast, are the most homogeneously liberal group in the American polity (Dawson 1994a; Tate 1993). They are more supportive of redistributive policies and government intervention in the economy than are most whites (Dawson 1994a). They are also more ambivalent about the American Dream (Hochschild 1995), more cynical about the American justice system (Kennedy 1997), and so on. These significant political differences remain even between African Americans and whites of the same socioeconomic background.

There are other striking inconsistencies between the political incorporation patterns of African Americans and the predictions of the pluralist model. Recall Dahl expected the political salience of ethnic or racial group identity to decline as individuals move into the middle class ranks and begin to base their political decisions on socioeconomic calculations. One perhaps would expect this predicted pattern to be especially pronounced among African Americans, with the deepening economic divisions between middle- and lower-class segments of the population over the last three decades. Counter to Dahl's formulation, however, group identity among African Americans does not decline in political salience as group members attain middle-class status.

Public opinion data, in fact, suggest middle-class African Americans are more attached to their racial group identity than their lower-class

---

[9] Despite their liberal leanings on questions of economic policy, African Americans display more conservative tendencies on a number of social issues (Dawson 2001). Also see Fogg-Davis 2005.

counterparts. Moreover, they continue to rely on their group identity to make a variety of political judgments (Dawson 1994a; Tate 1993). They do not appear to find group politics "embarrassing or meaningless," as Dahl would have predicted. Indeed, African Americans inevitably must reckon with the fact that race has a disproportionate influence on their civic, social, and economic standing in the United States. Consequently, one of the major lessons they learn during the incorporation process is to use their ties to other blacks – their racial identity – as a heuristic for making political decisions about issues likely to affect their lives (Dawson 1994a). Becoming politically active for African Americans, then, often means learning to emphasize and give political weight to racial identity. More generally, group identity seems to hold far greater political and ideological significance for African Americans than it does for white Americans.[10]

African-American political incorporation patterns differ from those of European immigrants in one other important respect. As middle-class arrivistes, the formerly stigmatized European immigrants and their children overcame prejudice and other initial barriers to individual socioeconomic success and melted almost imperceptibly into the American mainstream. They enjoyed mobility in practically all arenas of American life (e.g., Alba and Nee 2003; Lieberson and Waters 1988; Allen and Farley 1987; Lieberson 1980). This pattern was fully in keeping with the predictions of Dahl's model. Not so for African Americans. Although they have achieved a measure of political incorporation in many cities across the United States, African Americans have not been able to escape racial considerations. Some of the earliest studies of black life in American cities, such as the classic *Black Metropolis* by St. Clair Drake and Horace Cayton (1945), concluded that a seemingly impenetrable color line blocked African-American mobility in housing, employment, and other areas. Despite the reforms of the civil rights movement, barriers remain.

Even the most upwardly mobile African Americans today find their social and economic progress stymied. Middle-class African Americans often have a difficult time transferring their success from one arena to another. So their increased incomes, for example, do not translate readily to asset accumulation and stable wealth (Oliver and Shapiro 1997). Similarly, middle-class earnings and occupational status do not give African Americans an automatic pass into high-quality, residentially integrated

---

[10] See Chapter 6 for more discussion.

neighborhoods. Their difficulty in turning such advantages into residential mobility contrasts sharply with the case for white ethnics, among whom middle-class status typically translates into higher levels of residential integration with other groups. Despite their advances, however, middle-class African Americans have remained residentially segregated, excluded from whole sectors of the housing market by active antiblack discrimination (e.g., Massey and Denton 1993). All in all, middle-class African Americans have had difficulty bolstering and enhancing their socioeconomic status.

Even more strikingly, political incorporation has failed to translate into steady socioeconomic improvements for the poorest African Americans (e.g., Stone and Pierannunzi 1997; Wilson 1996; 1987; Reed 1988). Incorporation has not generated the resources or policy influence necessary to eradicate the severe social and economic problems that have ravaged poor black central-city neighborhoods in recent decades. It is a perverse irony, in fact, that many of the most vexing issues associated with inner-city black neighborhoods – commercial disinvestment, population loss, joblessness, weak schools, violent crime, drugs, AIDS, and so on – actually either surfaced or deepened just as African Americans gained political control in many cities. In sum, political incorporation has proved to be a somewhat "hollow prize" for African Americans. Even the most sanguine accounts concede the incorporation process is at best incomplete for the population (e.g., Bobo and Gilliam 1990). Whatever the interpretation, the path to political incorporation has been difficult for African Americans, leading some to speak despairingly of the "permanence of racism" and the "impermanence" of black gains in the post–civil rights era (Bell 1992). (See Figure 1.2 for a schematic model of the process.)

Most scholars of African-American politics believe severe racial discrimination and inequality explain why the group has been unable to follow the same neat path to political incorporation as whites in this country. They reject attempts by Dahl and others to shoehorn African Americans into the pluralist mold. Recall some researchers have attempted to preserve pluralism for African Americans by casting the group's bid for incorporation as a variant of the traditional European immigrant experience that was simply stalled by temporary racial obstacles. In their view, the African-American experience is largely an anomaly in a political system that gives all groups a fair chance for full incorporation.

Many scholars of African-American politics, however, reject the standard pluralist recitation about the structure of the American polity (e.g.,

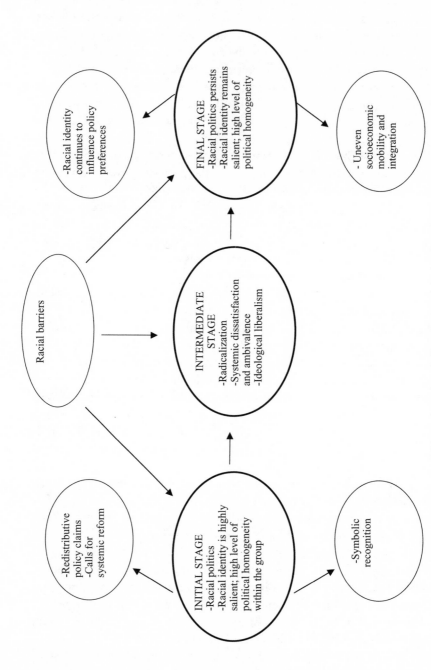

Racial barriers

Racial identity continues to influence policy preferences

FINAL STAGE
-Racial politics persists
-Racial identity remains salient; high level of political homogeneity

- Uneven socioeconomic mobility and integration

INTERMEDIATE STAGE
-Radicalization
-Systemic dissatisfaction and ambivalence
-Ideological liberalism

-Redistributive policy claims
-Calls for systemic reform

INITIAL STAGE
-Racial politics
-Racial identity is highly salient; high level of political homogeneity within the group

-Symbolic recognition

FIGURE 1.2. African-American/Minority Model of Political Incorporation

Pinderhughes 1987): that is, the belief that inequalities are dispersed, and the obstacles to incorporation few, transitory, or otherwise insignificant. On the contrary, studies on African-American political incorporation suggest this group, unlike European immigrants, has faced cumulative inequalities and long-standing barriers to integration. Some scholars, in fact, insist "[r]ace unlike ethnicity is so distinct as to make the process of political integration considerably more difficult for African Americans than it was for European immigrants" (Pinderhughes, 20).

III. NON-WHITE IMMIGRANTS

The fact that the majority of today's newcomers to American cities are non-whites like African Americans has led many to worry their path to political incorporation also will be tortuous, incomplete, and complicated by the rigors of American racism. Indeed, many researchers have used the African-American experience to develop an alternative model to pluralism to explain the difficult, uncertain road to incorporation that lies ahead for most non-white minority groups (e.g., Kim 2001; Hero 1998; 1992; Browning et al. 1997; Takaki 1989). Paul Peterson (1981, 158–159) summed up this minority group perspective in his 1981 study on urban politics.

Color changes the character of ethnic politics. The visibility of the minority group is much greater and therefore group members are assimilated into the larger society more slowly and more painfully . . . African Americans have been the most militant minority ever to surface in urban areas . . . Only the particularly severe economic and political deprivations of black Americans would account for a radicalism more characteristic of Europe than North America.

Exponents of the minority group view believe recent non-white immigrants are likely to encounter some of the same racial barriers and challenges to political incorporation as African Americans. Accordingly, they predict these minority newcomers will follow the same strategies as their native-born black counterparts in their own bids for political inclusion: collective grassroots mobilization, demands for government reform and resource redistribution, heavy, sustained reliance on group identity to make political decisions, and so on.

Other scholars, however, believe the United States over the last half-century has leveled most of the racial obstacles that once stymied minority group progress. In their view, the reforms of the civil rights era ultimately have helped to validate Dahl's pluralist model for racial minority groups, including African Americans. Dahl himself might argue the 1965 Voting Rights Act, affirmative action, and the other antidiscriminatory remedies actually have made racial minority status a potent political resource, rather than the disadvantage it used to be. According to this line of thinking, majority-minority electoral districts, minority government contract set-asides, and the like, all give African Americans and other minority populations even better prospects for descriptive and substantive representation. These reforms have cleared the way for non-white minorities, the argument goes, to follow the former European immigrants into full political incorporation.

Neopluralist researchers therefore contend recent non-white newcomers are likely to follow the pluralist path marked out by early European immigrants. Several studies on contemporary migrants from Latin America and Asia have looked to resuscitate Dahl's pluralist model and apply it to these new arrivals (e.g., Portes and Rumbaut 1996; Skerry 1993; Portes and Stepick 1993; Chavez 1991). They expect these immigrants to overcome any initial barriers, achieve upward mobility, and melt into the American mainstream much as their European predecessors did. In short, they predict full political incorporation for today's non-white newcomers.

The Limitations of the Pluralist and Minority Group Models

Although the minority group and neopluralist perspectives furnish important insights to help make sense of the political incorporation patterns of contemporary immigrants, they both also have serious blind spots and weaknesses. Each model is informed by normative assumptions that do not quite hold up under scrutiny. Both also fail to give enough weight to immigrant status as an independent analytic category that has bearing on how foreign-born groups navigate the political incorporation process. With these limitations, neither of these models can be expected to predict or capture fully the political incorporation patterns of today's newcomers.

First consider the minority group perspective. This model is built on the premise that non-white minorities, both native- and foreign-born, share in a common predicament that is bound to make political incorporation difficult and uncertain: subordinate racial status and vulnerability to discrimination. Peterson (1981, 158–159), for example, observes, "minorities of color seem to have a greater sense of grievance and deprivation. Their demands for social innovation have been more encompassing and all-embracing than past [white] ethnic demands ... minority group politics has taken a more virulent form than older forms of ethnic politics."

The logical conclusion from this premise, then, is that non-white minority groups will have similar political responses to the racial barriers they inevitably encounter in this country. The assumption is that foreign-born minorities will follow the same reformist strategies as African Americans in their pursuit of political incorporation and acceptance in the wider society.

It is a reasonable first approximation to place all minorities into the general category of subordinate groups and to contrast their disadvantaged structural position and even their subjective perspective with those of whites. But buried within the common situation of minority populations are important differences of history, experience, numbers, and so on. The minority group perspective tends to overlook those differences. Yet they are bound to influence minorities' political behavior, the subjective meanings they attach to their experiences with discrimination, and their strategies for navigating the incorporation process.

One of the most significant differences between African Americans and minorities from Asia, Latin America, and the Caribbean is that the latter groups, unlike their native-born counterparts, are immigrants. As I show in my examination of the Afro-Caribbean case in the following chapters, the fact that these groups are immigrants with ties to other countries has considerable influence on their political attitudes and behavior – including their responses to the discriminatory barriers the minority group perspective rightly emphasizes.

Some minority group scholars might argue that minorities' shared racial predicament tends to trump the differences among them and dispose them to pursue similar reformist political strategies. But "color" or subordinate racial status does not confer ipso facto uniform modes of political thinking. The experience of discrimination by itself does not necessarily compel a group to radical or reform-minded political attitudes or behavior. More formally, discrimination is a necessary, but hardly sufficient, condition for the emergence of radical or reformist political demands. After all, early European immigrants were once "racially" marked victims of discrimination; they were subjected to considerable prejudice. Yet, as Dahl and others have shown, they, unlike African Americans, made no significant radical claims on the political system and only occasional demands for redistribution (e.g., Erie 1988; Wolfinger 1965).

The fact that African Americans suffered more discrimination than European immigrants also does not explain the difference in their political responses. Sociologists and social psychologists have long argued that groups who suffer significant discrimination will demand political remedy or mount resistance only insofar as they find their situation unfair, illegitimate, or unjust.[11] The political response of a group is thus determined by the subjective meanings they attach to the racial hardships they encounter. Those subjective meanings are likely influenced by the background factors that differentiate minority groups.

African Americans, for instance, often make political sense of their repeated encounters with discrimination and inequality through the cognitive lens or frame of a specific historical memory sustained over the generations they have spent in a subordinate position in this country. This historical memory informed the subjective meanings they attached to their experiences with discrimination in American cities and, in turn, influenced the choices they made in their bids for political incorporation. As recent arrivals to this country, most of today's non-white immigrants do not have the same long-standing historical memory of racial suffering in the United States. But in contrast, they may draw on their home country experiences and ties to make political sense of their encounters with discrimination here. The minority group view overlooks these differences by placing exclusive analytic focus on the predicament of racial disadvantage shared by most non-whites.

Neopluralist arguments, in contrast, are too quick to ignore or gloss over the potentially complicating impact of racism on the political incorporation process. Racial discrimination against blacks and other non-whites has diminished significantly in the last five decades, to be sure. The rawest forms of bigotry have mostly receded from American life. But racial discrimination persists, albeit often in more subtle forms. Numerous studies indicate Latinos, Asians, and blacks all continue to experience racial prejudice and exclusion to varying degrees (e.g., Chong and Kim 2004; Hochschild and Rogers 2000). It is reasonable to assume, then, that discrimination might affect the prospects of political incorporation for non-white immigrants from Asia, Latin America, and the Caribbean, although it is difficult to predict exactly how.

The pluralist perspective, like the minority group model, also does not give enough analytic weight to the immigrant status and home country ties of foreign-born groups during their political adjustment to the United States. Traditional pluralist accounts of political incorporation assumed immigrants were usually eager to gain acceptance in the wider society

---

[11] Sociologists and social psychologists call this "cognitive liberation" (Brown 1986; Conover 1984; McAdam 1982).

and melt into the mainstream. Consequently, they often underestimated the effect lingering home country attachments might have on the foreign born as they navigate the political incorporation process. But recent studies have shown home country ties have a strong emotional hold on contemporary immigrants from Asia, Latin America, and the Caribbean and perhaps had a similar effect on their European predecessors as well (e.g., Foner 1997; Pessar 1995; Basch et al. 1994). What is more, this emotional pull influences how these newcomers regard the prospect of becoming American citizens and getting involved in politics in this country (Jones-Correa 1998).

As I demonstrate in my analysis of Afro-Caribbean incorporation patterns in the chapters to come, the pluralist perspective would do well to give more consideration to how these ties affect the political experiences of today's non-white immigrants. It is not only that they have an emotional hold on these newcomers. Home country attachments and experiences are also likely to have a cognitive effect on immigrants' political attitudes and behavior. Indeed, as I discover in the Afro-Caribbean case, these ties affect not only how the foreign born see themselves, but also how they view the political world and how they navigate racism and the other challenges they encounter in their adjustment to American life. Home country ties, experiences, and memories serve as a frame, a cognitive structure, that helps foreign-born newcomers make sense of the issues and choices that animate American political life.

The potentially significant effect of home country ties and experiences on the political thinking and choices of the foreign born suggests researchers in both the pluralist and minority group traditions ought to give more weight to immigrant status as an analytic category. Their failure to do so is a major limitation of both models of political incorporation. The growing numbers of minority populations from abroad in the United States are an invitation to make immigrant status a key variable, along with race, class, and so on, in our studies of how new groups navigate the political incorporation process.

Although neopluralist and minority group accounts of the political incorporation patterns of recent non-white immigrants have their respective strengths, many fail to give this variable sufficient independent analytic attention. Of course, many surveys include this variable with a simple item asking whether a respondent is foreign born or not. But the influence of immigrant status extends well beyond the fact of foreign birth. It goes to matters of home country experience and the accompanying cognitive outlook that often influences immigrants' political life in the United States.

IV. CONTEMPORARY RESEARCH ON NON-WHITE IMMIGRANTS

Much of what we have yet to learn or understand about the new wave of immigrants, in fact, may be informed by these home country factors. Ignoring them produces limitations and blind spots that show in some of the recent minority group and neopluralist studies on contemporary immigrant populations. A brief consideration of notable examples from the existing research highlights a few of the problems.

The Minority Group Approach

Rodney Hero's study of Latino politics (1992) falls in line with the minority group perspective. His compelling analysis reiterates many of the insights developed in the research on African-American political incorporation but extends them to Latino immigrants. Hero contends the American political system is based on a "two-tiered" form of pluralism. This two-tiered pluralism allows full incorporation for whites, in keeping with Dahl's original formulation, but only marginal inclusion for Latinos, African Americans, and other minority groups. Minorities, Hero argues, face unique racial barriers and inequalities that stall their integration into the political process. "Their efforts to wield political influence seem inevitably to require explicit political activity, taking the form of redistribution, and to appear as demands (or complaints)" (193).[12] His description practically echoes the standard account of African-American political incorporation.

But Hero offers some important new insights as well. He posits a continuum of racial disadvantage for the non-white groups relegated to the second tier of American pluralism, with African Americans on the far end and Latinos in the middle. Hero concedes African Americans are saddled with more severe racial disadvantages than Latinos. Further, he observes, Latino immigrants have a more "tenuous" relationship to the United States than African Americans. But he does not spell out the analytical

---

[12] Hero (1992, 204) asserts, "While dominant [white] groups use the political system to maintain and enhance their power and status, minorities pursue politics to try to achieve a modicum of equality, to realize equal opportunity in the first place."

implications of these differences or how they might inform the political incorporation patterns of the groups.

Without those distinctions it is difficult to predict how Latinos will differ from African Americans in their bids for inclusion. We are left with an undifferentiated category of minority groups sharing in a common racial predicament and without clear analytic clues for understanding how their political responses to this condition may differ. Again, subordinate racial classification may render groups vulnerable to prejudice and exclusion, but the experience of discrimination does not necessarily lead them to similar political responses. By generalizing from the African-American case to those of recent non-white immigrants, the minority group perspective sometimes may miss or fail to give sufficient consideration to key differences in the experiences of African Americans and their non-white foreign-born counterparts. Most significantly, African Americans are involuntary immigrants with a long history of racial subordination in this country. Many other non-white groups, such as Latinos, Afro-Caribbeans, and Asians, are recent voluntary immigrants with ties to their home countries.[13]

What is more, Latino and Asian immigrants may not even be subject to the harsh forms of discrimination African Americans have tended to encounter. Just as racism assumes different manifestations over time, it also may take different forms for different groups.[14] The critical question prompted by this fact is whether the political experiences of predominantly immigrant groups, such as Latinos, and those of African Americans are likely to differ as a result. If the forms of prejudice Latinos encounter differ from those faced by African Americans, this predominantly immigrant population also may opt to pursue alternative strategies for responding to these challenges and achieving political incorporation. Add to this complexity the fact that foreign-born Latinos hail from different countries, each of which might provide its own distinct cues for dealing with discrimination, and it becomes all the more untenable to lump them with African Americans.

The discrimination experienced by recent Latino or Asian immigrants, in fact, may prove to be less like the systematic racial barriers encountered by African Americans, and more analogous to the temporary prejudices

---

[13] Transnational attachments likely account for the "tenuous" relationship some Latino immigrants have with the United States (Jones-Correa 1998).

[14] See Kim 1999 for a discussion on how the forms of racism Asians encounter differ from those African Americans face.

faced by Southern and Eastern European immigrants earlier in the last century.[15] If so, these two groups ultimately might be incorporated into the "first tier" of the pluralist political process, while African Americans remain confined to the "second tier." This would certainly stand the minority group interpretation on its head. Whatever the case, this line of argument cannot be ignored by those who take the minority group perspective seriously.

Although much of Hero's analysis turns on the non-white racial status of Latinos, he acknowledges Latinos preponderantly identify as white, and some nationality groups such as Cubans show a greater inclination to do so than others. Some white Americans even view Latinos as another white ethnic population. This country's official racial enumerator, the census, treats Hispanics as an ethnic group and so leaves room for them to identify with the black, white, or Asian racial categories, or none at all. In short, the group does not fit the simple black-white or white–non-white analytic binary typically employed by the minority group perspective. This distinction alone vitiates any easy comparisons between Latino immigrants and African Americans, who have been rigidly subject to classification as blacks.

A similar qualification can be made for Asian Americans. Unlike Latinos, Asians are considered a separate racial group under the classifying scheme used by the census. Aside from a few scholars who have labeled Asians in the United States "honorary whites" (e.g., Hacker 1997; Ignatiev 1996), most observers believe they belong to the non-white minority category along with African Americans and are subject to racial discrimination and prejudice as a result (Kim and Lee 2001). Yet careful scholarship on the population suggests Asian Americans "occupy a distinctive 'third' position in the American racial hierarchy somewhere between black and white" (ibid., 633).

Accordingly, a number of researchers have concluded Asian Americans' experiences are likely to be distinct from those of African Americans. Some believe Asians suffer from the stigma of perpetual foreignness in the eyes of other Americans. Others argue they have been valorized relative to African Americans and yet marginalized as "strangers in the land" (Kim

---

[15] I doubt this will prove to be the case. Asian Americans, for example, have been in this country for as long as some European immigrant groups and yet are viewed as "perpetual foreigners" by many whites (Kim 1999). Still, this is an open empirical question worth considering. For an alternative view on Asian Americans contra the "perpetual foreigner" perspective, see Ignatiev 1997 and Hacker 1992.

1999). Whatever the case, Asians appear to suffer a different form of racial subordination than African Americans. Add to this distinction again the fact that Asian immigrants are from a number of different countries, which may provide distinct cues on how to respond to discrimination in the United States, and simple analogies between them and African Americans collapse.

Finally, some Latino and Asian immigrants are making confident strides into the socioeconomic mainstream. In fact, some of these newcomers arrive on American shores with far more economic resources than earlier European immigrants had. Early-twentieth-century immigrants from Europe were predominantly poor and working class. Today's immigrants, in contrast, show a diverse range of socioeconomic backgrounds: some exceed the average native-born American on individual-level resources, such as education, whereas others have higher rates of poverty than African Americans (Rumbaut 1999; Portes and Rumbaut 1996). It is thus a mistake to portray non-white immigrants as uniformly disadvantaged relative to whites. Minority group accounts that make this assumption paint with much too broad a brush.

The Neopluralist Approach

Most attempts to resuscitate pluralism and apply it to non-white immigrants make the same analytical mistake. Consider the study on Cuban politics in Miami by Alejandro Portes and Alex Stepick (1993). The authors largely reaffirm Dahl's account of the political incorporation process, albeit with a few intriguing distinctions. In keeping with the standard pluralist formulation, they contend ethnic politics among Cuban immigrants has facilitated the group's incorporation into a local political system that had once been the exclusive province of Anglos. Further, they conclude the process has unfolded in much the same way as it did for European immigrants. Ethnic politics among Cuban immigrants has centered on allocational policies and issues of symbolic group recognition, rather than on redistribution and systemic reform. As Portes and Stepick point out, Cuban group politics bears no resemblance to the radical-reformist politics of African Americans.

The most significant amendment the authors make to Dahl's model is on the question of cultural adaptation. Dahl argued acculturation – the process whereby an immigrant group loses its cultural distinctiveness and adapts to dominant cultural norms – accompanies political incorporation.[16] Portes and Stepick, however, claim "biculturalism" has emerged as an alternative adaptive project to acculturation. Biculturalism is "acculturation in reverse." "Foreign customs, institutions, and language are diffused within the native population." In Miami, for example, Cuban immigrant influence has resulted in the "Latinization" of the city's political economy.

Nevertheless, Portes and Stepick also observe signs of convergence in Miami. Following Dahl's pluralist formulation, they assert the political mobilization of group identity is a critical but temporary phenomenon that eventually leads to incorporation. They (8) write, "[I]mmigrants become Americans by elbowing their way into the centers of power through the political mobilization of ethnic group solidarity. The very success of the strategy leads to its obsolescence." Their discussion of biculturalism notwithstanding, Portes and Stepick largely endorse the pluralist model of political incorporation for recent non-white immigrants.

There are too many glaring exceptions in the Miami case, however, to make this model the rule for new immigrants. For example, Portes and Stepick are hard pressed to explain why Miami's Haitian immigrants and African Americans remain largely excluded from the local political structure and economic mainstream. Their exclusion is all the more troubling because, at 17 percent of the population, their numbers make them a potentially crucial bloc of swing voters in local elections. Nor are blacks the only exceptional case. Some of the more recent Latino immigrants from Central America have not been incorporated as readily as their Cuban counterparts and are nearly as marginalized as blacks from Miami's "Cuban miracle."

If we take a broader view, then, we might easily conclude the Cuban trajectory is exceptional, rather than predictive of the political incorporation patterns of most recent non-white immigrants to Miami (Moreno 1996). After all, most new immigrants do not have the unique advantages of the first wave of Cuban exiles to the city, an affluent group of refugees, whose incorporation was in part facilitated by the generous resettlement grants issued by the federal government. Yet the Cuban experience described by Portes and Stepick does have generalizable implications in one important respect. Their account suggests Cubans' home country ties and memories

---

[16] Sociologists and historians long have challenged the acculturation thesis, arguing ethnocultural identities do not decline; see Handlin 1941. Nevertheless, recent scholarship (Waters 1990; Alba 1990) insists ethnocultural identities among white Americans are largely symbolic and voluntary.

have had considerable influence on the immigrants' political choices and orientations in the United States. Home country ties and experiences are worth emphasizing because they are likely to matter for other immigrant groups as well.

Peter Skerry's study on Mexican immigrants (1993) is another attempt to resuscitate pluralism; in this case, however, the author does so by raising objections to the minority group view. Skerry argues incorporation no longer unfolds in the neat linear fashion sketched by Dahl and other early pluralists. He contends that today it is a far more complicated process. In his view, the civil rights reforms of the 1960s fundamentally changed American political institutions and, consequently, bifurcated the path to incorporation. He (1993, 6–7) theorizes that recent non-white immigrants are now faced with two options for integration: they may press for incorporation as "individual citizens or as members of an oppressed racial group." Skerry claims American political institutions have adopted the group-based logic of the civil rights and black power movements established by African Americans and are thus tutoring new immigrants to define themselves as "victimized racial claimant groups." This, he (29) laments, has become "an obvious and accepted way to get ahead . . . [D]efining themselves as a minority group may be the way this new wave of immigrants assimilates into the new American political system."

Unlike those who subscribe to the minority group perspective, Skerry does not argue that racism impedes the incorporation process for non-whites, although he does concede discrimination is at issue in the case of African Americans. Rather, his contention is that the country's political institutions encourage new immigrants to magnify the inevitable discontents that accompany mobility and interpret these as legitimate group grievances worthy of government redress, even when "assimilation" is progressing well along most dimensions. He insists these "discontents" are not very different from those faced by European immigrants in the early twentieth century. But in his view the country's political institutions are encouraging immigrants to adopt a militant racial group perspective, much like that of African Americans, which he believes ultimately makes for a more divisive political culture.

Skerry's argument is interesting, because it correctly suggests immigrants consider strategic imperatives as they negotiate the incorporation process. Yet the thesis has some limitations. First, it implies immigrants, following the African-American model, willfully exaggerate group grievances or pass themselves off as "racial claimants" to procure government favor. Most observers, however, would agree the question of whether African Americans have "gotten ahead" politically is still an open one. Moreover, immigrants' passing themselves off as "racial claimants" hardly seems a sure prescription for political success these days, with the affirmative action rollbacks of the past two decades and the rightward shift of the American electorate.

Survey data indicate new Latino immigrant communities, far from being hotbeds of liberalism and racial group consciousness, are often more conservative than earlier-generation immigrants and their native-born counterparts (e.g., Hochschild and Rogers 2000; Uhlaner 1991). Some researchers further argue immigrants actually seek to distance themselves from disadvantaged African Americans (e.g., Waters 1999). In short, they are not especially eager to cast their lot with other "racial claimants" or aver racial minority status. As Skerry himself concedes, Latino immigrants show considerable ambivalence and "in-betweenness" about their racial status and place in the country.

V. THE POLITICAL LEARNING APPROACH: HOME AND HOST COUNTRY CUES

Skerry's attention to how political institutions influence non-white immigrants in their bids for incorporation is useful. As I noted in my account of the political incorporation process at the beginning of this chapter, institutions are a dominant source of cues to immigrants on how the American political system works and how they can influence its outcomes. But foreign-born newcomers are not a *tabula rasa*. They arrive with experiences and ties to their home countries that also inform the political choices they make in the United States. Recall political incorporation is not simply about outcomes: it is also a learning or socialization process. Recent foreign-born arrivals draw on cues from both their home countries and their new host country to navigate this process.

It is likely many non-white immigrant groups encounter discrimination in their political and social adjustment to the United States. Whether they in turn think of themselves as racial minorities, opt to pursue affirmative action benefits, or make radical political demands in their bids for incorporation are all decisions that are likely to be affected by their home country experiences, as well as the cues they receive from American political institutions and elites. Home country attachments, in fact, often serve as the dominant cognitive lens or perceptual frame through which these newcomers make judgments about politics in the United States, if only because these ties are already intact, whereas the cues from their new American political culture are still coming into focus. Immigrants' home country perspectives interact with the cues and frames they receive from American political institutions and elites to shape the choices they make in their bids for incorporation.

The cognitive influence of home country norms and attachments on how the foreign born adjust to American politics was evident in the experiences of early European immigrants as well. Consider the Irish, for example. The fact that they became the leading practitioners of machine politics in the late nineteenth and early twentieth centuries was certainly due to the historical timing of their arrival and the emerging institutional dynamics of the American party system. But it was also attributable in part to political advantages they brought with them from their old world, home country experiences. The Irish were already steeped in the practices of mass political organization, local electoral manipulation, English literacy, and a strong sense of group solidarity when they arrived on American shores (Erie 1988). These home country skills and values translated into political resources that gave the Irish an edge in the competition to dominate the fledgling political machines of the Northeast. It is no wonder, then, the Irish were more inclined than some of their European immigrant counterparts to use machine politics as a vehicle for incorporation and mobility. Their home country experiences provided them with some of the cues to do so.

Neopluralist and minority group interpretations that fail to take the cognitive influence of home country experiences and ties into account are likely to miss important aspects of the political incorporation experiences of contemporary, non-white immigrants. Many of these newcomers are unlikely to conform to the predictions of the pluralist model, because it fails to anticipate how racial obstacles complicate the incorporation process for non-white groups. Nor, however, will these immigrants necessarily follow the path traced by African Americans simply because they too encounter racism, as the minority group perspective predicts. Many of these newcomers will have political responses to racial discrimination that differ from those of African Americans. As voluntary immigrants with ties to other countries, they are likely to view the political world differently than native-born blacks.

Nowhere is that more clear than in the case of Afro-Caribbean immigrants. Although these foreign-born blacks share a common racial classification and the bitter historical legacy of enslavement with African Americans, their home country ties and experiences make for important differences in how they and their native-born counterparts make sense of the political world. To be sure, racial discrimination complicates the immigrants' adjustment to American life and their bids for political inclusion. But their home country ties largely explain why they have not exactly followed the path to political incorporation marked out by African Americans. I turn to their experiences in the chapters that follow.

2

"Good" Blacks and "Bad" Blacks?

The accident that my ancestors were brought as slaves to the islands while black mainland natives were brought as slaves to the United States is not really that important compared to the common heritage of black brotherhood and unity in the face of oppression.

Shirley Chisholm

The vast gap in the history and worldviews of immigrants from . . . impoverished Third World count[ries] and long-term citizens of a First World nation can[not] be entirely papered over.

Alejandro Portes and Alex Stepick

The classical community studies literature does little to draw analytical distinctions – for instance gender, ethnoregionism, age, and especially ethnicity – among blacks.

John H. Stanfield II

Brooklyn is awash with signs of the Caribbean. All along Flatbush Avenue signals of a vibrant Caribbean immigrant presence shout at even the most casual observer. Storefronts advertise Caribbean nostalgia – the bright green, yellow, and black colors of a Jamaican flag, a palm tree, a stack of island newspapers in the window. But this is not empty symbolism – the Caribbean has come to New York. Small, garrulous groups of men and women congregate in front of Caribbean bakeries and restaurants to discuss the news from back home. Their animated conversations are thick with the inflections of Caribbean dialect. Jitney vans and dollar cabs perilously jockey for position as they compete for fares along the busy thoroughfare. Above the din, the sounds of calypso, reggae, and reggaeton music ring out. This is black New York.

Only a short train ride away is Bedford-Stuyvesant, one of the city's older African-American neighborhoods. Newly refurbished brownstones sit only blocks away from decaying tenement buildings. Mixed in with the brownstones are

TABLE 2.1. *New York Population by Race and Hispanic Origin,*
2000

	Population		% of Population	
Total	8,008,278		100	
White	2,801,267		35	
Black	2,037,887		25.4	100
African American		1,445,181		70.9
Afro-Caribbean		524,107		25.7
African		68,599		3.4
Hispanic	2,160,554		27	
Asian	889,642		11.1	

Source: U.S. Census Bureau.

venerable African-American churches. Some stand stoically amid changing neighborhoods; others cling tenuously to deteriorating buildings and declining memberships comprised mostly of an older, faithful generation. Young African-American men stand on street corners or sit on stoops, playing spirited rounds of "the dozens." They exchange clever barbs in an endlessly inventive form of American English vernacular. Cars speed by pulsing with the aggressive beats of rap and hip-hop on souped-up stereos. This too is black New York.

These two vignettes together provide a snapshot of an increasingly diverse group of black New Yorkers. Within the past three decades, the cleavages within the city's black population have multiplied at a dizzying pace – a pattern reflected generally among blacks throughout the United States. The divisions are many: economic, regional, generational, and so on. But the most pronounced sign of diversification among black New Yorkers is the division between the native and foreign born. Native-born African Americans predominate, but their numbers are in relative decline. The proportion of black immigrants from the Caribbean, in contrast, is on the upswing; their numbers have increased dramatically over the last few decades. Recent estimates put their numbers at roughly 524,000 – that is, more than a quarter of the city's black population (see Table 2.1). If the current immigration and demographic trends persist, first- and second-generation Afro-Caribbean immigrants will soon outnumber African Americans.

In light of this growing diversity, monolithic categorizations of the city's black population have become increasingly untenable. Yet much of the early influential scholarship on racial and ethnic politics in the United States tended to treat the black population as if it were a homogeneous lot. Traditional studies routinely ignored or elided intragroup differences, tensions, and conflicts among blacks. Such treatments simplistically assumed or implied an undifferentiated black community, bound by common experiences and wedded to a unitary vision of a political agenda. Consequently, researchers were often left with lamentably superficial, one-dimensional analyses of black politics and the suggestion of a rather uncomplicated essential racial community. To posit an undifferentiated black population, however, is to ignore how class, gender, and ethnic divisions within race may shape reality differently for members of the group. As Omi and Winant (1986) have noted, "Blacks in ethnic terms are as diverse as whites." Sophisticated analyses of black politics then are obliged to take note of this diversity.

The rapidly expanding Afro-Caribbean population in New York makes black ethnic diversity hard to ignore. Despite their growing numbers, however, the immigrants have mostly been overlooked in studies of black politics in New York City and elsewhere.[1] Indeed, the group was ignored for many decades in much of the social science literature, prompting one observer to dub Afro-Caribbean immigrants "the invisible minority" (Bryce-Laporte 1972). Most studies simply lumped the immigrants with African Americans, rendering the two groups of blacks a monolithic whole. This analytic myopia was undoubtedly the result of the overdeterminacy of dichotomous racial categorization in the United States. Much like the larger society itself, scholarship on blacks often reflected a "biracial rather than a multicultural mode of analysis." As one researcher (Halter 1993) noted, "The peculiar but widely held belief that whites – whether Anglo-Saxon, Polish, or Greek – [were] defined by ethnicity, while blacks [were] defined by skin color alone, persist[ed]."

But this approach has become increasingly outdated and inadequate as the country's racial classification system has been destablized by immigration from Asia, Latin America, and the Caribbean. Immigrants from these regions have prompted researchers finally to look beyond black and white to divisions within non-white minority populations. Scholars in disciplines such as sociology, anthropology, and economics have turned their attention in the last two decades to ethnic divisions among blacks, particularly to Afro-Caribbean immigrants.[2] Political scientists, however, have yet to focus on this group.

---

[1] Philip Kasinitz's (1992) study on Afro-Caribbean New Yorkers and Winston James's (1998) historical account of Caribbean radicalism are notable exceptions. But neither is situated in the political science literature.

[2] There is now an established, steadily expanding literature on Afro-Caribbean immigrants in the United States (e.g., Waters 1999; Vickerman 1999; Watkins-Owens 1996; Kasinitz 1992; Model 1991; Woldemikael 1989; Foner 1987; Thomas Sowell 1978; Bryce-Laporte 1972; Reid 1939).

Afro-Caribbean immigrants warrant serious analytical attention from political scientists not simply because the group has been overlooked or because they allow us to take a more differentiated account of black politics. These foreign-born black ethnics also provide a uniquely instructive case for revisiting some of the most stubborn and significant racial conundrums in American life. Recall from the Introduction that Afro-Caribbeans share a common racial classification with African Americans as blacks yet also lay claim to a distinctive ethnic background as voluntary immigrants. They thus furnish a rare, natural case study for exploring the relative importance of race, ethnicity, and immigrant status in American life.

The immigrants' experiences, when put in comparative perspective alongside those of African Americans, promise to help illuminate the nature of racism in the United States. Chiefly, does race still matter and if so, how? Is racism a crude, indiscriminate weapon that hobbles all blacks, native and foreign born alike, subjecting Caribbean immigrants to the same unfortunate constraints as African Americans? Or is it alert to ethnic distinctions, exempting these foreign-born blacks from some of the disadvantages that have been imposed on their native-born counterpart? It may be that Afro-Caribbeans' immigrant status and ethnic background insulate them from some of the discrimination African Americans have faced.[3] Or the immigrants' experiences might demonstrate racism is no longer the obstacle it once was for African Americans. Still, there is the grim possibility that racism has yet to decline enough to spare blacks – whatever their background – from its perverse effects. Afro-Caribbeans allow researchers to consider each of these hypothetical possibilities. In short, they furnish a rich case for getting at the heart of contemporary racial patterns in the United States.

The question in this study is whether racism is such a looming obstacle for blacks it compels Caribbean immigrants to follow the same tortuous path to political incorporation marked out by African Americans, as the minority group perspective anticipates. Or do these foreign-born black ethnics manage to replicate the far neater patterns of early European

---

[3] Stephen Steinberg has made an analogous argument about class. He (1995) writes, "Racism has never been indifferent to class distinctions, and it may well be the case that blacks who have acquired the right status characteristics are exempted from stereotypes and behavior that continue to be directed at less privileged blacks." Following Steinberg's line of reasoning, contemporary racism may not be indifferent to *ethnic* distinctions among blacks.

immigrants, in keeping with the predictions of the pluralist model? Before delving into the political experiences of Afro-Caribbean New Yorkers, however, this chapter provides a socioeconomic profile of these black ethnics. It catalogs and analyzes data on the immigrants' economic, residential, and social mobility patterns to gauge the extent of their integration into American life.

The aim is to determine whether the immigrants' socioeconomic trends are consistent with a pluralist pattern of steady inclusion into the mainstream or a racial pattern of exclusion and disadvantage. Although the chapter focuses on strictly socioeconomic indicators of well-being, these patterns nonetheless have implications for the immigrants' political life. Pluralist and minority group models share the assumption that social and economic trends influence a group's political incorporation patterns. A consideration of Afro-Caribbeans' socioeconomic trajectory is therefore a logical starting point for this study.

Afro-Caribbean socioeconomic patterns have been compared fairly routinely with those of African Americans to gauge the significance of race in American life today. Economists, sociologists, and historians all have written about the mobility trends of the two groups, comparing them to make inferences about whether racism is still a barrier to black achievement in the United States. But their works have drawn different, sometimes contradictory conclusions, and there is no clear consensus on what the comparisons tell us about the nature of American racism. Some researchers believe Afro-Caribbeans are faring better than their native-born counterparts and thus argue racism no longer severely limits blacks' life chances in the United States (e.g., Sowell 1978). Others, however, reject this inference as overly sanguine. Or, worse, they suggest it is incorrect insofar as it overstates how well Afro-Caribbeans are doing relative to African Americans (e.g., Farley and Allen 1987).

How these two groups of blacks are faring and whether race has any influence on their respective mobility patterns are not just academic queries. The answers to these questions bear on ongoing public debates about the aims, applicability, and appropriate target groups for antidiscrimination policies, such as affirmative action. If Caribbean-born blacks are doing better than their native-born counterparts, some observers will take this as evidence racism no longer inhibits black mobility and proof it is time to curtail or end affirmation action efforts in employment and education. Others, however, might see the same evidence and conclude affirmative action is still a necessary remedy; only it ought to be limited to African Americans who continue to need and deserve such measures to compensate for ongoing and past discrimination.

Indeed, a few leading African-American public intellectuals have argued it is a perverse misapplication of policy that Afro-Caribbean immigrants and their children have benefited disproportionately from affirmative action admissions to some elite universities while African Americans have received short shrift (Rimer and Arenson 2004). They point out African Americans have been disadvantaged by decades of discrimination, Jim Crow segregation, poverty, and inferior schools, and thus these native-born blacks, rather than new arrivals from the Caribbean or Africa, ought to be the principal beneficiaries of such policies. But if the goals of affirmative action extend beyond compensating for historic discrimination – say, if they include promoting diversity or remedying the effects of continuing racism – then exactly who should be targeted for its benefits is an open question. All in all, there is much at stake in this issue of how Afro-Cariibbeans are faring relative to their African American counterparts.

My conclusion on reviewing the data is Afro-Caribbeans have had a slight edge over African Americans on several indicators of socioeconomic well-being over the last few decades. Yet their advantage over their native-born counterparts has evaporated on some of these dimensions in more recent times. Even more importantly, Afro-Caribbeans, despite their edge over native-born blacks in areas such as employment, are not exempt from race-based discrimination. They, like African Americans, seem to encounter racial barriers in arenas of American life that provide opportunities for mobility. More precisely, race appears to constrain residential and economic outcomes for the immigrants no less than it does for African Americans. Both groups ultimately are disadvantaged relative to whites.

After highlighting the patterns in the socioeconomic data, I discuss their implications for both the ongoing debates over affirmative action and the theoretical question of incorporation at the heart of the book. Most of the data reviewed in this chapter are not new. I conclude, however, with a descriptive overview of the fifty-nine respondents interviewed for the analysis of Afro-Caribbean political incorporation patterns, which follows in the next five chapters.

I. THE CARIBBEAN COMES TO NEW YORK

Ride the IRT to Central Brooklyn or stroll along the streets of Cambria Heights, Queens, these days and see why many observers insist that the

Caribbean has come to New York. Even the most casual observer is likely to notice the lilting Caribbean accent of the tired black women in rumpled nurse uniforms chatting as they ride the late night train to Flatbush. The distinctive sound of their quiet conversation is an unmistakable signal of Caribbean ancestry. Likewise, the men arguing about sports in the backyard of a middle-class home in Queens are not raging about American baseball, but rather its close British cousin cricket. This favorite Caribbean pastime is unfamiliar to most Americans but a staple for men who grew up on the islands. These are unequivocal signs of the ever-expanding presence of Caribbean immigrants in New York City.

Afro-Caribbeans have been immigrating to the city since the turn of the twentieth century. During the first half of the century, their numbers were small, if not insubstantial, sometimes rendering them invisible. The size of the population began to increase at an almost exponential rate, however, with the passage of the 1965 Hart-Cellar immigration reforms.[4] The flow of Caribbean migration to the United States in the ten years following the reforms exceeded that of the previous seventy years (Kasinitz 1987a, 46). Since the 1970s, well over a million Afro-Caribbeans have entered the country. The population grew by more than 600,000, an increase of almost 70 percent, over the last decade alone. Today more than 1.5 million Afro-Caribbeans who have legal immigrant status live in the United States (Logan and Deane 2003).

More Afro-Caribbeans make their home in New York than in any other American city. In fact, New York has long been the leading entrepot for Caribbean newcomers to the United States. The 1990 census numbers revealed that 48 percent of all individuals reporting Afro-Caribbean ancestry were living in the New York metropolitan area. Consider the figures in Table 2.2. In 1980, there were just over 250,000 Caribbean immigrants living in New York. By 1990, the number had grown to just about 400,000, an increase of almost 50 percent.[5] By 2000, their numbers had grown by another 40 percent or almost 200,000 (see Table 2.1). It is no exaggeration, then, to declare that the Caribbean has come to the city, especially in light of these numbers and the relatively small populations of the nations that make up the region. Three of the largest Caribbean

---

[4] See the Introduction for a brief description of the 1965 immigration reforms.

[5] These census figures are conservative estimates at best. First, the official tabulations likely miss the large numbers of illegal, undocumented Caribbean immigrants living in New York. These undocumented newcomers are no doubt eager to avoid the ambit of official government agencies such as the U.S. Census Bureau. Second, it is well known the census routinely undercounts black and Latino populations in cities.

TABLE 2.2. *Distribution of Caribbean Population, New York City,*
1980 and 1990

	1980		1990	
	Population	%	Population	%
Jamaican	106,073	41.4	140,024	37.5
Haitian	43,468	17	84,011	22.5
Trinidadian and Tobagonian	24,072	9.4	37,052	9.9
British Caribbean	20,215	7.9	41,310	11.1
U.S. Virgin Islander	1,653	0.6	2,162	0.6
French Caribbean	819	0.3	837	0.2
Other Caribbean	59,850	23.4	67,535	18.1
Caribbean total	256,150	100	372,931	100

Source: U.S. Census Bureau.

countries each sent almost 10 percent of their respective populations to
the United States in the 1980s (Waters 1999, 52). The flow of immigrants
from the Caribbean to New York has been so heavy that the city now
boasts a larger Afro-Caribbean population than well over half of the
countries in the region.

The majority of the immigrants hail from the largest Caribbean nations:
Jamaica, Guyana, Haiti, and Trinidad and Tobago. Jamaicans predominate, constituting roughly 40 percent of the city's Caribbean population (Table 2.2). Haitians constitute just over 20 percent. Guyanese and
Trinidadian immigrants both make up sizable cohorts as well. There are
also significant numbers of Barbadians, Grenadians, and Vincentians. But
all the nations of the Caribbean have sent their share of immigrants to
the city.

Today their numbers in New York are so large Afro-Caribbeans
are impossible to miss on the city's streets and subways. Observers of
Caribbean life report that the immigrants are making a strong imprint on
the city. It is obvious in the neighborhoods where they have settled, the
occupations in which they cluster, the small businesses they have opened,
the cultural celebrations they stage, and so on. They are, to put it suc-
cinctly, no longer invisible. I will not detail the breadth of their impact
here; suffice it to say, the growth of the population has been reflected in the
social and economic life of the city.[6] I turn instead to their socioeconomic
patterns.

---

[6] For details, see Kasinitz 1992.

II. "GOOD" BLACKS AND "BAD" BLACKS?

The long-standing view – rooted in popular opinion and sustained by some social science research – is that these foreign-born blacks are doing quite well. The common perception, in fact, is they are faring much better than their native-born black counterparts (e.g., Fears 2003). According to this view, Afro-Caribbean immigrants are better educated, work harder, earn more money, live in better neighborhoods, and have stronger families than African Americans. By comparison with their native-born counterparts, the thinking goes, these immigrants are "model minorities" living out the American Dream. They are, in the words of one writer (Gladwell 1996), "good blacks." The much-touted successes of prominent blacks of Caribbean ancestry, such as Colin Powell and Kenneth Clark, reinforce and lend credence to this view. It is now a widely circulated stereotype in the United States.

But this view of the Afro-Caribbean as a kind of "superior" black dates back many decades. The earliest depictions of the first wave of Caribbean immigrants to New York emphasized their business acumen, work ethic, ambition, and overrepresentation among the city's black professional elite (Reid 1939). These accounts of Afro-Caribbean success were not always laudatory. Some American blacks and whites derisively dubbed the immigrants "Jewmaicans" for their thrift, hard work, and preoccupation with making money (Hellwig 1978; Reid 1939). In short, this view of Afro-Caribbeans as very successful became a prevalent stereotype that now passes for common sense. Today the image is so entrenched in popular opinion, people use it to make judgments and draw distinctions between the immigrants and their native-born black counterparts. Indeed, researchers have found the stereotype even has cachet with employers, many of whom reportedly prefer to hire Caribbean immigrants instead of African Americans (Waters 1999; Kasinitz 1992).

The stereotype has not only been perpetuated by employers or other groups. It also has been reinforced by the immigrants themselves. Researchers find Afro-Caribbeans often cite their reputation for hard work and success as a point of pride and even rely on it to distinguish themselves from African Americans or gain favor with whites in positions of power, such as employers. Both Kasinitz (1992) and Waters (1999) contend the immigrants strive to hold on to their accent to telegraph their Caribbean ancestry for this very reason. The emphasis Caribbean-born blacks place on their foreign ancestry does not square with the conventional view of immigrants, which suggests new arrivals are always keen to cover up any and all evidence of their non-American origins. Early

European immigrants, for instance, were thought to be eager to assimilate and conceal any telltale signs of their foreign background.[7] This research suggests Afro-Caribbeans, in contrast, are only too eager to embrace and project their foreign ancestry. By doing so, they can capitalize on the popular stereotype that casts them as "good blacks" and reap the economic and social rewards that result from this perception.

The Empirical Evidence on the Afro-Caribbean Success Story

Thomas Sowell gave this idea of Afro-Caribbeans as "good blacks" serious intellectual imprimatur in the 1970s. Sowell was not the first to make a scholarly claim for Afro-Caribbean success – this distinction probably should go to Reid. But Sowell's work had the most far-reaching impact. His research offered statistical proof the immigrants were more successful than African Americans. Sowell (1978) marshaled selected 1970 census data to show first- and second-generation Caribbean immigrants had greater income, higher occupational status, and a higher rate of business ownership than their native-born counterparts. The evidence was limited, but his findings gained wide currency, not so much for their scientific reliability as, for their ideological implications.

Sowell argued the success of Caribbean immigrants relative to African Americans was proof racism alone did not impede black socioeconomic mobility. If a group of foreign-born blacks such as Afro-Caribbeans could immigrate to the United States and succeed, he reasoned, then the source of African-Americans' disadvantages could hardly be racial discrimination. Sowell concluded cultural differences largely account for why African Americans continue to be mired in poverty, whereas their Caribbean counterparts move steadily up the socioeconomic ladder. He hypothesized the immigrants' superior cultural values – their ambition, emphasis on education, strong family bonds, and propensity to work hard and save – were the key to their mobility. The less prosperous economic fate of their native-born black counterparts, in his view, was the product of a maladaptive culture. Sowell's conclusion was that African Americans' cultural shortcomings left them ill equipped for success in American life.

Conservative ideological implications fairly shout from Sowell's conclusions. By his logic, African-American disadvantages are best addressed not through antidiscrimination or systemic reform but, rather, through

---

[7] See Chapter 5 for a challenge to this traditional assimilationist view of European immigrants.

a focus on the group's bad cultural habits. During the fierce affirmative action debates of the 1980s, many conservative observers pointed to Sowell's evidence and the "model" example of Afro-Caribbean immigrants to question the advisability of the policy or call for its end.[8] The implication was obvious: if a group of foreign-born blacks could get ahead under their own steam, African Americans' demands for "special help" or "preferential treatment" to overcome racial hardship were illegitimate and excessive. The immigrants thus were valorized "model minorities" relative to African Americans. It was not uncommon to hear pundits and policymakers urging American-born blacks to rid themselves of their maladaptive habits and adopt the "model" cultural values of their Caribbean-born counterparts.[9] Sowell's arguments gave powerful ammunition to conservatives in these debates and lent intellectual support to the long-standing view of Caribbean immigrants as highly successful, "good blacks."

Afro-Caribbeans would appear, on the basis of Sowell's evidence, to be on the pluralist path to full integration into the American mainstream. By his account, the immigrants are making the steady climb up the ladder of the American opportunity structure, in keeping with the predictions of the pluralist model. They thus would appear to have more in common with the white ethnics of America's melting pot ideology than with their native-born black counterparts. Yet a careful review of more recent research on Afro-Caribbean socioeconomic trends reveals a more complicated and less sanguine picture. These studies suggest the case for Afro-Caribbean success made by Sowell and others has been overstated. The available evidence qualifies, and in some cases disputes, the accounts of the immigrants' outperforming their native-born counterparts.

Self-Employment

First, the accounts of the impressive entrepreneurial success of the earliest wave of Afro-Caribbean immigrants to New York appear to have been mostly impressionistic and greatly exaggerated. Data on the business

---

[8] Asian Americans were perhaps the most commonly cited "model minorities" of this period. Their successes and reputation for diligence, discipline, and family solidarity were frequently invoked to make the same ideological point about the illegitimacy of affirmative action demands by African Americans (Kim 1999). The Afro-Caribbean example, however, may have been even more ideologically potent because these black immigrants are ostensibly vulnerable to the same kinds of racial hardships as African Americans.

[9] Glazer and Moynihan (1963) make a similar argument.

TABLE 2.3. *Class Distribution of New York Males in the Labor Force, 1925*

	% Afro-Caribbeans	% African Americans	% All New York Men
Employers	0.24	1.03	4.67
Own account[a]	1.45	3.21	12.00
Workers	78.41	76.77	74.58
Uncodable	19.91	18.99	8.75
N of unweighted cases	340	419	3001
N of weighted cases	8,294	26,473	637,788

[a] Own account = self-employed without employees.

Source: Reprinted with permission from Suzanne Model, "Where West Indians Work," in *Islands in the City: West Indian Migration to New York*, ed. Nancy Foner (Berkeley: University of California Press), © 2001 The Regents of the University of California.

activities of this first cohort of black immigrants are quite scant. But the available statistical evidence from the early twentieth century suggests Afro-Caribbeans were no more likely than African Americans to be self-employed. What is more, both groups had very low rates of self-employment relative to whites. Afro-Caribbeans and African Americans were, in fact, mostly concentrated in low-wage jobs (Gutman 1977). In a recent study based on 1925 census data, Suzanne Model (2001) finds African Americans actually showed a slightly higher propensity for self-employment than their Caribbean-born counterparts. Still, as Table 2.3 indicates, the rates of self-employment for both groups paled in comparison to those of whites. The overall self-employment rate for all New York males was nearly four times higher than that of African Americans, and over eight times higher than that of Afro-Caribbeans.

A welter of recent research also has raised doubts about the magnitude of the much-heralded Afro-Caribbean socioeconomic advantage over African Americans in the last few decades. The findings from this body of research are too voluminous and complex to recount in detail here. I thus briefly review only the most salient patterns in the recent data. By and large, the immigrants' edge remains on some indicators, disappears on others, and varies sharply by gender, immigration cohort, generation, and length of residence in the United States.

Earnings

First, 1970 census figures did reflect an earnings advantage for Afro-Caribbeans who had lived in the United States for at least ten years. The immigrants tended to have higher annual incomes than their African-American counterparts (Chiswick 1979). The Afro-Caribbean earnings advantage appears to have evaporated, however, by 1980. In separate analyses of 1980 census data, Suzanne Model (1995) and Kristin Butcher (1994) each found Afro-Caribbeans did not hold a significant earnings advantage over African Americans who had similar social background. In fact, Model discovered a modest, but significant earnings deficit for Afro-Caribbean men relative to their African-American counterparts. There were also notable variations for different Caribbean nationality groups. Men from Trinidad and the Virgin Islands were at parity with African-American men in earnings. Men from other Caribbean countries showed the same earnings disadvantage relative to native-born black men found in the overall sample. But swamping the earnings disparities between Afro-Caribbean and African-American men was the larger black-white difference. Both groups of black men earned considerably less than their white counterparts.

Model found an altogether different and intriguing pattern among women. Afro-Caribbean and African-American women had very similar earnings. The immigrant women had slightly lower income than the native born, but most of this small disparity could be explained by differences in social background characteristics. More surprising were the author's findings on black-white comparisons. Caribbean-born women's earnings were, at a minimum, equivalent to those of white women. In fact, Afro-Caribbean women actually had a modest earnings advantage over their white counterparts with similar social background characteristics. The same pattern held in comparisons between African-American and white women.[10]

Analyses of 1990 census data have yielded similarly complex results on the earnings patterns of Afro-Caribbeans and African Americans. Again, Model's work (1995) is instructive. She finds the gross earnings of first-generation Afro-Caribbean immigrants are lower than those of African Americans.[11] There is, however, an important caveat. It turns out the earnings of Afro-Caribbeans catch up with those of African Americans when year of arrival and length of residence in the country are taken into account. Moreover, the earnings of second-generation Afro-Caribbeans are consistently higher than those of both their first-generation

---

[10] Model's findings on white and black women's earnings parallel those of Farley and Allen (1987).

[11] Model finds more variation from this pattern in comparisons of net earnings.

predecessors and African Americans. A couple of late 1990s studies (Dodoo 1997; Kalmijn 1996) also concluded English-speaking Caribbean immigrants show higher earnings than African Americans. All told, then, the data indicate the earnings advantage Afro-Caribbean immigrants had over African Americans three decades ago has since mostly evaporated. Although this trend is less pronounced or non-existent for particular Afro-Caribbean subgroups, one pattern has remained consistent over the last three decades: both native- and Caribbean-born blacks earn less than their white counterparts in the United States.

Education

The data on educational outcomes reflect an even clearer pattern of a disappearing edge for Afro-Caribbean immigrants than the earnings statistics. Roger Waldinger's analyses of census data (1996) show a trend toward declining educational attainment for foreign-born blacks and increasing attainment for their native-born counterparts. In 1970, black immigrants were one and a half times more likely to have graduated from college than all other New Yorkers. African Americans, in contrast, were 70 percent less likely to have a college degree than the rest of the city population. By 1980, the number of college degree holders among foreign-born blacks had declined. The immigrants were 35 percent less likely to have a college degree than all other New Yorkers. Yet they were still more likely to have one than their native-born black counterparts. By 1990, however, black immigrants were no more likely to have graduated from college than native-born blacks. Both groups were roughly 50 percent less likely to hold college degrees than all other New Yorkers. Furthermore, although the two groups had roughly the same high school dropout rates in 1970 and 1980, a serious disparity had turned up by 1990. The census data for that year show black immigrants were twice as likely to have dropped out of high school as native-born blacks. It is clear Afro-Caribbeans, in New York at least, no longer boast an edge over their native-born African-American counterparts in high school educational attainment.

Employment

Although Caribbean-born black immigrants no longer hold a clear earnings or education advantage over African Americans, they have retained an edge over their native-born counterparts on other socioeconomic indicators. Studies consistently find the immigrants have higher rates of labor force participation and lower rates of public assistance receipt than their African-American counterparts (e.g., Waters 1999; Model 1995, 1991). In 1990, Afro-Caribbean men were 12 percent more likely to be employed than African-American men. The disparity was even greater among women. The labor force participation rate for Afro-Caribbean women was 14 percent higher than that of their African-American counterparts (Model 1995). Caribbean-born black women were more likely, in fact, to be in the labor force than any other demographic group in New York.

Equally as striking, Model found Afro-Caribbean female household heads were more likely be employed and less likely to be on public assistance than their African-American counterparts. More generally, though, Afro-Caribbeans had fewer single-earner households than African Americans. Put another way, Afro-Caribbeans had higher marriage rates, and thus more two-earner households, than their native-born black counterparts. Caribbean-born black men were 14 percent more likely to be married than American-born black men; Afro-Caribbean women were 8 percent more likely to be than their American-born counterparts. All told, Afro-Caribbeans have an edge over African Americans on a few indicators of socioeconomic well-being but fare about the same or worse than native-born black counterparts on others.

III. RECONSIDERING THE AFRO-CARIBBEAN SUCCESS STORY

What conclusions might we draw from this brief review of socioeconomic data on Afro-Caribbeans and African Americans? First, it is clear the popular stereotype of Afro-Caribbean success relative to that of African Americans has been overstated on several counts. The Caribbean advantage in education and earnings has diminished over time, and their edge in business enterprise perhaps never existed. The decline in earnings and education advantages for Afro-Caribbeans is a clear contravention of the standard pluralist trajectory, which predicts steady socioeconomic progress over time.

The disappearance of the educational advantage, in particular, suggests today's Afro-Caribbean newcomers are not as highly selected as those who immigrated to New York before the 1970s. Afro-Caribbean immigrants who entered the United States before 1965 were drawn predominantly from the middle classes of their home countries. Those who migrated between 1900 and 1932 had much higher literacy rates than their compatriots back home (Holder 1987). The small cohort who arrived between the late 1930s and 1965 included many "young professionals who [entered] on student visas and stayed after completing their degrees" (Kasinitz 1992, 26). Others immigrated for certain occupations, such as nursing. These early immigrants therefore had clear educational advantages over African Americans, who were predominantly poor, rural, and undereducated for most of the first half of the twentieth century.

Today's Afro-Caribbean immigrants, however, exhibit a much wider range of educational and class backgrounds upon entering the United States. Some continue to migrate to this country for certain occupations. There is still, for instance, a modest but steady influx of nurses from the Caribbean to New York City hospitals. But many more immigrants enter the country under family reunification provisions and are not selected on educational or occupational criteria. As a group, then, these more recent immigrants have proportionally fewer educational advantages than their predecessors.

The fact that today's Afro-Caribbean newcomers also work more than African Americans, but have no appreciable earnings advantage to show for it, is consistent with the classic immigrant story. Immigrants are typically more willing than natives to accept low-status jobs, low wages, and long work hours.[12] Most migrate in search of whatever economic opportunities they can find. This often means they are willing to accept low pay and less than ideal working conditions in the secondary labor market. The data on Afro-Caribbeans' earnings and labor force participation appear to conform to this standard immigrant profile. These foreign-born blacks, on average, are probably more willing than their native-born counterparts to work long hours in low-status jobs, for little pay. Afro-Caribbean women, for example, are far more likely than their African-American counterparts to work as domestics in private households (Model 1995, 549).

This pattern of hard work for little pay raises questions about whether employers actually prefer Afro-Caribbeans rather than African Americans because of the immigrants' superior cultural values, as some researchers have argued. Employers' purported preference for Afro-Caribbean values on the job translates into very limited remunerative benefits for the

---

[12] Immigrants may evaluate jobs according to how they compare with employment opportunities back home. Even a low-paying job may appear desirable from this perspective. The immigrants also may assess their status from this transnational frame of reference. See Chapters 5, 6, and 7 on ways the transnational lens informs the immigrants' political thinking and sense of themselves.

immigrants themselves. Judging from the patterns in the data, employers do seem to prefer Afro-Caribbean workers, but they stop short of paying the group higher wages for their superior cultural values. What employers actually might prefer about Afro-Caribbeans, then, are not their distinctive cultural attributes per se; rather, it might be their immigrant status – that is, their willingness to work long hours for little pay. What employers prefer about Afro-Caribbeans is perhaps what they appreciate in immigrant workers in general. The Afro-Caribbean values Sowell has heralded and employers are said to esteem could be the standard immigrant ethos, only dressed up as culture.

White employers' reported preference for Afro-Caribbeans also might be a convenient camouflage for racism. On its face, choosing the immigrants over their native-born counterparts announces these employers have no problem with blacks. They simply prefer "good blacks" with the right set of cultural attributes – Afro-Caribbeans – to "bad blacks" with the wrong set – African Americans. But this subtle racial hairsplitting is racism just the same, because it relies on prejudice and negative cultural stereotypes to make evaluative judgments about these two groups.[13] The positive standing Afro-Caribbeans have with white employers is based not only on their high regard for the immigrants' values but also on their more cynical views of African Americans.

Still, the data do lend support to several "positive" cultural stereotypes about Afro-Caribbeans.[14] Recall they are more likely to be employed, less likely to be on public assistance, and more likely to be married than their African-American counterparts. These findings hint at a distinctive set of Afro-Caribbean cultural tendencies, some of the very ones Sowell and others have emphasized. Whether they are products of historical legacy or structural conditions, these hints of culture have beneficial social consequences for the immigrants and cannot be simply dismissed or glossed over.[15]

---

[13] For a similar argument, see Kirschenman and Neckerman 1991.

[14] I use scare quotes to remind readers that whether cultural patterns are deemed positive or negative is a matter of social context. This might seem a deceptively simple point, but it bears noting. For example, in the United States, single-parent households are much more negatively stigmatized in the context of impoverished, black inner-city neighborhoods than they are in middle-class, suburban enclaves.

[15] Arguments about how history produces cultural tendencies in groups are quite common. Sowell (1978), for example, asserts Afro-Caribbean and African-American cultural differences stem from the contrasting slave histories of the Caribbean and the United States. Although I am unconvinced by Sowell's thesis in this particular case, I recognize that history mediated by institutions can inform group attitudes and behavior, an

What is more important than the source of these apparent cultural tendencies, however, is their impact on Afro-Caribbeans' overall prospects for social mobility and access to opportunities for enhancing or shoring up their socioeconomic status. These cultural resources, whether distinctive to Afro-Caribbeans or common to most immigrants, probably help these black ethnics secure some forms of employment and also may even help diminish the potential for racial friction in their dealings with whites in some settings. Yet the data show Afro-Caribbeans' cultural attributes do not give them a consistent ethnic economic advantage over African Americans. For all their cultural resources, these foreign-born blacks neither earn more, nor are they much more likely to have a high school diploma than their native-born counterparts. Even more significantly, both groups of blacks remain at a pronounced socioeconomic disadvantage relative to whites in this country.

The fact that Afro-Caribbeans' propensity for hard work and high labor force participation do not translate into economic parity with whites or any other clear-cut socioeconomic advantages for the immigrants is worth underscoring. Some of the keenest observers of American political culture have argued that "work" or the "willingness to work" confers civic standing to groups in the United States (e.g., Shklar 1991). Although this claim has not been validated with anything like systematic empirical testing, it is certainly a reasonable proposition consistent with the broad outlines of American history. Immigrants from Europe, for example, seem to have been able to overcome the hostilities and suspicions of established Americans and win acceptance into the mainstream by dint of their hard work and sacrifice in pursuit of the American Dream (e.g., Hochschild 1995).[16] On the other hand, public opinion data indicate lingering antiblack prejudice among whites stems in part from their belief that blacks are lazy and unwilling to work hard (Gilens 1999).

Afro-Caribbean immigrants confound this stereotype, have a reputation for hard work, and yet are unable to achieve the same level of

insight reflected in some of the analyses developed later in this study. See Chapters 6 and 7 especially.

Structural conditions that shape culture may be economic or institutional. Consider how legal institutions in this country might affect Afro-Caribbean marriage rates. The family reunification provisions under which so many of them migrate to the United States may possibly account for why Afro-Caribbeans are more likely to be married than their native-born counterparts. Who has not heard anecdotes about immigrants marrying American citizens to secure permanent legal residency?

[16] Their European backgrounds and non-black phenotypes may have helped ease their path to ultimate acceptance as well.

economic security and social acceptance as whites. Their inability to win such rewards suggests hard work and good cultural habits do not ensure blacks full or firm civic and social standing in the United States. They, like African Americans, are disadvantaged relative to whites on a number of socioeconomic dimensions. This stark, black-white empirical reality virtually dwarfs the ethnic socioeconomic differences between African Americans and Afro-Caribbeans. It suggests whatever cultural advantages Afro-Caribbeans have, they are not completely spared the racial disadvantages their native-born counterparts have suffered. This proves "even 'good culture' is no match for racial discrimination" (Waters 1999, 10).

IV. AFRO-CARIBBEAN RESIDENTIAL PATTERNS

Nowhere is this trend more apparent than in the residential patterns of these black immigrants. Afro-Caribbean New Yorkers live predominantly in three areas of the city: central Brooklyn, the northern Bronx, and the southeasternmost edge of Queens. Brooklyn is home to the largest numbers of Afro-Caribbeans. The immigrants are concentrated in the Crown Heights, East Flatbush, and Flatbush sections of the borough. Afro-Caribbeans in the Bronx live in neighborhoods around Eastchester and along Gun Hill Road to Williamsbridge. In Queens they have made their homes in Jamaica, Laurelton, Cambria Heights, and Queens Village. These three areas – central Brooklyn, the northern Bronx, and east Queens – are not only centers of Caribbean settlement; they are also the location where the vast majority of black New Yorkers live in mostly segregated neighborhoods.

Residential Segregation

The main areas of Caribbean residential settlement all fall within solidly black sections of New York City. As Crowder and Tedrow (2001) show, these three areas form a solid core of contiguous census tracts in which blacks constitute between 80 and 100 percent of the population (see Figure 2.1). All three had even higher levels of black residential concentration in 2000 than they had in 1980, suggesting a trend toward deepening segregation. The total number or percentage of blacks in an area is not an exact measure of segregation. Segregation is actually an index of a group's residential distribution relative to that of other groups: that is, a measure of the likelihood of residential contact between individuals from different groups. By this index, Afro-Caribbeans and African Americans

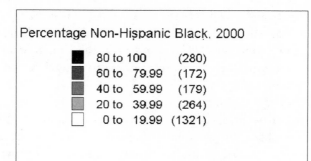

Percentage Non-Hispanic Black, 2000

■	80 to 100	(280)
	60 to 79.99	(172)
	40 to 59.99	(179)
	20 to 39.99	(264)
□	0 to 19.99	(1321)

FIGURE 2.1. Distribution of Non-Hispanic Black Population in tracts in New York City, 2000. Numbers in parentheses are numbers of census tracts.

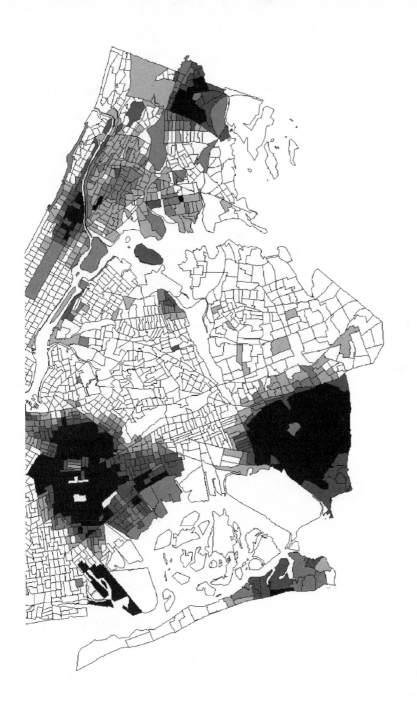

TABLE 2.4. *Indices of Dissimilarity between Selected Groups, New York City,*
1980 and 1990

Group	Afro-Caribbeans			African Americans		
	1980	1990	Difference	1980	1990	Difference
Afro-Caribbeans	—	—	—	0.432	0.401	−0.031
African Americans	0.432	0.401	−0.031	—	—	—
Non-Hispanic Whites	0.817	0.831	0.014	0.83	0.84	0.01
Japanese	0.9	0.916	0.017	0.896	0.907	0.011
Chinese	0.832	0.856	0.024	0.854	0.861	0.008
Filipino	0.842	0.848	0.006	0.852	0.865	0.013
Korean	0.904	0.908	0.004	0.914	0.913	−0.001
Asian Indian	0.761	0.763	0.002	0.786	0.797	0.012
Vietnamese	0.949	0.901	−0.048	0.964	0.919	−0.046
Other Asian	0.833	0.791	−0.043	0.827	0.803	−0.024
Mexican	0.703	0.772	0.07	0.628	0.746	0.118
Puerto Rican	0.678	0.674	−0.004	0.571	0.551	0.02
Cuban	0.735	0.727	−0.007	0.727	0.699	−0.028
Other Hispanic	0.676	0.671	−0.005	0.648	0.631	−0.017
All others	0.612	0.605	−0.007	0.69	0.631	−0.032

Source: Reprinted with permission from Kyle D. Crowder and Lucky M. Tedrow, "West Indians
and the Residential Landscape of New York," in *Islands in the City: West Indian Migration to
New York*, ed. Nancy Foner (Berkeley: University of California Press), © 2001 The Regents of
the University of California.

TABLE 2.5. *Neighborhood Exposure to Other Racial Groups, 2000*

Population	% Same Population	% Blacks	% White
African American	45	60.7	9
Afro-Caribbean	25.4	65.8	9.9
All blacks	61.6	61.6	9.4

Source: Lewis Mumford Center for Comparative Urban and Regional Research.

almost never have residential contact with whites and only occasionally
share neighborhoods with other groups. They are, in short, the two most
residentially segregated groups in New York City.

Tables 2.4 and 2.5 show different dimensions of the residential segregation African-American and Afro-Caribbean New Yorkers have experienced over the last three decades. Consider the indices of spatial dissimilarity for 1980 and 1990 presented in Table 2.4. Without delving into too
much technical detail, the index of dissimilarity compares the residential
distribution of two groups and is commonly interpreted as the proportion

of either group's population who would have to change census tracts in order to be evenly distributed across the city (ibid., 88). High indices mean high levels of residential segregation, and hence little contact between the two groups. In 1980 and 1990, Afro-Caribbeans and African Americans were both quite segregated from most Asian New Yorkers. Each had notably more contact with the city's Latino residents, although there was nonetheless a considerable degree of black-Latino segregation. But the most severe segregation in New York over the last three decades has been between blacks and non-Hispanic whites. Afro-Caribbean and African-American indices of spatial dissimilarity from whites in both 1980 and 1990 were roughly 83, indicating very high levels of segregation. Their level of segregation from whites remained high in 2000, still hovering in the low eighties (Logan and Deane 2003).

Table 2.5 presents 2000 census data on the racial composition of Afro-Caribbean and African-American neighborhoods in New York. More precisely, it shows the degree of neighborhood exposure to whites and other blacks for the average Afro-Caribbean and African-American New Yorker. The exposure indices for both African Americans and Afro-Caribbeans to whites are under 10 percent. Their likelihood of exposure to the city's white residents is markedly lower than that of Latino and Asian New Yorkers. On the other hand, the average Afro-Caribbean and African American have greater exposure to other blacks in their neighborhoods than Latinos and Asians have to their own coethnics in theirs.

All in all, Afro-Caribbeans and African Americans have more residential contact by far with each other than with any other single group in the city. Indeed, the level of Afro-Caribbean segregation in New York rivals that of their native-born black counterparts. They are, in short, the two most segregated groups in the city. African Americans are known to be the most segregated group in the country (Massey and Denton 1993). In light of these data, Afro-Caribbeans also can claim this dubious distinction.

Of course, one could argue the high level of Afro-Caribbean segregation is to be expected for a new group of immigrants. The degree of Afro-Caribbean segregation in 1980 was consistent with the standard concentrated residential patterns researchers predict for immigrants in the early phase of their settlement and adjustment to the United States. By 1980, Afro-Caribbeans had been immigrating to New York in the tens of thousands for only ten years. By 1990, however, the level of Afro-Caribbean segregation from whites had not diminished. On the contrary, it had increased, and it has continued to inch upward since (Logan

FIGURE 2.2. Percentage Caribbean in Tracts in New York City, 2000. Numbers in parentheses are numbers of census tracts.

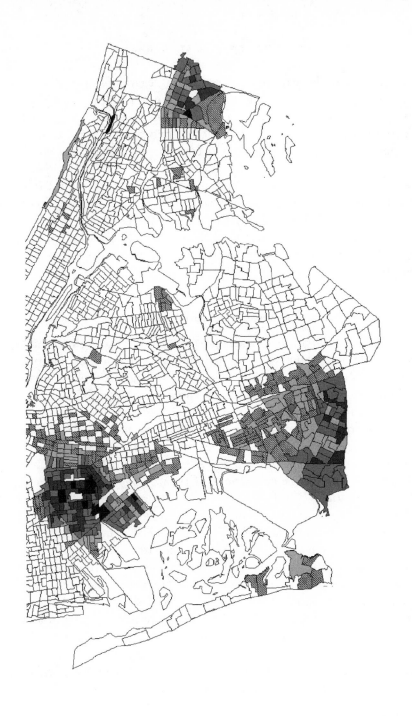

and Deane 2003). This pattern of increasing segregation is another clear contravention of the assimilationist predictions of the pluralist model.

Racial barriers seem to prevent Afro-Caribbeans from achieving greater residential integration with whites and other non-black groups. Despite their apparent cultural and slight socioeconomic advantages, the immigrants have been no more able than African Americans to set up house in majority-white neighborhoods or leave majority-black ones. On the job, whites may prefer to hire Afro-Caribbeans rather than African Americans. But it is clear that they are not eager to live alongside either of these groups. The distinction between "good blacks" and "bad blacks" may be meaningful for whites in the office or the factory, but it does not extend to their front stoop.

Afro-Caribbean Residential Enclaves

Afro-Caribbeans' slight socioeconomic edge over African Americans does show plainly in one aspect of the immigrants' residential patterns. Census data indicate Afro-Caribbeans have carved out their own distinctive ethnic residential enclaves within the three predominantly black sections of New York (see Figures 2.2, 2.3, and 2.4). "The clear conclusion to be drawn from these maps is that [Afro-Caribbeans] are clearly not evenly distributed across the areas of the city. Instead, by 1980 they were highly concentrated in distinctly [Afro-Caribbean] neighborhoods constituting highly discernible subsections of each of the city's three large black agglomerations and these distinct [Afro-Caribbean] enclaves persisted into the 1990s" (Crowder and Tedrow 2001, 95). Indeed, the data show these Caribbean enclaves not only have persisted, but also have expanded and become more consolidated in the last decade.

The presence of distinct Afro-Caribbean enclaves would be unremarkable for any group of immigrants, but for the fact these residential areas tend to be of higher socioeconomic standing than the surrounding African-American areas. Tables 2.6, 2.7, and 2.8 compare Afro-Caribbean and African-American neighborhoods – census tracts with significant concentrations of each group – on several socioeconomic indicators over the last few decades. The Afro-Caribbean neighborhoods have higher median household incomes, higher levels of home ownership, and higher proportions of college-educated residents than the African-American neighborhoods.[17]

---

[17] Of the three major areas of Afro-Caribbean residential concentration, the neighborhoods in east Queens show the highest socioeconomic quality by far.

The disparity in homeownership levels between Afro-Caribbean and African-American neighborhoods is particularly striking. In 1990, almost half of the housing units in neighborhoods where Afro-Caribbeans constituted 50 to 60 percent of the population were owner occupied (Table 2.6). In contrast, only about a quarter of the units were owner occupied in neighborhoods with comparable proportions of African Americans. In 2000, the homeowner disparity between Afro-Caribbean and African-American neighborhoods remained (Tables 2.7 and 2.8). It is worth noting the average homeownership rate for black New Yorkers as a whole is lower than the national average for the black population. The disparity is due to the fact that black New Yorkers are heavily concentrated in inner-city areas (Logan and Deane 2003).

Poverty is thus a significant problem in New York's Afro-Caribbean and African-American neighborhoods but is notably more pronounced in the latter (Tables 2.7 and 2.8). Almost one-third of the residents in Brooklyn's mostly heavily African-American neighborhoods live below the poverty line. In contrast, only one-fifth of the residents in the borough's most Afro-Caribbean neighborhoods live in poverty. New York's Caribbean-born blacks appear to live in more economically stable environs than their native-born counterparts. Crowder and Tedrow (2001) are careful to note they do not know exactly why Afro-Caribbean neighborhoods exhibit stronger socioeconomic characteristics than African-American areas. As they (101) point out, it could be the socioeconomic advantages of the immigrants themselves, or it could be their greater ability to gain access to neighborhoods with higher-status residents.[18]

This last observation brings me to one other important point about Afro-Caribbean residential enclaves in New York. Quite a few of these neighborhoods are located on the "fringes of larger black agglomerations." As Crowder and Tedrow (100) explain, these enclaves are near long-established black areas but also encompass neighborhoods that not long ago were home to significant numbers of whites. This is especially true of central Brooklyn, where white exodus was followed by black succession in the 1970s. Several observers of Afro-Caribbean life in New York (Kasinitz 1992; Foner 1987) have noted the immigrants may have been among the first black pioneers in the succession process. The 1980 census data confirm the most heavily Afro-Caribbean residential areas had

---

[18] The authors hypothesize these ethnic residential enclaves act as a social buffer for the immigrants, providing "protection from relegation to those largely African-American neighborhoods where access to quality public services is most limited."

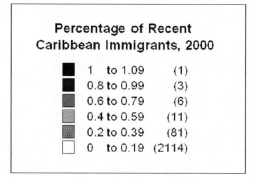

FIGURE 2.3. Percentage of All Recent Caribbean Immigrants to Tracts in New York City, 2000. Numbers in parentheses are numbers of census tracts.

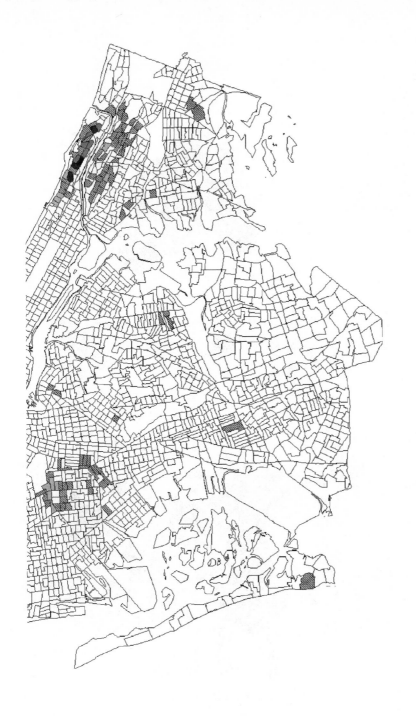

Map 1: North Bronx Enclave

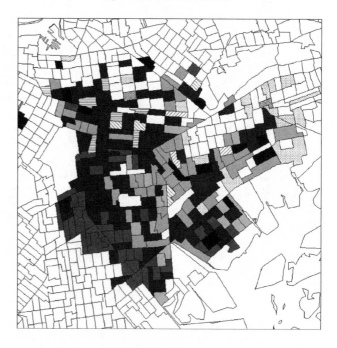

Map 2: North Bronx Enclave

FIGURE 2.4. Composition of Caribbean Population in New York City Enclaves, 2000. Numbers in parentheses are numbers of census tracts.

Composition of Caribbean Population
Caribbean Enclaves in New York City, 2000

	< 10% Caribbean	(1668)
	Ethnically mixed	(153)
	Haitian	(64)
	Jamaican	(122)
	Jamaican & mixed comp.	(69)
	Jamaican & Haitian	(28)
	Jamaican & Trin.-Tob.	(8)
	Jamaican & Guyanese	(9)
	Jamaican & other Caribbean	(5)
	Trinidadian-Tobagonian	(9)
	Guyanese	(78)
	Other Caribbean	(3)

Map 3: East Queens Enclave

TABLE 2.6. *Characteristics of Tracts by Concentration of Afro-Caribbeans and African Americans, Weighted by Total Group Population in Tract, 1990*

	Group Presence in Total Tract Population (in %)										
	20–29.99		30–39.99		40–49.99		50–59.99		60 and above		Total Five Boroughs
Mean Tract Characteristics	Afro-Caribbean	African American	Afro-Caribbean	African American	Afro-Caribbean	African American	Afro-Caribbean	African American	Afro-Caribbean	African American	
Socioeconomic											
% housing units owner occupied	37.48	17.70	29.24	18.94	29.44	18.00	41.68	27.39	–	24.91	34.67
Median household income ($1,000s)	32.42	21.95	31.96	24.10	32.24	22.57	35.92	27.62	–	22.16	31.48
% of adults with some college	39.34	29.68	38.72	33.17	38.65	30.38	41.09	36.21	–	30.48	38.62
% of adults college graduated	14.85	11.84	13.70	13.22	13.58	10.50	14.09	13.52	–	9.64	19.53
Racial composition											
% non-Hispanic white, 1980	24.18	27.13	15.41	24.04	14.24	12.92	15.84	12.05	–	3.07	53.31
Change in % non-Hispanic white, 1980–90	–12.33	–10.99	–9.43	–10.31	–10.57	–6.04	–12.93	–5.82	–	–1.29	–8.53
% Asian, 1980	1.85	2.50	2.43	1.95	1.64	1.50	1.51	1.18	–	.50	3.05
Change in % Asian, 1980–90	1.41	1.88	–.57	.97	.02	.19	–.56	.26	–	.06	3.52
% Hispanic, 1980	13.10	42.49	11.28	31.21	9.34	25.49	7.58	15.94	–	9.15	18.98
Change in % Hispanic, 1980–1990	.93	5.05	–.79	4.67	–2.92	2.89	–2.78	1.10	–	2.03	3.10
N	110	143	57	116	38	114	7	107	–	283	2,106

Source: Reprinted with permission from Kyle D. Crowder and Lucky M. Tedrow, "West Indians and the Residential Landscape of New York," in *Islands in the City: West Indian Migration to New York,* ed. Nancy Foner (Berkeley: University of California Press), © 2001 The Regents of the University of California.

TABLE 2.7. *Characteristics of New York City's Afro-Caribbean Neighborhoods, 2000*

	Flatbush	Jamaica	Williamsbridge
Total population	693,944	384,629	200,787
% white	8.2	4	8.9
% black	77.8	75.7	65.5
% African American	44.5	51.3	38.6
% Afro-Caribbean	32.1	23.3	25
% Hispanic	10.4	10	21.8
% Asian	2.8	7.5	2.6
% immigrants	48.5	37	37.8
% recent immigrants	33	27.6	33.5
% non-citizen, blacks	23.1	14	19.2
% home owners	28.2	67	39.8
% below poverty line	21.3	10.4	17.1
% college educated	15.7	18.8	17.6
% unemployed	12.7	9	10.4
Median income, total	$34,221.00	$49,382.00	$37,930.00
Median income, white	$39,298.00	$38,695.00	$30,296.00
Median income, black	$34,960.00	$50,971.00	$41,069.00
Median income, Hispanic	$27,564.00	$47,823.00	$32,484.00
Median income, Asian	$34,533.00	$52,511.00	$47,628.00

Source: John Logan and John Mollenkopf, "People and Politics in America's Big Cities," Drum Major Institute for Public Policy.

larger white populations than predominantly African-American sections of the city. This pattern has held over the last two decades.

It is not clear whether Afro-Caribbeans have an easier time gaining access to formerly white areas or whether they simply are more inclined than their African-American counterparts to push their way into them. Whatever the case, though, the eventual outcome for Afro-Caribbean immigrants is the same as it has been for African Americans: persistent residential segregation. Afro-Caribbean neighborhoods experienced a steeper decline in their number of white residents than any other neighborhoods in New York during the twenty-year span between 1980 and 2000. This trend suggests black immigrant encroachment was followed predictably by white flight, which is consistent with the historical pattern for African Americans. Although Afro-Caribbeans hold a notable residential advantage over their native-born black counterparts, it has failed to win them access to stably integrated neighborhoods. Residential segregation characterizes life in the United States for Afro-Caribbeans no less than it does for African Americans. It ultimately confines both groups of

TABLE 2.8. *Charactersitics of New York City's African-American Neighborhoods, 2000*

	Flatbush	Jamaica	Williamsbridge
Total population	876,699	294,767	119,338
% white	4.81	2.47	4.71
% black	77.44	86.68	74.31
% African American	53.3	61.4	41.35
% Afro-Caribbean	22.94	23.98	30.59
% Hispanic	14.94	7.02	17.65
% Asian	2.02	2.45	2.38
% immigrants	31.38	29.49	36.93
% recent immigrants	34.91	28.84	34.1
% non-citizen, blacks	13.95	11.43	18.14
% home owners	20.56	64.57	38.23
% below poverty line	30.74	13.34	19.81
% college educated	13.04	16.81	16.72
% unemployed	16.94	10.41	11.4
Median income, total	$28,737.11	$48,523.78	$38,190.57
Median income, white	$35,783.46	$36,237.21	$26,937.09
Median income, black	$29,796.63	$49,668.18	$40,967.62
Median income, Hispanic	$21,597.92	$45,682.82	$28,877.70
Median income, Asian	$31,649.17	$42,769.99	$45,774.74

Source: John Logan and John Mollenkopf, "People and Politics in America's Big Cities," Drum Major Institute for Public Policy.

blacks to neighborhoods of lower socioeconomic quality than their white counterparts in the city.

V. CONCLUSION

The research reviewed in this chapter suggests the early scholarly claims and still popular stereotypes of Afro-Caribbean success overstate the differences between the immigrants and their African-American counterparts. Caribbean-born blacks have an advantage over African Americans on several socioeconomic dimensions, to be sure: they show greater labor force participation, lower reliance on public assistance, better neighborhood quality, and higher marriage rates. On other important socioeconomic indicators, such as education and income, however, the immigrants do not have a clear edge. The differences between Afro-Caribbeans and African Americans on these other variables are either nonexistent or quite slight. So there is evidence both for and against the idea that Caribbean-born blacks are more successful than their native-born counterparts. At the very least, the ambiguity in the research findings counsels against definitive claims about an Afro-Caribbean edge over African Americans.

But these results reveal more than indeterminacy. They also show the immigrants share many of the same racial disadvantages as their American-born black counterparts relative to whites. When compared to whites, Afro-Caribbeans and African Americans both have income, education, and neighborhood quality deficits.[19] Both groups also appear to have difficulty translating their economic gains into residential mobility, and both experience uniquely high levels of segregation. As Kasinitz (1992, 91) notes, "if [Afro-Caribbeans] look like immigrants when compared to [American-born] blacks, they still resemble blacks when compared to whites." In sum, Afro-Caribbeans have an occasional socioeconomic edge on African Americans but have yet to make up the black disadvantage relative to whites.

This finding has important theoretical implications for this study and the ongoing debates over who should benefit from affirmative action policies. First, the latest incarnation of the affirmative action debate again casts Afro-Caribbeans as model minorities, a reprise of their role from the fierce 1980s ideological battles over the policy. But there is a new wrinkle this time around: it is not conservatives, but rather progressive African-American public intellectuals who are casting Caribbean immigrants in the model minority role. Although the names and ideological affinities of the actors have changed, the script is still the same. When these intellectuals suggest Afro-Caribbeans are taking away affirmative action slots from more deserving African Americans, they run the risk of several troubling and misleading interpretations they probably do not intend.

First, their position implies African Americans have encountered more racial hardships in the United States than their Caribbean-born counterparts. Although this may be true enough as a matter of historical experience, it nonetheless obscures the racial disadvantages Afro-Caribbeans currently suffer. The empirical evidence may be ambiguous on whether the immigrants have a socioeconomic edge over their native-born counterparts, but what it does make clear is that Afro-Caribbeans and African Americans both are hobbled by racial obstacles and both lag behind whites on practically every indicator of socioeconomic security. Both groups, for instance, have difficulty moving into predominantly white neighborhoods with good schools and high-quality public services. Debates over whether

---

[19] The finding on women's earnings is the lone exception.

one or the other group of blacks has borne the greater share of racial hardship deflect attention from this larger, persistent pattern of black-white inequality.

Second, arguing African Americans are more fitting or deserving beneficiaries of affirmative action than Afro-Caribbeans potentially recasts the policy debate along lines that could undermine the overall antidiscrimination cause. The formulation pits African Americans against Afro-Caribbeans in a competition for affirmative action benefits. It suggests Afro-Caribbean gains in elite university admissions, for instance, are at the expense of deserving African Americans. What used to be a fight mostly between whites and non-whites over the moral legitimacy and practical value of the policy thus becomes a conflict between two groups of non-whites over who should reap its rewards.[20] The danger in this turn is that it could lead affirmative action supporters blindly down a slippery slope.

Conservatives might agree with these African-American intellectuals that foreign-born blacks should not receive affirmative action benefits, either because they have not faced as much discrimination as native-born blacks or because they do well enough in spite of it. The argument is not much of a stretch from the usual conservative stance. There is little analytical distinction or logical difference between this position and the old conservative line that affirmative action has exceeded its shelf life insofar as discrimination has diminished and blacks are doing better in this post–civil rights era. Both positions minimize ongoing discrimination against blacks and weaken the overall antiracist justification for affirmative action. The socioeconomic data showing a pattern of continuing African-American and Afro-Caribbean disadvantage relative to whites, however, prove there are still grounds for affirmative action and other policies aimed at diminishing racial inequality.

Whether Afro-Caribbean immigrants are inclined to demand such reform policies and follow in the political footsteps of their African-American counterparts or not is another question and the focus of this book. The socioeconomic data reviewed in this chapter lend some empirical support to the minority group perspective on political incorporation. The clear socioeconomic evidence of Afro-Caribbean disadvantage relative to whites suggests the immigrants face some of same racial challenges that complicated and shaped African Americans' bid for political

---

[20] See Kim (1999) for a similar argument on conflicts over affirmative action between African Americans and Asian Americans.

incorporation. It is plausible, then, that the immigrants might follow the same strategies African Americans employed in their own bid for incorporation, as the minority group model predicts. This trajectory would suggest incorporation is still a difficult enterprise for blacks in this country.

But the more ambiguous evidence of an Afro-Caribbean socioeconomic edge over African Americans suggests the pluralist path is also a possibility for the immigrants. If Afro-Caribbeans are facing discrimination yet making socioeconomic progress and bypassing their African-American counterparts in some cases, it is possible these black ethnics could follow the mold established by the former European immigrants turned white ethnics, as predicted by the pluralist model. It would be an ironic instance of historical repetition, to say the least, if these Caribbean-born blacks managed to overcome discrimination, leapfrog over African Americans, win acceptance into the mainstream, and achieve incorporation without significant demands for systemic reform. They essentially would be replicating the pattern established by European immigrants in the last century.

VI. A NOTE ON THE RESEARCH SAMPLE

The coming chapters unravel the political incorporation patterns of Afro-Caribbean New Yorkers to determine whether there is strong evidence for either of these perspectives. Before I move on to these empirical chapters, however, I want to provide a brief descriptive overview of the interview sample for this study. In many ways, the respondents resemble the Afro-Caribbean achievers evoked by the model minority stereotype. The fifty-nine interview subjects – thirty-five women and twenty-four men – were from various English-speaking Caribbean nations. Jamaican, Guyanese, and Trinidadian immigrants made up the majority of the sample (see Table 2.9). Fifty-one of the respondents were residents of Brooklyn. The

TABLE 2.9. *Distribution of Sample by National Origin*

Country of Origin	N
Jamaica	21
Guyana	12
Trinidad	10
Barbados	5
Grenada	4
Other	7

remaining eight lived in Queens. As a group, they had an average length of residence in the United States of twenty-three years.

The majority of the immigrants claimed a middle-class background, but a handful identified as working class. Thirty-eight were married, and of those, thirty-two had children. Twenty-nine of the respondents were homeowners, twenty-one in Brooklyn and the remaining eight in Queens. Most of the immigrants also had at least some college education, and all had completed high school. Fifty-five were employed, and the remaining four were retired. Most of the employed respondents had a white-collar job in the service sector, and a few had a position in government. Five of the respondents, all men, were self-employed and had their own business.

These interview subjects had more socioeconomic security than the average Afro-Caribbean New Yorker. But as I explain in Appendix A, the fact that these respondents as a group were perhaps better off than the average Afro-Caribbean immigrant proved to be an analytic virtue for this study. Following the literature on political behavior, I reasoned these solidly middle-class Afro-Caribbeans would be more politically active than the average newcomer to the United States. Middle-class individuals tend to be more civically engaged and prone to participate in politics than their lower-class counterparts (e.g., Verba, Schlozman, and Brady 1995). A close look at the political experiences of a group of middle- and working-class Afro-Caribbean immigrants thus promises to shed light on the dynamics of the incorporation process for these foreign-born blacks (refer to Appendix A for more details on the sample and methods). I also interviewed fifteen elites or leaders from the Afro-Caribbean community for the same reason. I turn to the immigrants' political experiences in the following chapters.

3

Letting Sleeping Giants Lie

Afro-Caribbean immigrants are the sleeping giant of New York City politics – a stirring Goliath not yet quite awakened to its full strength. This is a common lament among Afro-Caribbean community leaders. They complain low rates of political participation have prevented Afro-Caribbean immigrants from achieving a level of electoral and governing influence commensurate with their growing numbers. One leader, long active in the city's political life, fretfully observed, "In our community, we have too many aspiring leaders, and too few followers" (Sengupta 1996a, 8). He and other elites believe Afro-Caribbean political mobilization has been slow, halting, and frustratingly out of pace with the group's increasing numerical strength and the ambitions of its politically minded leaders. These worries about the relative political quiescence of Afro-Caribbean immigrants inevitably prompt questions about the group's long-term prospects for incorporation.

Under both the pluralist and the minority group perspectives, the incorporation process begins with new groups' mobilizing and participating in formal – and sometimes informal – politics. These first steps toward political integration are measured typically in increased rates of registration, voting, and – in the case of first-generation immigrants – naturalization. These basic political acts are all taken as indices of a group's growing engagement with the American democratic process. They often serve as building blocks for other forms of political participation. That is, engagement in one arena, say, voting in local elections, is usually correlated with participation in other arenas (Verba et al. 1995). These early actions are thus stepping stones to deeper engagement in the political process. Groups who show little or no growth on these measures appear disengaged and at risk of remaining on the margins of political life.

Recall from Chapter 1, however, Dahl and other pluralists were certain mobilization and participation in local politics would occur inevitably – as a matter of course – in all groups. Even if the groups themselves did not aggressively pursue electoral representation and influence, Dahl surmised the institutional workings of urban democracy would ultimately draw them into the political process. Traditional pluralist interpretations portrayed parties – political machines more specifically – as vital institutions for encouraging participation among immigrants and other groups on the margins of urban political life. Driven by their need for votes, parties courted new groups and drew them into the political process through naturalization and voter registration efforts, ethnic politicking, and patronage (e.g., Banfield and Wilson 1963; Dahl 1961). Parties thus functioned as immigrant mobilizers par excellence. By this account, the anxious worries about low participation rates and quiescence among Afro-Caribbean immigrants in New York may be unfounded. Although the city's Democratic machine languished decades ago, parties nonetheless remain strong in New York. Perhaps, then, Afro-Caribbean New Yorkers will be mobilized and drawn into the formal political process by these party organizations, in keeping with Dahl's predictions.

Yet recent scholarship, challenging the conventional pluralist view and its teleological assumptions, advises against such hope. Erie (1985; 1988), Jones-Correa (1998), Mollenkopf (1992b), and others have shown political machines are rarely the mobilizers described in Dahl's account. Instead, they argue, parties typically function as gatekeepers.[1] Dominant parties, such as New York's Democratic organization, are usually reluctant to expand the electorate, for fear of destabilizing entrenched coalitions. They thus tend to protect the status quo: focusing on core constituencies, monopolizing access to the political process, and ignoring new groups. Contrary to the standard pluralist view, this interpretation suggests the normal institutional workings of urban politics do not lead inevitably to incorporation for new groups.

Hegemonic parties do not routinely encourage mobilization and participation among immigrants and other groups on the political margins. In the rare instances when they do, it is usually because they are faced with stiff party competition, insurgency, or crises that disrupt politics as usual. In short, parties leave newcomers to fend for themselves. By this

---

[1] Also see Shefter 1986; 1985; and Lin, n.d.

logic, immigrant groups will be slow to naturalize and participate in formal politics. Indeed, Erie (1988) concludes non-incorporation or slow, limited incorporation has been the norm for most groups in local politics.

This chapter considers recent patterns of political mobilization and participation among New York's Afro-Caribbean immigrants. The picture that emerges lends support to the revisionist view that parties more often ignore than court newcomers to the United States. Although hundreds of thousands of Afro-Caribbeans have been migrating to New York since the 1960s, the city's parties have played almost no proactive role in encouraging their political participation. New York's Democratic Party has been more inclined to ignore Afro-Caribbean newcomers, even in the face of their growing numbers, expanding residential enclaves, and obvious potential for electoral influence, in boroughs such as Brooklyn and Queens. Party elites mostly have turned a blind eye to the immigrants and sometimes even blocked their entry into the political system.

Adding to what revisionist scholars have found, I also show dominant parties neglect newcomers even when faced with the prospect of a serious threat from another party organization or insurgent politicians. In such cases, the self-interest of party insiders in holding on to power may prevent dominant organizations from responding to the strategic incentive to mobilize new voters. Even when competition increases, then, parties still tend to ignore immigrants. The data presented in this chapter show evidence of such neglect: naturalization, registration, and voting rates among the immigrants are relatively modest and group mobilization has been slow in coming. My conclusion is the normal institutional workings of New York's electoral and party politics are not enough to mobilize these black newcomers.

I. SIGNS OF MOBILIZATION AMONG AFRO-CARIBBEAN ELITES

Afro-Caribbean immigrants ought to be showing strong signs of political mobilization. On almost all of the prima facie indicators used to predict mobilization at the group level, Afro-Caribbeans would appear to be on track to make significant inroads into the political system. First, their historical presence in New York City dates back to the turn of the last century. More importantly, their numbers have increased dramatically in recent decades. Indeed, the Afro-Caribbean population since the 1980s has been large enough to make them a potentially important voting bloc in local elections. Recall also the immigrants have established distinct residential enclaves in Brooklyn, Queens, and the Bronx. They constitute, in fact, 20 percent or more of the total population in 180 of New York City's roughly 2,200 census tracts. Their geographic concentration gives them potential voting majorities, and thus distinct political advantages in a number of election districts in these three boroughs.[2]

The data cataloged in the previous chapter also suggest Afro-Caribbean residential enclaves have emerged in some of the most socioeconomically stable sections of New York's larger black neighborhoods. On average, these enclaves have better-educated, more affluent residents with higher rates of home ownership than surrounding African-American neighborhoods (Crowder and Tedrow 2001). This finding combined with data on individual socioeconomic outcomes suggests Afro-Caribbeans are not a desperately poor group of immigrants. The population boasts a modest middle-class cohort with time and money to devote to political life.[3] Finally, both the pluralist and minority group perspectives view the emergence of a shared sense of group identity as a critical first step in the path to political incorporation. It often binds newcomers together and prompts them to mobilize as a group. By this index, too, Afro-Caribbeans should be well on their way to political mobilization. These black immigrants have evinced strong feelings of group identity since the 1970s, when their numbers began to grow exponentially.[4] All told, these factors augur well for Afro-Caribbean political mobilization.

Beyond these promising predictors, there also have been what look like outward signs of incipient political incorporation. Increasingly since the 1970s, Afro-Caribbean elites have begun to use explicitly ethnic cues as a basis for political organization – a break with earlier historical patterns. There is a long tradition of Afro-Caribbean elite participation in New York's black political establishment. Some researchers (Kasinitz 1992; Holder 1980; Lewinson 1974), in fact, contended Afro-Caribbeans were disproportionately "overrepresented" among New York's black politicians between 1935 and 1965. Yet despite maintaining strong private ties to their home countries, these Afro-Caribbean elites made no special

---

[2] Although geographic concentration is a potential source of electoral advantage for Afro-Caribbean immigrants, it is, ironically enough, the result of their high rates of residential segregation. Among non-whites in New York, only African Americans experience comparably high or higher levels of spatial isolation. For more on the residential patterns of Afro-Caribbean immigrants, see Chapter 2. Also see Crowder and Tedrow 2001; Waldinger 1987.

[3] As Rokkan (1966, 105) famously observed, "Votes count but resources decide."

[4] See Chapter 6 for an analysis of Afro-Caribbean group identity and its political implications.

ethnic appeals to the small immigrant community. On the contrary, they tended to downplay their ethnic attachments in public and opted instead to market themselves as representatives of the black population at large. With the growth of the immigrant population in recent decades, however, a new generation of Afro-Caribbean leaders are promoting themselves specifically as representatives of this expanding ethnic constituency. Over the last two decades there has been a proliferation of self-consciously Afro-Caribbean political and civic organizations, aimed at appealing to the immigrants' ethnic group loyalties.

The first such organizational effort, in 1977, was the formation of "Caribbeans for Sutton," a group established to support the mayoral candidacy of Manhattan borough president, Percy Sutton. "It was the first time such a group had publicly declared itself to be Caribbeans for anything. The new strategy asserted, if perhaps not completely intentionally, that a Caribbean constituency existed and was able to use the political process to support Afro-Caribbean interests" (Kasinitz 1992, 223–224). It also marked the first time Afro-Caribbeans had articulated a group identity apart from African Americans in the electoral arena.

There has been since then a literal flowering of Afro-Caribbean ethnic organizations and voluntary associations. Although island-based voluntary associations have been a perennial fixture in New York's Afro-Caribbean community, they have assumed a far more public role in the lives of community leaders since the 1970s. Enterprising elites also have established a number of panethnic organizations that seek to unite immigrants from the entire Caribbean region. The Caribbean Action Lobby (CAL), the Caribbean Women's Health Association, and the Caribbean American Chamber of Commerce and Industry are some of the most well-known examples. These organizational efforts announce the presence of a distinctive Afro-Caribbean ethnic constituency in New York City politics (Kasinitz 1992).

Even more striking than the proliferation of ethnic organizations is the growing presence of Afro-Caribbean leaders in electoral politics. Parting with the pre-1965 pattern, Afro-Caribbean politicians have begun to make bids for elective office specifically as representatives of the Afro-Caribbean population. The first forays were in the early 1980s when reapportionment decisions created a number of predominantly black districts – a few of them encompassing some of the most heavily Afro-Caribbean neighborhoods in Brooklyn and Queens. Although these early campaigns proved unsuccessful, they nonetheless signaled the emergence of an Afro-Caribbean ethnic constituency.

In the past decade, there have been even more bids for elective office in the name of this growing black ethnic population, and better results. Redistricting decisions in 1991 again created several predominantly Afro-Caribbean legislative districts in Brooklyn and Queens, marginally enhancing the group's prospects for descriptive representation. Afro-Caribbeans have secured two seats in the city council and three in the state legislature over the past decade. They also have held positions on school and community boards in both Brooklyn and Queens. Although the group has yet to achieve a level of descriptive representation proportionate to their numbers and remain outside the city's governing coalition, they have nonetheless made notable inroads in the electoral arena. Several immigrant leaders also now play nominal roles in Brooklyn's Democratic Party organization.

Taken together, these electoral and organizational efforts by Afro-Caribbean leaders look like evidence of group mobilization. Indeed, a casual observer might take them as promising signs of Afro-Caribbean political incorporation and confirmation of Dahl's pluralist predictions. One writer (Dugger 1996, 28), for instance, asserted Afro-Caribbeans "have achieved more political power than any other immigrant group in New York City."

Yet such conclusions are premature at best, and perhaps even misleading. The signs of mobilization among Afro-Caribbean immigrants have been confined largely to the elite stratum. To be sure, there has been no shortage of Afro-Caribbean political elites – what Kasinitz (1992) calls ethnicity entrepreneurs – running for office, establishing ethnic organizations, and otherwise seeking to capitalize on the growing numbers of Afro-Caribbean immigrants in New York. Their activities have heightened the profile of the immigrants in city politics and give the impression Afro-Caribbeans are mobilizing rapidly and well on their way to full incorporation in keeping with Dahl's model.

II. NON-PARTICIPATION AMONG AFRO-CARIBBEAN IMMIGRANTS

Broadening the focus to the wider Afro-Caribbean immigrant population, however, reveals a different picture. Although the activities and ambitions of Afro-Caribbean political elites might give the impression of imminent group incorporation, the immigrants themselves actually have been slow to mobilize and participate in the political process. Non-participation is, in fact, the norm among these first-generation newcomers. For all their activity and ambition, Afro-Caribbean elites speak for the interests of a

TABLE 3.1. *Naturalization by Country of Origin, Top Sending Countries,*
1990

Country of Origin	Citizen %	Non-citizen %	Total
Anglophone Caribbean	37.20	62.80	332,024
Dominican Republic	25.20	74.80	221,620
China	42.60	57.40	114,565
Haiti	30.20	69.80	70,077
Colombia	24.50	75.50	67,429
Korea	27.00	73.00	56,446
Mexico	17.10	82.90	33,876
Phillipines	42.40	57.60	36,277
Eastern Europe and Russia	65.20	34.80	56,446

Source: 1990 Census Public Use Microdata Sample.

population that appears mostly disengaged from formal politics. As one immigrant leader (interview, November 22, 1996) complained, "There are many Caribbean Americans who don't participate or get involved in politics. They're not even citizens. They prefer to sit on their butts at home and not come out and vote, work in a campaign, and all the rest. They're pretty removed from politics." This is the frustrating reality elites have in mind when they complain the Afro-Caribbean immigrant community has "too many leaders, and too few followers."

The data on political participation bear out their complaint. For immigrants, the first step toward participation in the formal political process is the decision to become a United States citizen. Since the repeal of alien suffrage around the turn of the twentieth century, citizenship has been a requirement for voting in national, state, and city elections. To participate in the electoral process, immigrants must first pledge their allegiance to the United States. Naturalization rates are thus a good ground-floor measure of mainstream political mobilization among first-generation immigrants (Jones-Correa 1998).

By this index, Afro-Caribbean mobilization has been relatively slow and halting. Table 3.1 presents 1990 naturalization rates for New York's largest immigrant groups. With a 37 percent naturalization rate, the vast majority of Afro-Caribbeans – almost two-thirds – are not United States citizens. This relatively low figure is consistent with the overall naturalization patterns for recent first-generation immigrants, most of whom are not naturalized (Mollenkopf et al. 2001). Afro-Caribbeans, in fact, fall in the modest middle range of the overall naturalization trends for New York's foreign born. They are much more likely to become citizens than most

TABLE 3.2. *Naturalization by Country of Origin, Top Sending Countries: Post-1965 Voting-Age Immigrants in United States More Than Five Years, 1998*

Country of Origin	Citizen %	Non-citizen %	Total
Dominican Republic	38.40	61.60	306,047
Guyana	48.70	51.30	145,714
Mexico	2.10	97.90	111,777
Jamaica	45.90	54.10	103,315
China	54.50	45.50	101,185
Trinidad and Tobago	49.60	50.40	94,765
Russia	50.00	50.00	91,402
Haiti	39.90	60.00	82,487
Colombia	36.30	64.20	57,543
All countries	40.50	59.50	1,925,124

Source: March 1998 Current Population Survey, compiled in Mollenkopf et al. 1999.

Latino immigrants but less likely to do so than immigrants from Eastern Europe, the Middle East, and several Asian countries. By comparison to that of other groups, the naturalization rate for Afro-Caribbeans is not disturbingly low. But in light of the group's profile – its numbers, its socioeconomic standing, the size and activity of its elite stratum, and so on – researchers might expect a much higher overall figure.

Table 3.2 offers a more precise measure of naturalization trends among Afro-Caribbeans. It focuses only on voting-age immigrants eligible to naturalize – those living in the country for at least five years. It presents figures for Afro-Caribbeans from Jamaica, Trinidad and Tobago, and Guyana, the three largest immigrant cohorts from the anglophone Caribbean. The naturalization rate for these voting-age immigrants is roughly 10 percent higher than the figure for all voting-age immigrants.

Still, the majority of these immigrants are not United States citizens, even after living in the country for more than five years. The group's naturalization rate is moderate in comparison to the figures for all other eligible, voting-age immigrants in New York. Low naturalization rates mean low levels of participation in electoral politics. The thousands of Afro-Caribbean immigrants who have yet to naturalize essentially remain outside the formal political process. Although these immigrants' large numbers could translate into considerable electoral clout in New York City politics, they have yet to realize this potential.

Table 3.3 puts this unrealized electoral potential in bold relief. It compares current population figures for New York's major ethnic groups

TABLE 3.3. *Estimated Political Eligibility for Major Ethnic Groups, New York City, 2000–2001*

	Population	% of Total City Population	% Voting-Age	% Voting-Age Citizens	Estimated Voting-Age Citizens	% of All Voting-Age Citizens
Whites	2,801,267	35	73.2	70.2	1,966,000	43
African Americans	1,445,181	18	69.5	66.1	955,000	20.9
Afro-Caribbeans	524,107	6.5	75.5	50.5	265,000	5.8
Puerto Ricans	829,519	10.4	85.7	69.7	578,000	12.6
Dominicans	576,742	7.2	72.8	34.5	199,000	4.4
Mexicans	196,171	2.4	64.5	5	9,800	0.2
Chinese	374,321	4.7	86.3	59.2	222,000	4.8
Indians	206,228	2.6	77.9	20.6	42,000	0.9
Koreans	90,208	1.1	76.9	32.4	29,000	0.6

Source: John Logan and John Mollenkopf, "People and Politics in America's Big Cities," Drum Major Institute for Public Policy 2000 Census; Voting Age and Citizenship from March 2001 Current Population Survey; Hispanic ethnic group estimates from Lewis Mumford Center for Comparative Urban and Regional Research.

with their numbers in the electorate. As the table shows, whites, African Americans, and Puerto Ricans each compose a larger share of the city's active electorate than their actual proportions in the total population. In short, these groups are essentially "overrepresented" in the electorate. In contrast, Afro-Caribbeans and other immigrant groups are "underrepresented" among the city's active voters. Their numbers in the electorate actually decline when compared to their share of the total city population. Although more than three-fourths of New York's Afro-Caribbean immigrants are voting age, only half are voting-age citizens and thus eligible to participate in the formal electoral process. This significant disparity between the population's potential and actual pool of eligible voters is the reason so many Afro-Caribbean elites believe their immigrant constituents have yet to realize their full capacity for electoral influence in New York City politics.

Socioeconomic Status and Citizenship

Political scientists have long associated political participation with socioeconomic status. It is practically a matter of scholarly consensus that higher socioeconomic standing is correlated with higher rates of participation.

Dahl, for example, argued upward economic mobility leads to greater involvement in political life. Scores of other studies have found the middle class show higher rates of participation in all forms of political and civic activity than their poor and working-class counterparts – from registration and voting to campaign fund-raising and donations (e.g., Verba et al. 1995; Wolfinger and Rosenstone 1980). Some researchers (Portes and Mozo 1988; Jones-Correa 1988) have hypothesized that the basic political act of naturalization by immigrants is no less influenced by socioeconomic status than other forms of participation. Hence, the relatively low rate of naturalization among Afro-Caribbean immigrants may be due to their socioeconomic standing. A group of predominantly poor immigrants might be expected to have low naturalization rates. But New York's Afro-Caribbean population is hardly a uniformly poor group. Although a significant minority of the immigrants are mired in poverty, recall the population also boasts a modest middle-class cohort.

Chart 3.1 shows how naturalization rates vary by income among these black immigrants. High-income Afro-Caribbean immigrants quite predictably naturalize at higher rates than their low-income counterparts. Nevertheless, their naturalization rates are modest, even at the highest end of the income scale. Afro-Caribbeans who have household earnings in the highest income bracket are more likely to be citizens than their counterparts in lower-income categores. For example, the naturalization rate for Guyanese immigrants with household income at or above $75,000 is almost 20 percent higher than that of those who earn $25,000–35,000. Jamaican immigrants in the same high- and low-income categories show roughly the same disparity in their respective naturalization rates. The positive correlation between citizenship and household earnings is not as pronounced, however, in the middle- and low-income range. Consider immigrants from Trinidad and Tobago. Those who earn $35,000–60,000 are no more likely to be citizens than their counterparts with income of $25,000–35,000. Similarly, Guyanese immigrants with household income between $35,000–60,000 have approximately the same naturalization rate as those who earn $15,000 or less.

In sum, the relationship between citizenship and income among Afro-Caribbean immigrants is neither perfectly positive nor consistently linear. Middle-income Afro-Caribbeans are not much more likely to take the oath of citizenship than those on the lowest end of the income scale. Even at the highest end of the income scale, Afro-Caribbeans' naturalization rates are modest at best. More than two-thirds of the immigrants from Trinidad and Tobago with income exceeding $75,000 are not United States citizens.

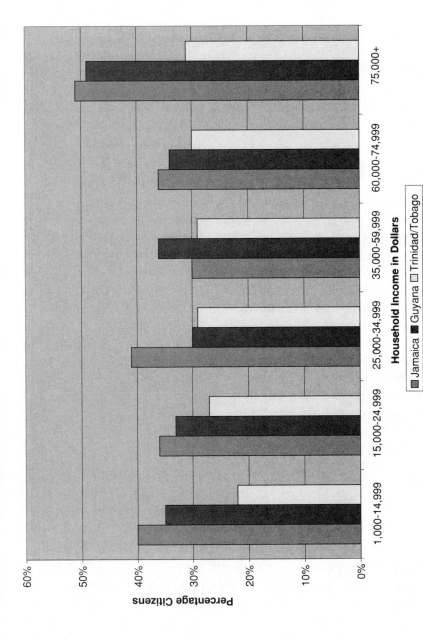

CHART 3.1. Percentage Citizens by Income. *Source:* 1990 Census Public Use Microdata Sample

Only about half of the immigrants from Jamaica and Guyana in the same income category have taken the oath of citizenship.

Length of Stay and Citizenship

Although income has only a slight positive relationship to naturalization rates among Afro-Caribbean immigrants, the correlation between length of residence and citizenship is quite robust. Chart 3.2 clearly illustrates Afro-Caribbeans are more likely to become citizens the longer they have lived in the United States. Longtime immigrant residents of the United Sates have higher naturalization rates than more recent newcomers. In 1990, almost 89 percent of the Afro-Caribbeans who entered the country before 1950 had become citizens, whereas only 14 percent of those who arrived in 1985 had done so. Naturalization rates among these black immigrants appear to increase with length of stay in the United States.

This finding is not surprising. Other studies have concluded length of residence is one of the most powerful predictors of naturalization among immigrants. Jones-Correa (1988, 62) asserts the "immigrants' year of entry into the United States is the best single predictor of the outcome of citizenship among first generation immigrants."[5] What is more revealing, however, is just how long it takes for Afro-Caribbean immigrants to decide to become United States citizens. By 1990, not even a solid majority of the cohort who entered the country between 1970 and 1974 had become citizens. Only 49 percent had taken the oath of citizenship after fifteen to twenty years of residence in the United States. A majority of the 1965–1969 cohort, roughly 58 percent, had become citizens by 1990; yet, there was a sizable minority who had not taken the oath of citizenship. These data suggest most Afro-Caribbean immigrants put off the decision to become citizens, or perhaps reject the idea altogether, for at least twenty years.[6]

III. PLURALIST PREDICTIONS AND THE REALITY OF NEW YORK PARTY POLITICS

Traditional pluralists would be hard pressed to account for why Afro-Caribbeans take so long to become citizens and why even the best-off among them have only modest naturalization rates. The pluralist view

---

[5] Also see Mollenkopf et al. 2001; Garcia 1981.
[6] Jones-Correa finds the same pattern among Latino immigrants in New York City.

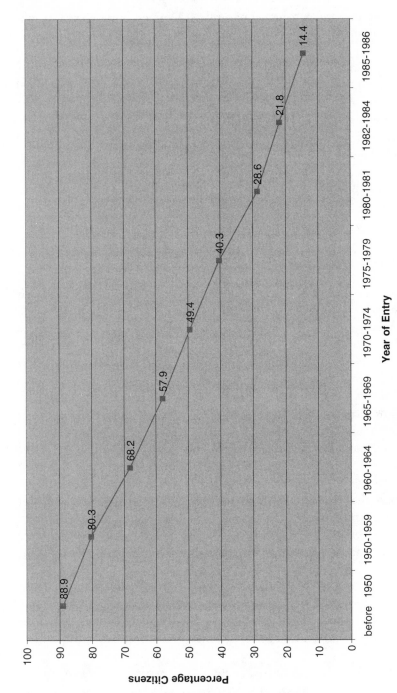

CHART 3.2. Percentage Citizens by Year of Entry. *Source:* 1990 Census Public Use Microdata Sample

actually would anticipate higher naturalization rates for the group, in light of their numbers, socioeconomic profile, and decades of residential settlement in New York City. Individual characteristics, such as income and length of residence, however, cannot alone explain why Afro-Caribbeans have been so slow to become citizens and participate in the formal political process. The data on these individual-level variables for Afro-Caribbean immigrants, in fact, only beg the question.

Individual characteristics may matter, but "the local [political settings] in which immigrants live are also likely to exert a strong influence on whether or not they become citizens and vote" (Mollenkopf et al. 2001, 7). Traditional pluralists predicted the institutional workings of urban democracy – specifically parties and incumbents – could be counted on to mobilize immigrants, whatever their individual characteristics. In the pluralist view, immigrants should not remain on the political margins for long in a city with strong, active parties and political elites eager for their votes.

New York is just such a city, and thus ostensibly would seem to favor the mobilization of Afro-Caribbean immigrants. The city looks like a relatively open political regime with ample incentives and structures for drawing Afro-Caribbeans and other immigrants into the electoral process. First, New York has a highly diverse population, fragmented by divisions of race, ethnicity, and nationality. Although whites constitute a bare majority of the active electorate, no one group can dominate city politics by virtue of their numbers alone. Winning electoral coalitions are therefore bound to be diverse and include a significant share of immigrant voters. In Brooklyn and Queens, where Afro-Caribbean immigrants make up a sizable proportion of the population, their numbers and potential votes ought to be an important consideration in any electoral calculus.

Second, the city is a "highly partisan, organized political environment with many offices representing small jurisdictions," such as community boards and city council districts (ibid., 9). This institutional structure potentially makes government much more accessible and the prospect of political engagement less daunting for newcomers to New York City. What is more, small jurisdictions concentrate the votes of groups who live in distinct residential enclaves such as Afro-Caribbean immigrants in Brooklyn and Queens. Their concentrated numbers would seem to make them hard to ignore in district-based races for lower-level political office.

Finally, New York has a relatively strong party structure. Although the last half-century has seen the atrophy and decline of political parties

and machines in most cities, New York has retained vital, if not altogether robust, Democratic Party county organizations, especially in the
outer boroughs. These regular Democratic organizations are not nearly
as strong or as influential as they were during the first half of the twentieth century, to be sure. The Tammany machine is a dim memory,
patronage has been significantly curtailed, and membership in constituent
political clubs has diminished (Ware 1985). Yet the county organizations still retain considerable control over ballot access, judicial appointments, and court jobs and wield significant influence in legislative and
school board elections. In short, Democratic machine politics has continued in New York's outer boroughs, albeit in attenuated form.[7] This
existing party structure provides a potential institutional vehicle for
bringing Afro-Caribbeans and other recent immigrants into the political
process.

With its traditional social base of lower-middle-class, white ethnic voters declining, the party appears to have a compelling strategic incentive for
reaching out to the growing numbers of recent immigrants to New York.
These newcomers could become an important source of constituent support for the party, replacing its dwindling traditional base and shoring up
its competitive advantage in city elections. Afro-Caribbean immigrants,
in particular, seem ripe for mobilization. The group is an obvious potential source of support for the party. Their naturalization rates are already
at modest levels, their numbers are substantial and concentrated, they
boast a solid middle-class cohort and a handful of prominent political
entrepreneurs, and those who are citizens and regular voters typically
cast their ballots for the Democratic Party.[8]

In light of these instrumental factors, the conventional pluralist wisdom
would expect the Democratic Party to be hard at work, making citizens
and active voters of New York's Caribbean immigrants. Yet this has not
been the case. On the contrary, the Democratic Party organizations largely
have ignored Afro-Caribbean immigrants. They have made no concerted
effort to encourage these newcomers to become citizens, register, vote, or
otherwise participate in the political process. One activist from Caribbean
Immigrant Services (CIS) (interview, November 29, 1996) observed, "The
Democratic Party has not pushed for Caribbean people to become citizens

---

[7] In fact, Mollenkopf (1992) notes the outer borough party organizations gained influence
during the 1980s.
[8] See Chapter 4 for more discussion on the high levels of Democratic partisanship among
Afro-Caribbean New Yorkers.

or for them to get involved in local politics. They've basically neglected us."

Several of my other elite respondents (interview, July 3, 1997) echoed this view.

Q: Has the Democratic Party played a role in the recent efforts to encourage Caribbean immigrants to become citizens or registered voters?
A: No. Not at all. Most of the work is being done by community agencies like CIS and Dr. Marco's organization [the Caribbean Women's Health Association].

Another interview subject (interview, April 7, 1997) complained the Democratic Party was shirking what he viewed as its traditional role of encouraging political participation.

Q: Has the Democratic Party encouraged Caribbean immigrants to become citizens and participate in city politics?
A: Absolutely not. You would think so, right? That they would want people to naturalize and vote for their candidates and so on. Isn't that what parties are supposed to do? But these folks here don't do a thing to push Caribbean people to get involved.

Most of the serious efforts to encourage citizenship and political participation among Afro-Caribbean New Yorkers, in fact, have been by service and non-profit organizations within the community (interview, July 3, 1997).

Q: Are you aware of any organizations engaged in formal efforts to encourage citizenship and political participation among Caribbean Americans?
A: Yes. There are quite a few. Most organizations, like the island benevolent associations, encourage that. But I think there are two or three major ones not connected with the island associations that go out and encourage Caribbeans to become citizens. There is Caribbean Immigrant Services, who've been doing a terrific job. Then there is the Caribbean Women's Health Association [headed] by Dr. Marco Mason, where they actually go out and recruit you to become citizens, and so forth. So you do have organizations that actually go out and do that. But I do think we need more coordination. For example, the National Association of Barbados Organizations, I think they usually have papers devoted to why Barbadians should become citizens. But then you could have the same paper and just change from "Barbados" to "Grenada" or "Guyana." Often, it's like one hand doesn't know what the other is doing. So, try as Barbados may try, or try as the Jamaican nationals may try, it's not as effective as when there is some type of central Caribbean American group.

Another respondent (interview, May 15, 1997) also cited the efforts of CIS and the Caribbean Women's Health Association.

Q: Are there any organizations to promote citizenship and political participation among Caribbean immigrants?

A: Yes. The organization of CARICOM [Caribbean Community and Common Market] nations tried to do that with Irwin Claire. Now he does it as a business for himself with CIS. It might well sustain itself over a long period of time. But I'm sure we need a lot more. The Caribbean Women's Health Association, their immigration program is also a good program for encouraging citizenship. And they have been there doing it for quite a while – ten to fifteen years.

The effort and resources these community-based organizations devote to promoting citizenship among Caribbean immigrants contrast starkly with the record of the Democratic Party.

The party's neglect of Afro-Caribbeans and other recent immigrants is hardly due to a lack of resources or party infrastructure. Although the elaborate patronage system and immense political club memberships of an earlier era are no more, the outer borough party organizations nonetheless retain a solid cadre of regulars to do the work of grassroots electioneering, mobilizing, and petitioning during primaries and elections. None of these resources, however, have been used to reach out to immigrants and draw them into the electoral process. The party simply has not played the mobilizing role described by Dahl and other pluralists.

Party Gatekeeping and Benign Neglect

Although the Democratic Party's neglect of Afro-Caribbean immigrants may confound pluralist expectations, it is fully in keeping with what Erie and a newer generation of scholars would predict (e.g., Jones-Correa 1998; Mollenkopf 1992b). Erie (1988) has argued convincingly that parties mobilize new voters only during their embryonic organizational stage or when faced with significant competition. Once party machines have secured control of the political system, they no longer have an incentive to court potential new voters. In fact, machines that no longer face serious competitive pressures, whether from other parties or from rival factions, tend to ignore these potential voters and focus only on mobilizing and satisfying their traditional core constituents.

Dominant party organizations typically are reluctant to draw immigrants and other newcomers into the electorate, for fear they might seek to oust party-backed incumbents, support rival factions, or otherwise disrupt entrenched coalitions (Shefter 1986). To maintain the political status quo and protect scarce resources, machines prefer to limit electoral participation to their traditional core voters and leave recent immigrants on the political periphery. Of course, contemporary parties do not employ the force, obstruction, and intimidation tactics used by parties in the early twentieth century to discourage electoral participation among new immigrants.[9] Rather, Jones-Correa (1998, 77) points out they simply practice benign neglect, leaving newcomers to fend for themselves. All in all, entrenched machines are not in the business of recruiting new actors into the political process.

Democratic Party organizations in New York's outer boroughs operate like entrenched machines. They have the allegiance of a solid majority of the city's registered voters; control a wide-reaching, machine-like apparatus in each borough; and almost never face serious competition from other parties. To be sure, Rudolph Giuliani's mayoral success in the 1990s breathed new life into the Republican Party, the only credible source of competition to the Democrats. But the former mayor was hardly a Republican Party standard bearer at the local level, and his success ultimately did not break the hegemony of the Democratic Party in New York City.[10]

Candidates supported by the Democratic county organizations still usually win elections for lesser offices (Mollenkopf 1997). In the Bronx, Brooklyn, and Queens, the Democratic Party is essentially the "only game in town." Democratic Party dominance removes much of the strategic incentive for the county organizations to mobilize immigrants and other potential new voters. Rather than introduce unpredictable new actors into the electoral process and risk losing their control over political outcomes, the Democratic organizations in the outer boroughs focus their limited resources on their longtime, traditional supporters.

Brooklyn

In Brooklyn, for instance, the Democratic county organization has made practically no effort to mobilize Afro-Caribbeans and other recent newcomers to the borough. Brooklyn has absorbed more immigrants over the last two decades than any other borough in New York City. In 1990, the foreign born constituted almost a third of Brooklyn's 2.3 million residents (1990 Census Public Use Microdata). Between 1990 and 1994, another 200,000 immigrants settled in Brooklyn neighborhoods (New York

---

[9] On the tactics of early-twentieth-century parties, see Erie 1988.
[10] For more on Giuliani, see Chapter 4.

City Department of Planning). Over 20 percent of these newcomers hailed from the anglophone Caribbean. Despite these dramatic demographic changes, however, the Democratic county organization has taken no systematic steps to expand the Brooklyn electorate to include these newcomers.

First, it has made no formal efforts to encourage these immigrants to become United States citizens. The party did not play a significant role, for example, in the late 1990s emergency campaigns to encourage citizenship among Afro-Caribbean immigrants. Launched in the wake of the 1996 congressional legislation limiting social services to unnaturalized immigrants, the drives were undertaken almost entirely by immigrant advocacy groups and other organizations within the Afro-Caribbean community.[11] Although a number of Brooklyn's Democratic incumbents gave their rhetorical backing to these campaigns, the party organization itself did not provide any serious institutional support to these efforts.

The party's neglect of Afro-Caribbean immigrants is reflected especially in the membership of its political clubs. Although the clubs are relatively open and easy enough to join, they generally do not recruit new members, even in the face of rapidly changing neighborhood demographics. Many political clubs in the heavily Afro-Caribbean neighborhoods of central Brooklyn have waning, older memberships. Yet quite a few have become defunct, rather than recruit new members from among the ranks of these recent immigrants. Consequently, the number of Democratic Clubs in this part of Brooklyn has dwindled considerably over the past several decades.

There are a few political clubs that have been started or colonized by small numbers of Afro-Caribbean immigrants – the New Era Democratic Club is one such example. These clubs, however, are almost never launched or actively fostered by the party organization itself. Rather, they are established by aggressive Afro-Caribbean self-starters who, without much invitation, have made their own incursions into the party. Such individual efforts are the exception. One of my elite respondents (interview, July 3, 1997) explained how the party's neglect prompted some Caribbean politicians to establish their own clubs.

Q: What about the Democratic Party machinery here in Brooklyn? Do you think that the party has tried to attract Caribbean immigrants and involve them in the political process?

---

[11] The congressional legislation triggered a wave of anxiety among unnaturalized Afro-Caribbean immigrants and a notable increase in petitions for citizenship. See Chapter 5 for more discussion and analysis.

A: No. In the Democratic Party machinery, especially in Brooklyn, tradition-
        ally the machinery has been controlled by whites. And then the few blacks
        who have been dominant within the machinery have been mostly African
        Americans. And, therefore, they used to have an unspoken type of declara-
        tion, "You don't bring anybody new into my territory, and I'm not going to
        put somebody in your territory." It's a kind of secret type stuff they have
        had. But I think what has happened now is that quite a few Caribbean
        Americans have created their own clubs. These are Caribbean clubs within
        the Democratic machine. So they now have a shot at having some influence
        within the party.

More generally, though, political clubs with significant Afro-Caribbean
membership are unusual. Most clubs in Brooklyn and the other outer
boroughs have smaller and more elderly memberships and do not reflect
the changing demographics of the borough.

The Democratic Party's neglect of Brooklyn's Afro-Caribbean immigrants is most pronounced at election time. Aside from presidential-
election-year efforts, party-sponsored voter registration drives aimed at
Afro-Caribbeans and other immigrants are practically non-existent. This
deliberate inattention to voter registration is in keeping with the party's
propensity to limit participation to a core of longtime, dependable constituents. Rather than register new voters, party resources and personnel are reserved instead for mobilizing traditional followers. The party
thus avoids the risk of drawing unpredictable new voters into the electorate and ensures its continued control of political outcomes. Brooklyn's
Democratic organization essentially counts on the "general nonparticipation of the public," particularly new groups, to maintain the status quo
(Mollenkopf 1992b, 79).

The results of this pattern of "benign neglect" show in the electoral
dynamics of some of the borough's most heavily Afro-Caribbean districts.
The Forty-second Assembly District (AD) in central Brooklyn is a clear
case in point. Encompassing parts of Flatbush, East Flatbush, and a small
section of Crown Heights, this predominantly black AD is home to large
numbers of Afro-Caribbeans and African Americans, and a much smaller
mix of Jewish and Italian ethnics, Latinos, and Asians. This part of central
Brooklyn was a virtual bastion of white ethnic neighborhoods, with very
few black residents until the 1970s. But with the process of succession –
that is, increasing black settlement and ensuing white exodus – the racial
and ethnic composition of the area has changed dramatically. The population is now roughly 72 percent black, 10 percent white, and 14 percent
Latino.

With the steady flow of immigration from the anglophone Caribbean over the last two decades, Afro-Caribbeans now practically outnumber African Americans and exceed all other groups in the AD. For all their numbers, however, Afro-Caribbeans have yet to elect a coethnic to the state assembly seat from this district. The seat has been occupied by the same white Democratic incumbent, Rhoda Jacobs, for the last twenty-five years. She has retained the seat and defeated both Afro-Caribbean and African-American challengers, even as the demographic characteristics of the district have changed to give both these groups numerical majorities.

The electorate that has ensured Jacobs's incumbency for so many years is a small subset of the district population, not reflective of its overall demography. Turnout in the district is typically quite low. Just 4,000 people – the equivalent of about five of the district's fifty-six election precincts – cast ballots in the 1994 race, most of them longtime registered Democratic voters (Sengupta 1996b, 8).[12] Jacobs won the race by a decisive two-thirds margin. The electorate that continues to return her to office, however, is disproportionately more white and native born than the actual district population.[13]

Afro-Caribbean immigrants, in particular, are highly underrepresented in this electorate. Most of them do not vote in AD elections. The immigrants are not simply apathetic voters who fail to show up at the polls. Rather, most adult Afro-Caribbeans in the district are not citizens and so are ineligible to vote. In fact, recent research (Mollenkopf et al. 2001) has revealed first-generation Afro-Caribbean immigrants who do vote have had higher turnout rates than their native-born counterparts in some city-wide elections. More generally, though, voting turnout tends to be low in heavily immigrant ADs, largely because so many residents are non-citizens. The Forty-second AD is no exception. More than 40 percent of the district's residents, most of them Afro-Caribbean, are non-citizens.[14]

In a telling, if inadvertent concession, Jacobs's chief aide noted in a 1984 interview that constituents in this heavily immigrant district "are docile" (Green and Wilson 1987, 58). What the aide described as docility or apathy may actually be the result of the large numbers of non-citizen immigrants in the district who are ineligible to vote. But whatever the case, the regular party organization has done nothing to stir these immigrant

---

[12] There are approximately eight hundred eligible voters in a New York City ED, the smallest electoral reporting unit (Mollenkopf et al. 2001).

[13] This same pattern obtains for the citywide electorate, as well (Mollenkopf 1992).

[14] New York State Legislative Task Force on Demographic Research and Reapportionment.

constituents from their apparent apathy and draw them into the formal political process. Jacobs's longtime incumbency is partly due to the "general nonparticipation" of a significant segment of her district's population. One respondent (interview, April 2, 1997) explained.

Q: What do you think of Rhoda Jacobs?
A: She should retire.
Q: Why?
A: Well, she has been in office for so long, and she hasn't served a great part of her constituency, the Caribbean community. Of course, it's our fault that she's in there because we don't get out there and vote her out. Many of the Caribbean Americans in the district aren't even citizens. And I'm sure she's not eager for them to get involved anyway. If one does not demand, you don't get much.

In 1996, Jacobs once again defeated a challenge to her incumbent seat – this time from an Afro-Caribbean, James Connolly.[15] Again, immigrant "non-participation" and the selective mobilization of longtime supporters helped produce her victory. One of my elite respondents (interview, November 22, 1996) expressed his frustration with this familiar outcome.

Q: What is your reaction to the recent reelection of Rhoda Jacobs in the Forty-second AD?
A: If you have 90 percent of an area that is Caribbean American and African American, and you have this woman representing that area for the past eighteen years, something is radically wrong. OK! She won with about three thousand votes. Three thousand, and you have thousands of Caribbean Americans who don't vote and thirty thousand registered Democrats who didn't bother to vote.

A Trinidadian political organizer (interview, December 15, 1996) further explained the calculus behind the election results.

If you're in a district with forty thousand registered voters, let's say twenty-five, thirty, forty percent of them are Caribbean. If you can get elected with three thousand votes, you're not going to reach out to the others. The three thousand are your votes. Somebody else has to organize the rest to challenge you. And if the organization is not there, you're not gonna do it. Why should you? It's not in your interest.

The only time these politicians reach out to you is when they . . . The way they reach out to you is if you have a bloc of votes, or you have a situation where they say, "If we don't go after these people, they may cause us some grief." But if they determine that, even though you have the potential for ten thousand votes you're not citizens or you're gonna stay at home, they don't care. Why should they reach out to you?

---

[15] See Chapter 7 for more discussion of this race.

The respondent neatly sums up the party's strategic rationale for ignoring thousands of potential Afro-Caribbean voters in the Forty-second AD at election time. The party focuses on constituents who are already mobilized and neglects those on the margins. The tactic worked predictably in 1996. The Jacobs campaign might have looked to best her opponent by appealing to the immigrants and undermining Connolly's ostensible ethnic appeal with Afro-Caribbeans. But self-interest likely stopped the incumbent from doing so.[16] Why risk mobilizing a new group of immigrant voters and potentially lose her seat to the insurgent opponent? Consequently, Jacobs's campaign made no such effort. Connolly's campaign, on the other hand, failed to draw significant numbers of Afro-Caribbeans into the electorate. As another Afro-Caribbean leader lamented, turnout for the race was low, and "Jacobs got most of her support from the predominantly white southern part of the district" (*New York Carib News*, September 14, 1996, 4).

Racial Bias?

Of course, this leader's observation prompts an obvious and important question. Is racial animus behind the party's practice of selectively mobilizing its core of traditional supporters, while neglecting Afro-Caribbeans and other newcomers? To be sure, party gatekeeping and selective mobilization can be explained as a purely rational, race-neutral strategy that allows Democrats to maintain their hegemony and the political status quo. But the practice does little to alleviate and arguably exacerbates patterns of racial stratification in the New York City electorate. The party's core of traditional voters is more white and native born than the overall population, whereas the non-voters on the political margins are mostly nonwhite immigrants from the Caribbean, Latin America, and Asia. Whites are roughly a third of the city population but nearly half of the voting-age citizens (Logan and Mollenkopf 2003; see Table 3.3).

There are, of course, sizable numbers of recently arrived white immigrants from Russia and Eastern Europe who are arguably also subject to the party's practice of benign neglect. Their presence would seem to vitiate the claim that there is a racial motivation to the party's gatekeeping strategy. Yet in a city marked by considerable residential segregation, these white immigrants are far more likely than their non-white counterparts to live in the same neighborhoods as the established white residents who

---

[16] See Chapter 4 for discussion of how the self-interest of African-American party insiders clashes with the prospect of Afro-Caribbean mobilization.

make up the majority of New York's active voters. Afro-Caribbeans, in contrast, tend to live near to other immigrants from the Caribbean who do not vote or near native-born blacks who vote less than whites. If the presence of active voters has any mobilizing influence on immigrants, as some researchers (Mollenkopf et al. 2001) have speculated, Russian and Eastern European newcomers are likely to become involved in the political process sooner than Afro-Caribbeans because they live in closer proximity to more active segments of the electorate.[17] European immigrants already have higher naturalization rates than Afro-Caribbeans.

Whatever the impetus for the party's practice of selective mobilization, then, it only reinforces existing racial disparities in political participation. New York's political insiders are predominantly white; the outsiders are mostly non-white.[18] These patterns likely will persist as long as Afro-Caribbeans and other non-whites are a disproportionate share of the new immigrants to New York and parties continue to ignore these newcomers. As Jones-Correa (1998, 79) observes, party mobilization is a matter of "preaching to the choir . . . [focusing only] on those constituents who are already active." Non-voting non-citizens, such as the thousands of Afro-Caribbean immigrants in central Brooklyn, are thus marginalized. Gone are days when party bosses and operatives would guide immigrants through the citizenship process. In fact, the truth may be these days never existed (Erie 1988). Today's Democratic Party functions more often as a gatekeeper than a mobilizer.

Preventing Countermobilization

The party's routine neglect of Afro-Caribbean immigrants necessarily raises questions about the potential political costs of this practice. How can the party continue to disregard so many potential voters with impunity, without fear of electoral retaliation? First, recall the Democratic Party in Brooklyn and the other outer boroughs almost never faces significant competition from Republicans or other parties. Afro-Caribbeans arguably have a pragmatic incentive to support the Democratic organization, as long as it retains its control of Brooklyn politics. Yet these recently arrived immigrants do not have the same long-standing ties to the

---

[17] Neighborhoods that have high concentrations of immigrants typically show lower voting rates than neighborhoods that have more native-born residents.

[18] See Chapter 4 for more analysis on the racial disparities in New York City politics and their implications for Afro-Caribbean political incorporation.

Democratic Party as some native-born minority groups, such as African Americans and Puerto Ricans. They therefore might be more inclined to give serious consideration to appeals from the Republican Party.

But Republicans have made very little effort to appeal to Afro-Caribbean immigrants – aside from the occasional symbolic gesture. True enough, the party has little organizational muscle in Brooklyn, where the potential for Afro-Caribbean electoral influence is most obvious. But the failure of Republicans to court Afro-Caribbeans is surprising, because the immigrants appear to be the kind of group the dominant conservative wing of the GOP would be eager to count among their constituents. Recall from Chapter 2 Afro-Caribbeans are popularly perceived as "good blacks," model minorities whose success lends credence to the conservative view racism is no longer a serious obstacle for blacks or can be overcome without government intervention. In the popular consciousness, Caribbean immigrants exemplify hard work, drive, ambition, self-reliance, values the Republican Party routinely emphasizes. Yet the GOP has not made a concerted effort to draw Afro-Caribbeans into their fold.

The absence of a serious competitive threat from the Republicans means Democratic organization can ignore non-voting Afro-Caribbeans, without any real fear this immigrant constituency will be mobilized against them by a rival party. Adding to the organization's strategic advantage, Afro-Caribbean immigrants who do vote are overwhelmingly Democratic.[19] In short, Democratic regulars need not be concerned that other parties will appeal to Afro-Caribbean immigrants on the political margins.

Although Democrats may not worry much about serious competition from other parties, there is the potential threat of insurgency from individual politicians or factions. After all, there are scores of Afro-Caribbean ethnicity entrepreneurs – community leaders and office seekers – with a stake in mobilizing Afro-Caribbean immigrants to participate in the political process as a self-conscious ethnic bloc. Afro-Caribbean political leaders conceivably could rally unnaturalized immigrants to become citizens, and then demand to be taken seriously by the party on the strength of their cumulative numbers and social capital. Indeed, this has often been a key line of rhetoric among the current generation of Afro-Caribbean leaders

---

[19] More than 90 percent of voters in election districts that were either predominantly African-American or heavily Afro-Caribbean were registered as Democrats in 2000. See Chapter 4.

and organizations (e.g., Sengupta 1996a). As one of my elite respondents (interview, December 14, 1999) noted, "The party has to take heed. They can count and our numbers are large and getting bigger all the time." There is the distinct possibility, then, that entrenched Democratic coalitions might be disrupted by an enterprising Afro-Caribbean group or politician who manages to mobilize the thousands of Afro-Caribbeans living in Brooklyn, Queens, or the Bronx.

The Democratic county organizations have several stock strategies for discouraging and responding to such insurgent challenges. First, the organizations and regular clubs are quite adept at manipulating the arcana of New York's state election laws to keep insurgents off the ballot (Jones-Correa 1998; Mollenkopf 1992b). To run for city council, for example, a candidate must compile a petition of nine hundred signatures. Producing a petition without the benefit of the party's organizational resources is difficult enough for insurgent candidates. But what is even more discouraging is their petitions are often subject to legal challenges from the Democratic county organizations and clubs. It is not unusual for an insurgent to be knocked off the ballot as a result of these challenges. The county organization occasionally even files legal briefs disputing final election results favoring insurgent candidates. With their superior resources and knowledge of the state's election laws, the party organization often can overwhelm an insurgent in court.

The former city council member Una Clarke, who hails from the Caribbean, saw her 1991 first-time election victory marred when the party-backed candidate threatened to challenge the voting results in court. The threats ultimately were dropped, and the county organization went on to make peace with Clarke. Nevertheless, her case demonstrates the way the Democratic organization uses the state's complex election laws to control ballot access and discourage challenges by insurgent candidates.

That Clarke went on to establish a fairly amicable relationship with the party, however, is also indicative of another strategy the county organization employs to contain the threat of insurgency from individual politicians and factions. The Democratic county organizations typically absorb insurgent candidates who win elections against them (Jones-Correa 1998; Mollenkopf 1992b). The organizations tend to incorporate a few ethnic elites – both insurgents and hand-picked party supporters – to forestall potential revolts and countermobilization against the party by new groups.[20] Not surprisingly, then, Brooklyn's Democratic county

---

[20] On how parties selectively incorporate potentially insurgent elites, see Shefter 1986.

organization has absorbed a handful of Afro-Caribbean elected officials, including Clarke; her former fellow Council member Lloyd Henry; and State Assemblyman Nick Perry. The organization's executive committee has also designated a few Afro-Caribbeans as district leaders.

Rather than mobilize the thousands of non-citizen Afro-Caribbean immigrants in Brooklyn, the party instead has incorporated this handful of elites to give the group symbolic recognition. The elites serve as power brokers for a heavily non-citizen constituency that has yet to mobilize fully. Whatever influence they wield in the party is therefore not based on the actual electoral strength of Afro-Caribbean immigrants. Rather, it derives from the potential impact this large and growing group of newcomers could have if they were to become citizens and vote.

The fact Afro-Caribbean leaders represent a population that is largely non-citizen and disengaged from the formal political process raises questions of democratic accountability. Their immigrant constituents hardly can ensure these elites are pursuing their interests if they themselves are unable to vote and otherwise participate in electoral politics. Without the vote, non-citizen Afro-Caribbeans cannot hold these elected officials' feet to the fire. Likewise the non-citizenship status of the immigrants also might engender doubts about the ability of their leaders to win concessions from the party without actual electoral firepower from their constituents to bolster their demands. Reliance on the threat their constituents could pose if only they became voting citizens seems a rather fragile source of political leverage.

Yet the possibility of Afro-Caribbean mobilization appears to carry some weight with party leaders. As Clarke has observed, "I think [the party leaders] understand and can count numbers. They understand the growing presence of the Caribbean community" (Sengupta 1996a, 8). By granting symbolic recognition, the party can acknowledge the huge presence of Afro-Caribbeans in Brooklyn, without taking any substantive steps to draw them into the political process. This strategy allows the party to maintain its limited store of material rewards and keep the political status quo largely intact.

For example, party regulars often appear at the Caribbean-American Labor Day Carnival and other ethnic celebrations to signal their support of New York's Afro-Caribbean community. Or they may give rhetorical backing to citizenship drives sponsored by Caribbean ethnic organizations and immigrant advocacy groups. These are all symbolic inducements, which take nothing away from the party's core supporters and leave prevailing political arrangements intact. Photo opportunities at the

Labor Day Carnival, supportive rhetoric, and other symbolic gestures by party regulars are simply "satisficing" devices: that is, they acknowledge the potential political strength of the Afro-Caribbean constituency but stop short of actually mobilizing or harnessing this untapped electoral power. One elite respondent (interview, December 14, 1996) elaborated this point.

Q: Does the party recognize the power in the growing numbers of Caribbean immigrants?

A: They recognize the power possibilities. But they know it's not there; it's still just a notion. They know the potential we have for political power. They know the potential economic power. But they also know it's not there yet. It hasn't been brought together where it could really impact on things. The party knows this. They also know that most of the Caribbean Americans who come out to events like the Labor Day Carnival are not registered voters. So they come to events like that for show and that's it. It is a photo op; that's all it is.

The only substantive steps the party has taken to encourage Afro-Caribbean political mobilization are in the area of reapportionment. Party regulars generally have supported efforts to enhance Afro-Caribbean representation through redistricting. The pressure to draw new districts favoring this immigrant constituency has come mostly from Afro-Caribbean elites. One respondent (interview, May 27, 1997) recalls the role of Caribbean advocacy groups.

At one point the issue was raised in our community about the lack of representation, political representation, in terms of political jurisdiction. There were no districts, no political districts where a Caribbean could run for State Assembly, City Council, or the Senate and get elected because the majority [of the residents] of that district were Caribbean. OK? So we put forth and we had a campaign during the time of reapportioning, the last reapportioning, where we actively waged a campaign to have Caribbean districts drawn in the Bronx, Queens, and Brooklyn. And we succeeded in getting those districts.

Party regulars more often than not have acceded to these demands. Although there has been occasional resistance from some traditional party insiders intent on maintaining the political status quo, legal imperatives coupled with changing demographic realities have made the party organization more amenable to these reapportionment efforts.[21] New districts,

---

[21] Party politicians often use the redistricting process to create or maintain "friendly districts" that will produce the continued reelection of incumbents – typically through gerrymandering. New York's City Charter, however, authorizes the creation of an independent commission on redistricting to limit partisan influence (Macchiarola and Diaz 1993).

in fact, have helped marginally to increase Afro-Caribbean representation in both the City Council and the State Assembly. With their high rates of residential concentration, Afro-Caribbean immigrants can benefit more readily from redistricting than other minority groups, such as Asians and Latinos, who are more dispersed

Yet reapportionment by itself is hardly enough to ensure immigrant participation. Redistricting decisions are matters for elite haggling and negotiation. Although districts drawn to enhance Afro-Caribbean representation may signal the incorporation and growing influence of a cadre of elites, they do not necessarily lead to more participation by rank-and-file immigrants. Indeed, as one elite (interview, May 2, 1997) observed, "What we have done is create the right number of districts. It is up to us to win those districts. There are still districts where we know that the majority of the residents are of Caribbean descent where they have not yet mobilized or organized in a fashion where we can win the district." Reapportionment, then, is hardly the most proactive step party organizations could take to encourage immigrant participation.

IV. CONCLUSION

Fully mobilizing Afro-Caribbean immigrants would require a commitment of institutional resources from the party organizations at the grassroots level. But this has yet to happen, and contrary to pluralist expectations, it is unlikely to occur without some pressure from Caribbean Americans. Parties tend to focus their resources on groups who are already mobilized. The entrenched machines in Brooklyn and the other outer boroughs have thus shown little interest in encouraging Afro-Caribbean immigrants to become citizens and participate in the political process. In short, they have left these black ethnics to fend for themselves. The party organizations' tendency to neglect and marginalize these newcomers helps to explain why naturalization rates for the group are so low.

Yet party neglect by itself is an inadequate explanation. Scholars who subscribe to the minority group perspective, for example, would not expect conventional parties to foster mobilization and participation among Afro-Caribbean immigrants, or any other racial minority group for that matter. Exponents of this view would anticipate that Afro-Caribbean immigrants are more likely to mobilize outside party channels. Minority group scholars have long argued political mobilization – for marginalized, non-white groups in particular – frequently begins outside established or formal channels of political engagement (e.g., Browning, Marshall, and Tabb 1997; Grimshaw 1992; Pinderhughes 1987; Kleppner 1985). Drawing from the African-American example, this view posits non-white groups who find themselves neglected or deliberately excluded by the parties invariably turn inward to their own social institutions, from which they can mount insurgent reform movements to secure incorporation. According to this line of thinking, Afro-Caribbean immigrants should be expected to begin a movement for reform and inclusion from their own social institutions, perhaps in conjunction with their native-born African-American counterparts.

As it turns out, however, the minority group perspective is no better than the pluralist framework at predicting and explaining some of the patterns of participation and incorporation among Afro-Caribbean immigrants. In the next chapter, I show African Americans have not joined Afro-Caribbean immigrants to mobilize for significant reform and greater racial inclusion, as the minority group view would predict. The seemingly natural coalition minority group scholars might expect between these two groups of blacks has not been easy to foster or maintain.

4

Afro-Caribbeans and African Americans

Racially Bound or Ethnically Splintered?

Although the Democratic Party's neglect of Afro-Caribbean immigrants may fly in the face of standard pluralist predictions, it would hardly surprise most exponents of the minority group perspective. Scholars who subscribe to this view believe exclusion from dominant political parties – and most mainstream institutions, for that matter – is an all too common shared reality for racial minority groups in the United States. According to this line of thinking, foreign-born minorities, no less than their native-born counterparts, are bound to encounter barriers to their participation in the many key arenas of American life. African Americans are, of course, the paradigmatic group in this regard. The history of their exclusion from the major parties and other mainstream American institutions is well known (e.g., Frymer 1999).

Yet the literature on urban political incorporation is replete with examples of African Americans' mobilizing from independent bases outside conventional party channels to demand racial inclusion, systemic reform, and sometimes a radical redistribution of resources – in cities such as Chicago and Atlanta (e.g., Grimshaw 1992; Pinderhughes 1987; Kleppner 1985; Carmichael and Hamilton 1967). Not surprisingly, then, minority group scholars would expect Afro-Caribbean immigrants to follow the example of their native-born counterparts and mount an insurgent movement for inclusion, in light of the unwillingness of the Democratic Party to draw them into the political process. Indeed, exponents of the minority group view arguably would predict a race-based alliance between Afro-Caribbean and African-American New Yorkers to press for greater black political incorporation.

One of the most widely considered questions prompted by the new wave of non-white immigration is how these newcomers will alter coalition dynamics in such demographically diverse cities as New York and Los Angeles, where alliances are a do-or-die fact of political life. Minority group scholars have speculated the non-white racial status of the immigrants and their vulnerability to discrimination will lead them to forge coalitions with native-born minorities, specifically African Americans (Jennings 1997; Marable 1994; Henry and Munoz 1991). Combating racial discrimination has long been a central political preoccupation for American-born blacks. Scholars who subscribe to the minority group view believe it will also be a chief concern for the new, non-white immigrants. Their conclusion is that this shared interest will become a powerful basis for interminority alliances, unifying African Americans and their foreign-born counterparts. In short, this perspective anticipates a grand rainbow coalition among native-born blacks and recent non-white immigrants from Latin America, Asia, and the Caribbean.

But in cities with significant numbers of African Americans and non-white newcomers, race-based alliances among these groups generally have proved to be an elusive political goal. Stable coalitions between native-born blacks and their foreign-born counterparts have not been much in evidence in cities around the country. In New York, for instance, political figures as varied as Al Sharpton and Fernando Ferrer have tried to foster an alliance between African Americans and Latinos with only the most limited results (Mollenkopf 2003; Falcon 1988). Black New Yorkers also have been at odds with Asians, most notably in a series of boycotts against Korean grocers in the early 1990s (Joyce 2003; Kim 2000). At the other end of the Atlantic seaboard in Miami, African Americans and Cubans have been at odds for decades (Warren and Moreno 2003). Tensions also have simmered between African Americans and Asians in Los Angeles (Sonenshein 2003a). In short, political relations between blacks and recent non-white immigrants have been marked more often by conflict than cooperation. Although race-based coalitions among native-born blacks and foreign-born minority groups are widely expected, as it turns out, they are actually quite rare.

The rarity of such alliances has led some researchers to speculate African Americans are more likely to find themselves in grim political isolation than in any grand rainbow coalition with non-white immigrants (Mollenkopf 2003). A few observers even dismiss the idea of race-based alliances altogether as a misguided and losing electoral strategy in increasingly diverse, multiracial cities, where immigration has scrambled the old black-white, biracial political calculus (Sleeper 1993). Whatever their future prospects, race-based coalitions between African Americans and non-white immigrants have not had much success to date. Indeed, even the most cursory review of the literature reveals intergroup coalitions of any stripe have been difficult to foster and maintain (Hochschild and Rogers 2000).

The fact that the rainbow coalition of non-whites predicted by the minority group view has not emerged in most cities begs the question, Why have such race-based alliances been difficult to foster? A number of studies have noted the political conflicts between blacks and non-white immigrants, to be sure. But very few have provided detailed analyses of why the racial commonalities they share have not been enough to override differences and produce stable alliances. Dominant theories of coalition building indicate strong leadership, common interests, and shared ideology are critical (Sonenshein 2003b; 1993). But few studies have explored whether the absence of any of these crucial girders or some other factor largely accounts for the rarity of alliances specifically between African Americans and recent non-white immigrants (Sonenshein 2003a; 2003b; Mollenkopf 2003). Rarely have any, in fact, closely analyzed political relations between these groups (Falcon 1988). In sum, the research literature does not offer much in the way of careful explanations for why the predictions of the minority group view have not been borne out in most cities.

This chapter takes up this question with an analysis of the political relations between African Americans and Afro-Caribbean immigrants. These two groups of black New Yorkers together furnish a uniquely instructive case for exploring why the race-based alliances anticipated by the minority group view have not come to fruition. By the logic of the minority group perspective, rainbow alliances among non-whites should be most likely when the racial commonalities between them are strong and the racial divisions separating them from whites are pronounced and politically salient. Afro-Caribbean and African-American New Yorkers meet those conditions and thus allow for a highly favorable test of the minority group hypothesis.

As blacks, the two groups share the same ascriptive racial category, encounter similar forms of discrimination and disadvantage, and have a number of political and economic interests in common. True enough, they also have a history of occasional intergroup tensions, which could undermine any potential for a race-based political alliance. Yet the minority group perspective would maintain racial commonalities, shared interests, and the potential benefits of a race-based coalition should override the intermittent interethnic conflicts.

The analysis reveals, however, that Afro-Caribbeans and African Americans in New York – like non-white groups elsewhere – have not had much success in fostering a sturdy race-based coalition. I find relations between Afro-Caribbean and African-American leaders typically have deteriorated in the face of interest conflicts over descriptive representation. The critical role interest convergence plays in coalition building has been well established by scholars (Sonenshein 2003b). When interests are at odds, alliances crumble or fail to develop, for that matter.

But rather than leaving the analysis at that conventional wisdom, the chapter explores why the racial commonalities the two groups share have not compelled them to settle these differences, as the minority group perspective would predict. It would be simplistic not to expect divisions of some kind among non-white groups. The challenge of any coalition is to overcome the inevitable intergroup differences and emphasize commonalities and compromises. Scholars who subscribe to the minority group view believe race provides much of the incentive to do so.

I offer evidence from my interviews with Afro-Caribbean political leaders that race is not always, however, the unifying category minority group scholars expect it to be. The interview data show race – despite its potential as a rallying point – has serious limits as a linchpin for coalitions among non-whites. In fact, it actually may heighten divisions among racial minority groups by emphasizing some interests over others. The analysis specifies the conditions under which such differences tend to be manifested, even in the face of strong racial affinities like the ones shared by Afro-Caribbean and African-American New Yorkers.

I then turn from the dynamics between these two groups to consider whether any external factors also may help to explain why they have been unable to capitalize on their commonalities to forge a stable alliance. I argue two key New York City political institutions – its parties and elections – have tended to undermine the intraracial commonalities of these two constituencies; these institutions, in fact, often have exacerbated the interethnic conflicts over descriptive representation between them. I also speculate the lack of an institutional vehicle to draw African-American and Afro-Caribbean elites together to emphasize shared racial interests, address disagreements, and find compromises has made it difficult for them to sustain a coalition.

In sum, the chapter draws two major conclusions. First, race has serious limits as a site for coalition building among non-white groups. Second, whatever potential it does hold may be undermined by a city's political institutions. More generally, the chapter suggests the literature on coalition building among non-white minorities in cities should be more attentive to how the complexities of race play out in intergroup relations and how institutions shape these dynamics.

The analytic inferences and conclusions at the heart of this chapter are based on my interviews with Afro-Caribbean political elites. They are supplemented with my analyses of key historical episodes and trends in the relations between Afro-Caribbean and African-American political elites. The chapter begins by spelling out the theoretical underpinnings of the minority group perspective. Next I lay out the prima facie case for a race-based alliance of Afro-Caribbean and African-American New Yorkers in keeping with the minority group view. I then turn to the discussion and analysis of their actual intergroup political dynamics and the reasons the predicted coalition between them has not emerged. The chapter ends with a consideration of conditions that might make coalitions among non-white groups more likely.

I. THE MINORITY GROUP THEORETICAL PERSPECTIVE

With so few cases of successful race-based alliances of non-white immigrants and African Americans in the literature, the question is why they are expected to develop at all. Why would scholars who advance the minority group perspective predict such a coalition in light of such limited empirical evidence? First, their expectations rest on the bedrock of dominant historical patterns in American politics. Race has been a long-standing and stubborn dividing line in local, state, and national politics in the United States. "Indeed, throughout American politics, the racial barrier redefined opinions, attitudes, and alignments" (Sonenshein 2003a). In urban politics, race has been a key axis for the ideological divisions and interest conflicts that dominate campaigns, make and break political alliances, and shape voting preferences. For much of this history, blacks and whites have been on opposite sides of the dividing line. But even when groups of blacks and whites have managed to forge alliances, racial issues often have been the touchstone for interest and ideological convergence between the two (Browning et al. 2003).

Although some observers believe the new non-white immigrants will blur and diminish the significance of the racial divide in urban politics, minority group scholars predict it will hold. Instead of pitting whites against blacks, however, it will divide whites and non-whites. Even with limited empirical evidence to date of race-based coalitions between blacks and the new immigrants, minority group scholars infer from the long history of racial division in this country that such alliances are still likely to develop. They reason that as non-white newcomers meet racial barriers like the ones African Americans have encountered, the probability of their making political common cause with their native-born black counterparts will increase.

Beyond the dominant patterns of racial division in this country, minority group scholars also take their analytic cues from theories of African-American politics. More specifically, the minority group view draws much of its inspiration from the literature on "linked racial fate" in African-American politics (Dawson 1994a; Tate 1993). Scholars have found African Americans remain a unified voting bloc in many cities, despite growing class divisions within the population (Stone and Pierannunzi 1997; Reed 1988). Dawson and others contend the persistence of the racial divide and antiblack discrimination in American life keep middle- and low-income African Americans in relatively close political step. African Americans, the argument goes, share a "linked fate" insofar as they all inevitably confront racial disadvantages. Race is, in short, a powerful political common denominator among African Americans, trumping the divisions between the middle class and the poor. It is essentially the linchpin unifying middle- and low-income blacks in an intraracial coalition. Similarly, minority group scholars predict race will override the differences between African Americans and the new immigrants and encourage them to forge political alliances.

II. THE PRIMA FACIE CASE FOR AN AFRO-CARIBBEAN AND AFRICAN-AMERICAN ALLIANCE

There are good reasons to expect this prediction to hold for non-white groups, particularly African Americans and Afro-Caribbean immigrants, in New York City. First, racial division and inequality have long been salient features of life in the city. Immigration has increased New York's demographic diversity in recent decades, to be sure: foreign-born minority groups from Latin America, Asia, and the Caribbean have proliferated, while the numbers of native-born whites and blacks have declined. But even in the face of these new patterns of population diversity, familiar racial divisions remain. The city's political and economic sectors are

TABLE 4.1. *Median Income by Groups in New York City*

Median Income	All Groups	Non-Hispanic Whites	Non-Hispanic Blacks	Hispanic	Asians
Income (2000)	38,293	50,920	35,629	27,881	41,338
Income (1990)	38,706	47,325	31,955	20,402	41,350

Note: Median income for both years adjusted for 2000 dollars.
Source: Lewis Mumford Center for Comparative Urban and Regional Research.

marked by a pronounced racial divide, with well-off whites often on one side and relatively disadvantaged non-white minorities on the other.

New York's Racial Divisions

New York's racial minorities have made significant advances in the last few decades. Blacks, Latinos, and Asians have advanced from having virtually no presence on the city council in the 1970s to a level of representation now almost proportionate to their numbers in the population. Racial minorities likewise have elected their own representatives to the state legislature and Congress, as well as to three of the city's five borough presidencies (Mollenkopf 2003). There are also signs of minority progress in the economy. Among the more notable trends from the last decade are the increases in black income, Asian educational progress, and Latino business growth (Lewis Mumford Center for Comparative Urban and Regional Research 2002).

But the picture is not altogether sanguine. Even with these advances by racial minorities, whites continue to enjoy a disproportionate share of the power, influence, and rewards in both the economic and political spheres of New York life. Table 4.1 indicates significant disparities remain between the city's white and minority populations on key indicators of economic well-being. For instance, white New Yorkers outpace their minority counterparts by a substantial margin in median income and homeownership. One recent study also uncovered a wide racial gap in neighborhood quality among New York residents (Lewis Mumford Center for Comparative Urban and Regional Research 2002). Whites tend to live in areas of the city that have higher incomes, more homeownership, greater numbers of degree holders, and lower poverty rates than their minority counterparts.

Similarly, although New York's minorities have enjoyed considerable gains in descriptive political representation in the last two decades, they nonetheless have much less substantive policy influence than whites. That is, they have less access to the political levers that actually control policy outcomes. Mollenkopf (2003, 121–122) notes, "With the exception of Congressman Charles Rangel . . . none of the city's minority legislators . . . wields great influence within their legislative bodies . . . The city's minority legislators can and do extract rewards from the white leaders of their bodies, but they do not exert a strong and independent influence on the overall allocation of public benefits."

At the mayoral level, minorities largely have been at the margins of or outside the electoral and governing coalitions assembled by New York's chief executive. Several of the elections for the top office have been racially divisive. What is more, the mayoralty has been occupied by a succession of white politicians. Aside from the short-lived administration headed by the African-American David Dinkins, minorities have not played a leading role in the city's mayoral regimes. Although several have relied on a modicum of minority support, they have been dominated largely by whites. Blacks, Latinos, and Asians mostly have occupied subordinate positions, if any at all.

In sum, non-whites are not as fully incorporated into New York's formal political structure as their white counterparts. As Mollenkopf (2003, 117) observes, "the key dynamic in New York City's political culture since the mid-1960s has been a series of reactions by white politicians and voters against failed or stalled bids for minority political power." The result is a significant racial disparity in political influence between whites and non-whites, mirrored by a similar divide in the city's economic arena.

The Racial Commonalities of Afro-Caribbeans and African Americans

Although the divisions separating whites and non-whites in New York are pronounced and politically salient, there is no reason to believe they alone would compel a race-based alliance among the city's minority constituencies. The minority group view holds that such divisions are necessary, but not sufficient to produce the predicted coalition. According to this perspective, alliances among non-whites are probable, not only when there is a sharp racial divide in the political system, but also when there are strong commonalities among the minority groups. By this logic, minority group scholars perhaps would not be surprised to find African Americans have not been able to forge a sustained alliance with the city's Latino or

Asian constituencies (Mollenkopf 2003; Falcon 1988).[1] After all, there
are notable cultural, ideological, economic, and even racial differences
between native-born blacks and these immigrant groups. Many Latinos,
for instance, do not identify as non-whites or racial minorities, unlike
African Americans, who largely do. In short, the racial commonalities
of African-American New Yorkers and their Asian and Latino counterparts are limited; the differences among these groups arguably match or
outweigh the similarities. It should not be surprising, then, that relations
between African Americans and these groups often have been riven with
conflict.

For African Americans and Afro-Caribbean immigrants, however,
there is a much stronger argument to be made for racial commonalities. The two groups of black New Yorkers appear to have considerable
mutual interests and incentives for forging a race-based alliance. Consider the prima facie case. First, Afro-Caribbeans and African Americans
obviously share the commonality of black skin color in a country where
discrimination against blacks has a long history. Sonenshein (2003a, 345)
has pointed out, however, "color is not necessarily an interest... [nor] a
unifying force." In this view, the commonality of race alone is not enough
to generate an alliance. In Sonenshein's formulation, shared interests and
ideology are also critical to successful coalition building. But race or color
is sometimes very much correlated with interests and ideology. It certainly
is in the case of Afro-Caribbean and African-American New Yorkers.

The two groups experience higher levels of residential segregation than
any other population in New York (Lewis Mumford Center for Comparative Urban and Regional Research 2003). Put another way, Afro-
Caribbeans and African Americans are both confined to overwhelmingly
black sections of the city.[2] The neighborhoods where the two groups
live tend to be more economically distressed than majority-white areas.
Afro-Caribbeans and African Americans are exposed to the same
neighborhood problems, whether they be failing schools, concentrated

---

[1] Scholars have puzzled over the absence of a strong minority coalition in New York. The
city would seem to be fertile soil for this kind of alliance. The fact one has yet to take root
makes New York a "great anomaly" in the urban politics literature (Mollenkopf 2003).

[2] Afro-Caribbean immigrants living in these overwhelmingly black areas have carved out
their own distinctive residential niches – often of marginally higher socioeconomic quality than surrounding African-American neighborhoods (Crowder and Tedrow 2001).
Yet this modest socioeconomic advantage has not won them access to more integrated
neighborhoods – a predicament they share with their middle-class African-American
counterparts. See Chapter 2 for more discussion.

TABLE 4.2. *Black Election Districts in New York City*

Democratic Vote and Registration	African American	Total	Afro-Caribbean	Total
2001 Mark Green (D)	38,825	51,379	43,855	63,829
%	75.6	100	68.7	100
2000 Al Gore (D)	83,649	87,431	97,823	108,135
%	95.7	100	90.5	100
2001 registered Democrats	143,013	174,356	140,851	183,848
%	82.0	100	76.6	100

Note: African-American election districts are less than 5% Afro-Caribbean and more than 40% African American. Afro-Caribbean election districts are less than 40% African American and more than 20% Afro-Caribbean.
Source: John Mollenkopf, CUNY Center for Urban Research.

poverty, or crime. These two groups thus often have overlapping interests in contests over the distribution of public services and resources to city neighborhoods.

Afro-Caribbeans and African Americans both also have had their share of neighborhood-level tensions with whites. Quite a few of New York's most serious cases of interracial conflict in the past two decades have involved either Afro-Caribbeans or African-Americans and white residents. In the late 1980s and early 1990s, the city was convulsed by a series of violent attacks against blacks by groups of whites. All but one of these incidents involved an Afro-Caribbean victim (Waters 1996). The two groups also have had turbulent relations with the city's mostly white police force. There is no need to rehearse individual instances of conflict here. But suffice it to say there have been complaints about police brutality and misconduct from both the African-American and Afro-Caribbean communities.

Finally, Afro-Caribbean immigrants and African Americans have similar partisan attachments. The two groups are more heavily Democratic than any other constituency – white or non-white – in the New York City electorate. Table 4.2 shows overwhelming attachment to the Democratic Party in both African-American and Afro-Caribbean election districts. Although first-generation Afro-Caribbean immigrants do not have the same long-standing historical ties to the party as their native-born counterparts, they nonetheless have favored the Democratic line almost as much as African Americans in their voting and registration patterns.

This shared party allegiance does not necessarily mean Afro-Caribbeans and African Americans have identical ideological outlooks.

Indeed, the table indicates Afro-Caribbean election districts are consistently several points less Democratic than African-American districts. Although voting statistics suggest both groups tend to be fairly liberal in their political outlook, there is evidence of some shades of difference between them on particular policy questions. Afro-Caribbeans, for instance, are supportive of liberal immigration policies, whereas African Americans are more ambivalent (Fuchs 1990). A few case studies also have suggested Afro-Caribbeans may be a little less supportive than their native-born counterparts of government solutions to social problems (Chapter 7; Waters 1999). Still, there is no evidence of deep ideological divisions between these two overwhelmingly Democratic constituencies.

Support for the party has led to gains for African Americans and Afro-Caribbean immigrants at the elite level. African Americans have secured leadership positions in the Democratic county organizations. The party also has incorporated a handful of Afro-Caribbean elites in recent years. Even with these gains, both groups have less power within the party than whites. In Queens and the Bronx, whites continue to control a disproportionate share of the leadership positions and influence within the Democratic Party; only in Manhattan, and in Brooklyn to a lesser extent, have African Americans been able to wield a decisive share of power in the party organization. After many decades of unwavering allegiance to the Democratic Party, then, native-born blacks still do not match their white counterparts in their level of influence over the organization. Afro-Caribbeans, on the other hand, are marginal players, as the party continues to ignore the vast majority of these immigrants.

All in all, the racial commonalities between African Americans and Afro-Caribbean immigrants are more than skin deep. The two groups have a number of experiences, interests, and partisan viewpoints in common. They also boast a solid cadre of leaders who regularly interact within New York's Democratic Party. All these factors – common interests, shared ideology, and familiar leadership – coupled with the pronounced racial divide in New York City politics would appear to pave the way for a race-based alliance of Afro-Caribbean immigrants and African Americans. This is not to say there are no potential divisions between the two groups. There are obvious differences of culture and ethnicity. Yet the minority group view would argue their commonalities and the strategic appeal of a race-based coalition should override such divisions. This perspective recognizes a clear imperative for these two groups of blacks to "close racial ranks" and forge a stable political alliance (Kasinitz 1992; Carmichael and Hamilton 1967).

Race-based mobilization represents an alternative route into politics for the thousands of Afro-Caribbean immigrants who have been neglected by the Democratic Party. Outnumbered by African Americans, these newcomers might find it hard to resist the strategic benefits of combining with their native-born counterparts to build a larger black constituency and thereby achieve incorporation. Likewise, such mobilization could also serve as a potent source of political leverage for African Americans seeking to enlarge their share of government resources and influence on the direction of public policy. With their combined numbers, the two groups could constitute a powerful minority bloc of voters with the potential to decide election outcomes.

III. A COALITION THAT NEVER FORMED

Yet Afro-Caribbean and African-American New Yorkers thus far have been unable to establish a stable coalition. For all their prima facie commonalities, the two groups have been no more successful at fostering a race-based alliance than their non-white counterparts in other cities. There have been instances of political cooperation and common cause between them, to be sure. In 1989, for example, Afro-Caribbean and African-American voters lined up solidly behind Dinkins in his successful first bid for the mayoralty. Together the two groups were the single largest bloc of voters to support Dinkins in the election (Arian et al. 1991). Since then, these two groups of black ethnics also have joined at the voting booth to support high-profile Democratic candidates for state- and citywide office, such as Senator Hillary Clinton and the unsuccessful mayoral candidate Mark Green.

Similarly, the episodes of police brutality in black neighborhoods in the late 1990s galvanized hundreds of Afro-Caribbeans and African Americans to take to the streets and demand greater police accountability. Both the Dinkins election and the protests against police brutality appealed to the sense of racial solidarity among African Americans and Afro-Caribbeans. The two instances might well have been viewed as promising precursors to the race-based coalition anticipated by minority group scholars. But these cases of mutual support were episodic and short lived.

Patterns of Conflict

Relations between Afro-Caribbean immigrants and African Americans over the last two decades more often have been marked by a stubborn undercurrent of tension, overshadowing the moments of cooperation.

My interviews with Afro-Caribbean elites reveal a pattern of friction in the political relationship between the immigrants and their native-born counterparts. The conflicts have not extended to rank-and-file Afro-Caribbean and African-American constituents. Nor have they revolved around anything like competing economic interests, substantive policy differences, or ideological disagreements. Rather, the conflicts typically have been confined to the elite level and have revolved mostly around matters of political turf. More specifically, African-American and Afro-Caribbean leaders have clashed over attempts by the latter group to secure descriptive representation and carve out political influence for a distinct constituency of Caribbean-born blacks. African-American leaders have resisted these efforts, whereas their Afro-Caribbean counterparts have complained about the opposition from their fellow black leaders.

My interview respondents noted African-American leaders long have been resistant to or lukewarm about the prospect of Afro-Caribbean mobilization. One interview subject (November 22, 1996) conjectured African-American opposition to Caribbean participation was one impediment to greater electoral representation for the immigrant group. As he explained, Afro-Caribbeans have yet to achieve a level of representation proportionate to their numbers, "[p]artially because there is, there has been, opposition from African-American leaders." The Caribbean Action Lobby (CAL) member and former state senator Waldaba Stewart (interview, May 2, 1997) recalled many African-American politicians were either slow or unwilling to acknowledge the emergence of an Afro-Caribbean ethnic constituency in the 1980s.

Ten, fifteen years ago, African Americans – many of them – took the position that the only relevant issues were African-American issues, and in many respects ignored the growing Caribbean bloc ... In the 1980s, they didn't even want us to run for political office.

Indeed, as Kasinitz (1992) has recounted in his study, African-American politicians consistently opposed or refused to support Afro-Caribbean candidates for elective office in the 1980s.

The pattern continued into the 1990s. Consider the former city councilwoman Una Clarke's account of her 1991 bid for a legislative seat. Clarke was seeking to represent a heavily Caribbean district in Brooklyn; her victory made her the first Caribbean-born member of the city council. Her account of the campaign underscores her perception that African-American leaders have often resisted Afro-Caribbean mobilization.

The Jamaican-born politician (interview, December 13, 20, 1996) recalled:

I helped to elect almost every African-American in central Brooklyn, and when my time came to run they were far and few in between that supported me . . . [T]here was not a single African American that considered themselves "progressive" that did not come to me and did not ask for my support, and for whom I gave it. So when my time came, I thought that everybody was gonna rally around me, that there would not even be a campaign . . . "Look, your time has come" . . . Nothing of the sort happened.

In a 1999 interview, the former city councilwoman lamented, "I never saw bias until I ran in 1991. When I entered office the street talk was, 'Why do these West Indians feel they have to be in politics?'" (Dao 1999). To be fair, Clarke did have the support of the African-American congressman Major Owens, who perhaps recognized backing her would carry important symbolic value in his own increasingly Caribbean district. But staunch opposition to Clarke's campaign arose from the African American Clarence Norman, Brooklyn's Democratic county leader. Norman ran his own candidate, a fellow African American, Carl Andrews, for the council seat and led an ultimately aborted legal challenge to Clarke's victory in the aftermath of the election. Clarke and Norman have managed to build a cordial, if somewhat delicate, relationship since then (*New York Carib News* 1996a).

The former city councilwoman and other elite respondents also noted African-American leaders generally have been slow to court Afro-Caribbeans as a distinct constituency. When asked whether African-American politicians reach out to Caribbean-American voters, one campaign organizer (interview, November 24, 1996) replied tersely, "Not enough. And when they do, they reach out halfheartedly." Another respondent (July 5, 1997) offered:

[Clarence] Norman has enormous political clout because he is the head of the Democratic Party in Brooklyn. From time to time, I've heard Caribbean leaders, including Una Clarke, [say] that he would support other people than them. I'm not sure if that's the case. But I would like to see him in more [Caribbean] events. I would like to see him reach out more to the community.

Clarke rated white politicians slightly higher than African Americans on outreach to the Caribbean population. She (interview, December 13, 20, 1996) elaborated, "I think white politicians [unlike their black counterparts] feel compelled to do that kind of outreach. Yes. Marty Markowitz is a well-known example. And I can give other examples, too."

More recently, some African-American leaders – Dinkins, Owens, Sharpton, and Rangel – have begun to make their own appeals to the immigrant community. Owens and Sharpton have been particularly vocal about incidents of police brutality involving immigrants from the Caribbean, Latin America, and Africa. Their efforts are clearly intended to acknowledge the growing numbers of foreign-born newcomers to the city and perhaps to prevent conservative interests from pursuing divide-and-conquer tactics among New York's minority constituencies. But some of my respondents still characterize these efforts by African-American leaders as begrudging or lukewarm. One (interview, November 22, 1996) recalled Dinkins's early outreach to Caribbean Americans. "Oh, we had a rough time getting Dinkins out into the Caribbean community... They say that there were some people in Dinkins's camp who were very anti-Caribbean – African-American people." In sum, many Afro-Caribbean elites remain convinced some African-American politicians still regard the prospect of Caribbean mobilization with ambivalence or resistance.

Key historical episodes in the relations between Afro-Caribbean and African-American political elites tend to support the views of these respondents. One of the most well-known instances of conflict between the two groups occurred during former mayor Ed Koch's 1985 bid for reelection. A group of approximately 150 politically active Afro-Caribbeans established "Caribbeans for Koch" to back the incumbent mayor's campaign. Support for Koch in the Afro-Caribbean immigrant community was hardly widespread or deep. But the group's aim was largely symbolic: that is, to secure greater access to the mayor and City Hall for Afro-Caribbean immigrants – especially since Koch likely would be reelected. Caribbeans for Koch was thus an early attempt by Afro-Caribbean elites to signal the emergence of their immigrant community as a distinctive ethnic constituency with its own aspirations to political power (Kasinitz, 253).

Whatever the motivation, Caribbeans for Koch was met with a torrent of angry criticism by African-American political leaders. Their outrage was fueled by two major concerns. First, anti-Koch sentiment was pervasive in the African-American community. African-American leaders accused the mayor of fomenting antiblack racism and exacerbating the city's racial problems with his incendiary rhetoric. In their view, then, Caribbeans for Koch showed complete disregard for the mayor's troubling record on race relations; that insensitivity was perhaps all the more incensing to African-American leaders because it was demonstrated by a group of black immigrants, who were expected to be as outraged by the mayor's record on race as their native-born counterparts.

Second, Caribbeans for Koch was established at the same time that African-American leaders were attempting to "close ranks" and mount an independent political initiative to replace Koch with a black mayor. The Coalition for a Just New York brought together scores of black politicians and activists to identify a candidate and support his or her campaign. The expectation by organizers was that the group would mobilize blacks and other minority New Yorkers to help ensure electoral victory. The coalition was riven by internal division, though; their African-American candidate ran a poor campaign and lost. Yet, many African Americans strongly criticized Caribbeans for Koch for working at cross purposes with the coalition, flouting the goals of African-American political leadership, and undermining the larger struggle for black empowerment. As one of my elite respondents recalled, the African-American leader of the Coalition for a Just New York, Al Vann, publicly reproached Afro-Caribbean leaders for pursuing divisive strategies. "They were not happy with us [Caribbean American leaders]. Al Vann called our attempts to organize on our own tribalism" (interview, November 22, 1996). The supporters of the Coalition for a Just New York essentially saw this attempt at independent Caribbean mobilization as a strain against the tether of racial solidarity.

There have been more recent political conflicts between the two groups involving issues of racial unity and representation. In fact, the tensions have become more palpable as growing numbers of Caribbean politicians run for elective office in the name of a distinct Afro-Caribbean ethnic constituency. As the numbers of Afro-Caribbean New Yorkers have increased steadily over the last two decades, so too have the political viability and likelihood of such ethnically targeted campaigns by Caribbean politicians. These attempts by Afro-Caribbean political entrepreneurs to organize their fellow immigrants into a distinct voting bloc still engender occasional criticism and resistance from some African-American leaders.

A number of Afro-Caribbean candidates joined the fray in recent New York City elections, making direct appeals to their coethnics. The most notable instance was the 2000 race for Brooklyn's Eleventh Congressional District seat between the then nine-term incumbent Owens and the former city councilwoman Clarke. Blacks constitute 55 percent of the district population; more than two-thirds of them trace their roots to the Caribbean. The large number of Afro-Caribbeans in the district is a striking example of the way immigration has transformed this stretch of central Brooklyn over the last few decades. Despite these demographic shifts, the African-American congressman, Owens, had held on to his seat since

1982 without a serious electoral challenge, that is, until he faced a fierce test from Clarke in the 2001 Democratic primary. Although Owens won the primary and went on to retain the seat in a lopsided general election victory, the race was one of the most bitter of the campaign season.

Practically none of the rancor between the two candidates was driven by actual issue disagreements; rather, it was fueled by two very emotionally charged factors. First, there was the underlying tableau of political betrayal. The two were longtime political allies before Clarke announced her candidacy. Owens described himself as a former mentor to the councilwoman (Hicks 2000b). He thus saw her bid to replace him as an act of political betrayal. Clarke, on the other hand, dismissed the talk of betrayal as a distraction from her true motivation for mounting her campaign: that is, to serve the district's constituents. As she put it, "Too much has been made of friendship. It's about leadership and effectiveness. I don't think he's kept up with the needs of the changing community" (Hicks 2000a). Clarke's mention of the "changing community" might be taken as a thinly veiled reference to the increasing numbers of Caribbean immigrants in the district. Her allusion hints at the other factor that fueled the rancor of the contest between these two candidates.

Even more significant than this personal tableau was the pall of interethnic conflict that hung over the race. Clarke made a point of trumpeting her Caribbean roots, appealing directly to her coethnics, and painting her opponent as anti-immigrant. Her goal clearly was to announce the presence of a distinct Caribbean constituency within the majority-black Eleventh District. Even more critically, she sought to emphasize her affinity with these immigrant voters and at the same time raise doubts about the incumbent's sensitivity to their concerns. Owens, in turn, condemned Clarke for couching her campaign in what he described as divisive ethnic chauvinism (Hicks 2000b). His complaint was echoed by a number of African-American leaders, who sent Clarke a letter urging her to abandon her candidacy. The congressman lamented Clarke's tactics would split Brooklyn's black community and undermine the larger cause of black empowerment. His complaints practically echoed those directed against Caribbeans for Koch by African-American leaders more than fifteen years earlier.

IV. THE LIMITS OF RACIAL SOLIDARITY

The conflicts over descriptive representation between Afro-Caribbean and African-American leaders are striking for the frequency with which the question of racial unity is invoked. The fact that racial solidarity has not provided the incentive for the two groups to overcome these differences belies the predictions of the minority group view. The steady recurrence of such conflicts suggests even racial commonality has its limits as a potential coalition linchpin.

The interviews and historical evidence indicate African-American politicians have had one dominant, prevailing criticism of their Afro-Caribbean counterparts in the conflicts over descriptive representation: they complain the immigrants' efforts to appeal to a separate Afro-Caribbean constituency are divisive and antithetical to the cause of racial solidarity and greater black empowerment.[3] This lament typically greets electoral campaigns by Caribbean politicians seeking to rally, mobilize, or acknowledge their coethnics as a distinct constituency. The logic behind this line of criticism is straightforward. Appealing separately to Afro-Caribbean immigrants, the complaint goes, is tantamount to splitting apart black New Yorkers, and doing that in turn undermines black political power. African-American political leaders have grown increasingly concerned about these potential divisions over the last decade, as the numbers of non-white immigrants in the city have expanded. Their worry is that conservative political interests will seek to exploit or even sow divisions between African Americans and these new immigrant constituencies, thereby dousing any potential for a liberal rainbow coalition led by blacks. It is the classic divide-and-conquer strategy. Divisions between native- and Caribbean-born black New Yorkers, they contend, might be put to those very political designs. In short, some African Americans argue the mobilization of Afro-Caribbeans as a distinct constituency is ultimately a threat to black racial solidarity and empowerment.

Afro-Caribbeans, on the other hand, insist the opposition from African-American leaders is unfair and appeals to racial unity are beside the point. More precisely, Afro-Caribbean politicians note the immigrant community is large enough to warrant its own representatives and has distinctive concerns that cannot be taken for granted or glossed over with appeals to black racial solidarity. My elite respondents were emphatic on this point. One (December 14, 1996) offered:

I think because we [Caribbean Americans] have some separate interests, we have a responsibility to be a distinct bloc, be it around immigration and immigration reform, be it around trade with the Caribbean. I think that we can play a pivotal

---

[3] The obvious irony of this complaint is that African Americans view attempts by a group of *black* immigrants to achieve political influence as a threat to black empowerment, rather than a step in that direction.

role...We have that obligation. And I think it's a mistake to use skin color to be the only criterion. To use skin color as the only criterion stifles both African Americans and Caribbean Americans.

Another respondent gave a more concise reply to the same question. He (interview, November 23, 1996) explained: "Caribbean Americans are a distinct bloc. Of course, we share many of the same concerns of African Americans. But we have our own needs and concerns that you just can't dismiss or take it for granted that they [African Americans] will understand." A community activist answered the charge that Afro-Caribbean mobilization promotes divisiveness within New York's black population this way:

Our comment is that you have different Caucasian or white groups, you have the Irish, the Italian, the this and that. What's wrong with us? Why can't we have that too? Just because we're originally, say, from Africa, does that mean we have to think and act the same way? Don't we [Caribbean Americans] have our own needs and issues? (interview, May 2, 1997)

Furthermore, many resent what they perceive to be African-American leaders' implicit assumption Afro-Caribbeans will be relegated to junior status in any alliance of the two groups. In a 1996 interview, for example, Clarke bristled when she was asked about the African-American county leader Norman's aim to consolidate black political power in the heavily Caribbean Forty-third AD. "There are over 300,000 Caribbean Americans in Central Brooklyn. What consolidation are we talking about here? Nobody will relegate us to second class status" (*New York Carib News* 1996b). It is clear Clarke's objection is not necessarily to the prospect of a unified black political bloc; in fact, she and many of the Caribbean-American leaders I interviewed were supportive of the notion of a coalition of the two groups. But her worry is that the political goals and interests of Afro-Caribbean immigrants will be subordinated in any such alliance.

Clarke's concern illuminates an important analytic point about alliances built around the idea of racial solidarity. The former city council-woman notes African-American leaders insist on serving as racial agents on behalf of Afro-Caribbean immigrants by appealing to the notion of group unity,[4] but in doing so, they often diminish or ignore the distinctive ethnic interests of their foreign-born counterparts. Appeals to racial group unity or collective racial interests – such as those made by

---

[4] I borrow the term "racial agents" from a conversation with Jack Citrin.

Vann, Norman, and Owens more recently – are almost always articulated in an effort to advance very specific agendas, which ultimately favor some interests over others. Vann's Coalition for a Just New York, for instance, invoked the goal of racial group unity to criticize and discourage independent mobilization by Afro-Caribbean politicians. The coalition's expectation was that all black New Yorkers, native and foreign born alike, should fall in line with their hand-picked candidates and issue positions. Their notion of group unity, then, was one in which their agenda took precedence over other interests within New York's black community, such as Afro-Caribbeans' desire for their own share of political influence.

Of course, racial solidarity in politics does not necessarily prescribe or authorize a particular agenda, set of positions, or slate of candidates. Indeed, calls to racial unity might well be seen as an invitation to discuss and reach negotiated stances on such issues. Yet appeals to racial solidarity often implicitly privilege one set of interests over others without any open debate. Even worse, the resulting bias takes cover beneath the rhetorical gloss of "natural" or "collective" racial interests that benefit the population as a whole. Consequently, interests that ought to be debated or evaluated for how they affect different constituents are instead deemed to be settled and beyond question. The case of African Americans and Afro-Caribbeans in New York demonstrates that the group that happens to have more influence – whether by virtue of numbers, longer political history, or whatever – has the advantage of framing the agenda in this way. African-American elites in New York thus often have taken the lead in prescribing what is required for a race-based alliance or minority empowerment, even if that agenda is not necessarily conducive to the interests of Afro-Caribbeans or other non-white groups.

Further, the case demonstrates that the notion of racial group unity not only favors specific interests and agendas, but also can be used to impose discipline and gatekeeping. Appeals to racial group solidarity are often made in the service of mobilization efforts. But the tensions between African-American and Afro-Caribbean politicians show racial group unity is a two-edged sword that can also be used to discourage mobilization by particular interests within the black population, or any minority constituency, for that matter.[5] To discipline specific constituencies within the population, dominant elites often stake out certain positions and label them as the ones most in keeping with the aims of racial empowerment and

---

[5] See Cohen 1999 on how this facet of racial group unity impeded grassroots campaigns to prevent the spread of AIDS in the African-American population.

the political preferences of blacks as a whole.[6] Any interests that appear to deviate from those positions are then conveniently challenged for threatening group unity, the "true" preferences of blacks, or the cause of empowerment. The criticisms lodged against Caribbeans for Koch by the leaders of the Coalition for a Just New York are an obvious example of this tactic.

Owens employed a similar strategy against Clarke in their 2000 primary battle. The congressman tried to portray the city councilwoman as a supporter of Mayor Rudolph Giuliani, who was notoriously unpopular among blacks during his tenure in office. He also charged Clarke had been silent on the issue of police brutality, about which the vast majority of black New Yorkers were acutely concerned. In contrast, he noted he had engaged in demonstrations to protest incidents of brutality and had even been arrested (Hicks 2000a). Owens essentially waved his civil rights credentials in support of blacks, while implying Clarke had none to show. The strategy served to brand the Caribbean-born candidate as a kind of race traitor, a politician out of step with black interests and the goal of black empowerment. Owens engaged, in effect, in a kind of implicit pro-black political communication.[7] His appeals all but announced he had deeper ties to New York's black constituents than Clarke and thus was more "racially authentic" than she. Tactics such as these are likely to play a role in the conflicts between Afro-Caribbean and African-American leaders, precisely because questions of racial unity and representation so often come into play.[8]

---

[6] The essentialist behavioral or cultural notions of racial identity that pervade everyday, commonsense thinking in this country follow the same perverse logic. That is, racial groups are deemed to "behave" or "act" in keeping with an identifiable mold. Blacks, say, are expected to be good dancers, or Asians good students. When group members deviate from the behavioral mold, they are labeled racially inauthentic. For a useful discussion of how this all-too-common essentialist conflation of racial identity and behavior nonetheless allows for an *antiessentialist* critique of racial categories, see Jackson 2001.

[7] See Mendelberg 2001 for a first-rate discussion of the use and effects of implicit racial messages in political campaigns. Although her analysis does not address pro-black racial cues, she contends this form of political communication circulates in majority-black areas and follows the logic she spells out in her study.

[8] Challenging the racial credentials or commitments of a fellow black politician in electoral competition is a strategy that surfaces even among African Americans themselves. The famously acrimonious 2002 race between the mayoral incumbent Sharpe James and young upstart Cory Booker in Newark is a recent example. Although both men are African American, questions of racial solidarity and authenticity emerged nonetheless. The James camp took the tactic to bizarre extremes when they began circulating rumors that Booker was actually white and passing as black to win the support of Newark's mainly black voters. Such strategies likely will become even more common as the black population becomes more diverse in cities around the country.

V. WHY INTEREST CONFLICTS OVER DESCRIPTIVE REPRESENTATION

The analysis demonstrates why race is not the ultimate unifying category minority group scholars expect it to be, even for two groups of blacks. Yet the question that remains is why the interest conflicts between Afro-Caribbean and African-American elites have focused on descriptive representation. Almost none of the major conflicts between these leaders have revolved around concrete policy interests, ideology, or the socioeconomic or cultural interests of their respective constituencies. They mainly have involved issues of political turf and representation.

African Americans have achieved higher levels of descriptive representation and influence in New York City politics than Afro-Caribbeans and other non-white groups. As the dominant minority group, in the Democratic Party, in fact, African-Americans have been able to control a significant share of the material rewards. Mobilization by Afro-Caribbean newcomers, or any other minority group, for that matter, potentially could threaten their hold on these political prizes and impede their socioeconomic mobility. After all, government jobs have helped foster the expansion of the African-American middle class. Entrenched African-American elites thus have a rational interest in maintaining the status quo and resisting Afro-Caribbean mobilization.

Afro-Caribbeans and African Americans are concentrated in many of the same election districts. The ascension of an Afro-Caribbean to political office could mean the displacement of an African-American incumbent. Several respondents explained this competitive intergroup dynamic.

> There definitely is competition and conflict between the two groups sometimes, especially in politics. Part of the problem is – if you want to call it [a problem] – we are fighting for the same political offices in the same election districts. We're fighting for the same piece of the pie. And African Americans probably think if Caribbean people get elected they will lose out on their share. (interview, November 28, 1996)

The result is often African-American resistance to Caribbean political initiative and organization. As Clarke (interview, December 13 and 20, 1996) put it, "The [African-American] attitude is 'Don't try passing me. I've been here.'"

Battles over political turf and representation between the two groups thus devolve into zero-sum struggles. The conflicts are not just about political office, but also access to the government jobs and other prizes that accompany it. For some African-American politicians, then, the interest in political self-preservation trumps any vision for race-based mobilization and coalition building by them and their Caribbean-born counterparts. Afro-Caribbean elites, on the other hand, worry their interest in greater descriptive representation and policy influence will be trumped by African-American political prerogatives.

The competition over political turf between African Americans and Afro-Caribbeans is arguably reminiscent of earlier historical conflicts among white ethnic groups. There were, for example, fierce battles over patronage and positions within the Democratic Party between Jewish and Italian New Yorkers. But there is an important distinction between those earlier interethnic conflicts and the current tensions between African Americans and Afro-Caribbeans. The earlier competition for patronage and public jobs among Irish, Italian, and Jewish ethnics was diminished, or at least moderated, as one or the other group moved into private sector employment and up the socioeconomic ladder. Italian politicians, for instance, had less of a stake in holding on to government jobs when their coethnics began to find success in private sector professions. They were thus gradually inclined to relinquish patronage positions in government to their Jewish rivals.

Today's African-American political elites, however, are much more reluctant to concede public sector jobs and positions to their Caribbean-born counterparts. Their determination to hold on to these forms of public patronage is not surprising. Discrimination historically has made it difficult for African Americans to find jobs and move up the career ladder in the private sector. Government, in contrast, has furnished them with fair and ample employment opportunities. Indeed, public sector jobs have helped foster the expansion of a stable African-American middle class in New York and other cities. The incentive to hold on to these public sector jobs is thus much greater for African Americans than it was for white ethnics in the past century. To put it more bluntly, the stakes are higher.

African Americans thus arguably have a legitimate reason to worry about Afro-Caribbean political mobilization. Their concern is likely compounded by the widespread perception that whites often view foreign-born blacks more favorably than they do African Americans (Waters 1999).[9] By this light, Afro-Caribbeans look less like a racial in-group and potential coalition partner for African Americans, and more

---

[9] For a thoughtful discussion on how white perceptions can engender conflict among subordinate minority groups, see Kim 1999; 2000.

like a competing out-group that could threaten these native-born blacks' share of political power and public sector resources. That threat of competition and displacement calls into question a key assumption of the minority group perspective: that is, that non-white groups are likely to find common cause and grounds for coalition building in their shared racial experiences. For all the galvanizing power race carries, this has not been the case with African-American and Afro-Caribbean New Yorkers. Clearly, even presumed common racial interests have their limits.

Electoral Institutions

Another weakness of the minority perspective is its failure to consider how institutional factors might influence the way groups perceive and frame their interests. Racial inequalities and divisions in the political system provide considerable impetus for African Americans, Afro-Caribbeans, and other non-whites to forge a race-based alliance, to be sure. But whether groups opt to coalesce and capitalize on common interests – racial or otherwise – or go it alone depends to some degree on the incentive structure of the political system. The prospects hinge on how political institutions frame group perceptions about interests, competition, rewards, and so on. Institutions structure the political learning process at the heart of the incorporation trajectory. They provide cues to new groups on ways to pitch their interests and fashion their political identities in the electoral fray. In the case of Afro-Caribbeans, the interviews make it clear the immigrants are inclined to elect their own coethnics to political office rather than have African Americans serve as their racial agents. The question is why these immigrants value ethnic over racial representation.

It turns out New York's electoral institutions may very well dispose them to do so. The city's electoral structure encourages groups to organize and think of themselves primarily as ethnic cohorts, rather than as racial constituents. Electoral jurisdictions in New York City closely follow the outlines of ethnic neighborhoods. The scores of community board, city council, and state assembly seats in New York are based on districts that often track the boundaries of residential enclaves and neighborhoods bearing the unmistakable stamp of particular ethnic groups. It is not much of an exaggeration, then, to conclude the basic political jurisdiction in the mind of New York politicians and perhaps its voters is the ethnic neighborhood. It is the fundamental unit of the city's political cartography. New York's "city trenches," to borrow Katznelson's (1981) famous phrase, are its ethnic neighborhoods.

Consider the Fortieth City Council District seat, formerly held by the Caribbean-born Una Clarke and now occupied by her daughter. The city created this district in 1991 specifically to accommodate the proliferation of Caribbean immigrant enclaves in central Brooklyn. Most of the pressure to establish the seat arose from Afro-Caribbean politicians. The new district essentially gave the ethnic group an opportunity to garner its own share of political representation. As Stewart of CAL (interview, May 2, 1997) put it, "We [Caribbean politicians] noticed that other groups had districts to represent their people; we felt we should have some too." His remark suggests the decision to push for a heavily Caribbean city council district was not merely the result of constituent pressure or elite initiative. Rather, it was encouraged by politicians' perceptions of the institutional logic of the city's electoral districts. Once institutional arrangements are in place, they tend to influence how elites understand their interests, their ties to constituents, and their relations with other groups. Sure enough, the Fortieth City Council seat has been held perpetually and predictably by a Caribbean politician, fulfilling the logic of the district's original design.

More generally, the city's electoral battles are waged from these ethnic neighborhood trenches. The most obvious way for an aspiring politician to build a constituent base in New York is to rally and mobilize voters in ethnic neighborhoods. If a politician can put together a sizable, cohesive bloc of ethnic votes at the neighborhood level, he or she essentially can become a serious player in New York's political game. Politicians thus often are encouraged to make appeals to particular ethnic groups. Ethnic politics has long been a staple of political life in American cities, to be sure. The ethnic and immigrant enclaves across New York City are a hard-to-miss source of votes. But the close continuity between the design of the city's electoral institutions and the pattern of its ethnic neighborhoods encourages and reinforces this ethnically conscious form of political organization and mobilization. Ethnically targeted appeals are practically dictated by the logic of the city's political jurisdictions.

Some researchers have argued convincingly that this neighborhood-based system of representation serves to regulate and perhaps mute interethnic tensions (Mollenkopf 1999; Skerry 1993). On this view, the system channels interethnic conflicts that might otherwise spill over into the streets and translates them to the bargaining table of the political process, where they can be resolved, or at least managed. This may explain why cities such as New York and San Antonio, which both boast this kind of neighborhood-based system, have been less susceptible to volatile intergroup clashes than Los Angeles, where no such system exists. Nevertheless, this electoral institutional design simply transfers the potential for interethnic tension from the neighborhood to the elite level, where leaders are often encouraged to position themselves and relate to each other as representatives of particular ethnic groups. The interethnic conflicts thus move from the neighborhood level to the political club, the party system, the campaign trail, and the legislature.

It is no wonder, then, relations between Afro-Caribbean and African-American political elites have been plagued by interethnic tensions over descriptive representation. The potential for interethnic conflict between these two groups of black leaders is fairly telegraphed in the pattern of black neighborhood settlement across New York City. Recall African Americans and Afro-Caribbean immigrants often live in adjoining neighborhoods or even share the same ones. When these areas are carved up into electoral jurisdictions, they readily become arenas for ethnically tinged, intrablack bickering over descriptive representation. When a district that was predominantly African American is somehow redrawn to give growing numbers of Afro-Caribbean immigrants a numerical advantage, the strategic incentive for Caribbean political entrepreneurs to make targeted appeals to their coethnics is hard to resist.

There are a few who avoid playing the ethnic card in campaigns. State Senator John Sampson is a good example. This second-generation Afro-Caribbean New Yorker has largely refrained from making exclusive appeals to his coethnics.[10] He instead campaigns to blacks generally and scrupulously avoids the interethnic schisms that have erupted among the city's black leaders. But most other Afro-Caribbean politicians have followed the ethnic strategy. The price of giving in to the temptation is the danger of engendering interethnic conflict with African-American political elites faced with the specter of electoral displacement. The primary battle between Clarke and Owens is just one of the better-known recent examples. But several cases fit this predicted pattern.

---

[10] Sampson's avoidance of the ethnic strategy may be due to his socialization in the United States. Born to Caribbean parents in New York, he has ties to African Americans that run deep. His second-generation experiences and how they color his political choices may be a precursor to the future of black politics in New York. He is part of a new, expanding population of second-generation Caribbean New Yorkers. These children of black immigrants likely will have a significant influence on the city's political future, as they become increasingly involved in the electoral process. It remains to be seen whether they will identify mostly as second-generation Caribbean ethnics or as African Americans. But whatever the case, they may find coalition building with African Americans easier than their parents if they interact regularly with their counterparts in institutional settings.

A simple historical comparison helps to demonstrate how the institutional design of electoral jurisdictions in New York shapes intergroup dynamics. It is no coincidence the tensions over descriptive representation between Afro-Caribbean and African-American political elites have emerged only in the last two decades. Prior to 1989, the city council did not have the fifty-one neighborhood-based seats it boasts today. Rather, it consisted of ten at-large districts, with two designated for each of the five boroughs (Macchiarola and Diaz 1993). Council members were elected on a boroughwide basis. Unlike the current neighborhood-based system, the at-large configuration compelled officeholders and candidates to make broad appeals beyond the boundaries of the city's ethnic enclaves.

An Afro-Caribbean politician with aspirations to the city council, for instance, could hardly afford to target only Caribbean voters in select neighborhoods. Minority candidates could win only by making wide cross-ethnic and sometimes cross-racial appeals. Earlier generations of Afro-Caribbean politicians thus refrained from marketing themselves as ethnic representatives of a distinct Caribbean constituency or appealing exclusively to their coethnics. Rather, they attempted to speak for blacks at large and did not draw a distinction between themselves and their African-American counterparts (Watkins-Owens 1996; Kasinitz 1992). Consequently, there were almost no interethnic tensions over descriptive representation between them and their African-American counterparts in that earlier era. This is not to say there were no conflicts at all between Afro-Caribbeans and African Americans: there were the inevitable cultural clashes and occasional conflicts over jobs when the immigrants first began migrating to New York (Vickerman 1999; Watkins-Owens 1996; Foner 1985; Hellwig 1978; Reid 1939).

Yet the friction between the two groups did not have much of a political dimension.[11] Ethnicity was simply not a major source of division or conflict among blacks in the electoral sphere. With the shift to neighborhood-based city council seats, however, there is greater electoral incentive for Afro-Caribbean politicians to engage in the kind of ethnically targeted appeals that lead to tensions with African-American leaders. The past two decades have thus seen a marked increase in political conflicts between

---

[11] African-American leaders at the time accused white party leaders of playing ethnic favorites by doling out the choicest patronage jobs to Afro-Caribbeans, who tended to be better educated than their native-born counterparts (Watkins-Owens 1996; Holder 1980; Hellwig 1978). But this was more job competition than political conflict, as the party structure was one of the few avenues of social mobility open to black New Yorkers.

the two groups. Although this historical shift is not conclusive evidence, it does suggest indirectly that institutional configurations have some causal impact on intergroup racial and ethnic dynamics.

A brief comparison across cities also makes the point. The city of Hartford, like New York, is home to a sizable minority population of American- and Caribbean-born blacks. Both groups, in fact, constitute roughly similar proportions of the minority population in both cities, although New York fairly dwarfs Hartford in absolute numbers. African Americans in Hartford, like their counterparts in New York, also have enjoyed greater levels of electoral representation and influence than the city's other minority constituencies. But in the last decade, the other groups have started to make their own serious bids for political power. Afro-Caribbean leaders in Hartford have begun to organize their coethnics to participate in politics, much as their fellow black immigrants in New York have been for the past two to three decades.

Yet these efforts by Hartford's Caribbean-born residents have generated considerably less friction and resistance from African-American leaders there than the attempts by their counterparts in New York. A number of factors may explain this difference in intergroup dynamics, to be sure. But one important variable may be the design of Hartford's electoral institutions. Unlike New York's neighborhood-based city council districts, Hartford's legislature features at-large seats. By the logic of the at-large electoral design, ethnically targeted campaigning must be balanced by broader appeals to other constituencies, which ultimately may serve to moderate or minimize interethnic conflict. The Hartford comparison is not conclusive support for the causal impact of electoral institutions on intergroup dynamics, but it is certainly suggestive.

In the New York case, it also should be noted the interethnic tensions between these two groups of black leaders have taken shape as Afro-Caribbean ethnic enclaves have developed and expanded to proportions large enough to leave an imprint or have an impact on the pattern of neighborhood-based electoral districts in boroughs such as Brooklyn and Queens. Prior to the 1980s, Caribbean settlements in these areas were too small to have much of an influence on the design of the city's system of political representation. What is more, African-American and Afro-Caribbean political leaders could talk of representing the city's blacks, without drawing any further ethnic distinctions. Representing blacks meant African Americans by and large. With the dramatic growth of the Caribbean immigrant population over the last few decades, however, intrablack ethnic distinctions have taken on political salience. The potential for interethnic conflict is now reinforced by the city's electoral institutions.

The Absence of an Institutional Mechanism

Still, a final question remains: why have the two groups been unable to resolve these interethnic differences over descriptive representation to build a coalition around their intraracial common interests and shared policy concerns? If New York's electoral institutions have encouraged or exacerbated the interethnic conflicts between Afro-Caribbean and African-American political leaders, the absence of certain other kinds of institutions have made those differences difficult to bridge. Sonenshein (2003) is correct: shared interests, ideological compatibility, personal ties, and strong leadership are all essential for forging sturdy intergroup alliances.

But his formulation overlooks one other important building block. Institutions are as important as interests, ideology, personal relations, and leadership for cultivating and sustaining coalitions. Viable institutions provide a framework for groups to engage in social and political learning: that is, articulate shared interests, acknowledge distinct ones, cultivate political identities, reinforce ideological commitments, solidify personal ties, and identify promising leaders.[12] Institutions, in fact, may be even more critical than ideology, personal relations, or leadership in coalitions involving immigrant populations. As newcomers to the American political system, immigrants are still engaged in political learning, trying to make sense of it all. Their ideological commitments may yet be evolving, personal relations may still be new and fragile, and leaders may not be obvious. Under such conditions, institutions may be especially vital for structuring and staging the political learning that can clarify and firm up these other coalition-building blocks.

Race-based alliances among non-white groups do not simply spring from some essential racial viewpoint or presumptive group interest. Rather, such coalitions require an institutional mechanism for expressing and mobilizing substantive, shared racial interests – a point proponents of the minority group view sometimes overlook. Blacks in Chicago, for instance, developed a network of community organizations in the early

---

[12] Social learning refers to the process by which potential coalition partners acquire knowledge and understanding of each other's interests (Stone 1989).

1980s that proved crucial to the election of the city's first black mayor in 1983 (Grimshaw 1992). This institutional framework allowed black Chicagoans to negotiate internal divisions, identify a strong mayoral candidate in Harold Washington, and muster the voter mobilization necessary to win the election. Similarly, institutional networks have been critical to successful intergroup coalition building in cities such as Atlanta (Stone 1989). The absence of such an institutional vehicle for New York's Afro-Caribbean and African-American political leaders largely explains their failure to override interethnic tensions and build an enduring race-based alliance.

The Democratic Party may appear, at first blush, to be a potentially viable institutional site for Afro-Caribbean and African-American elites to organize a race-based movement. By virtue of their combined numbers inside the party, the two groups have the makings of a powerful caucus capable of a reform. The overwhelming attachment of African-American and Afro-Caribbean voters to the Democratic Party also gives these leaders the electoral clout necessary for mounting such a challenge. In fact, a black reform impulse surfaced in the party's Brooklyn organization in the mid-1970s. But it faded as infighting erupted and many of the erstwhile insurgents made peace with the regular Democratic machine. Since then, there has been no major, viable movement for insurgency by blacks in Brooklyn or the other borough party organizations.

The failure of African Americans and Afro-Caribbeans to mount an insurgent movement from within the Democratic Party confirms the long-standing common sense of V. O. Key's (1949) fifty-year-old observation about one-party systems. Key argued one-party systems tend to be breeding grounds for factionalism. Factions, he noted, give rise to personality-driven politics that focuses on invidious status or group distinctions and drowns out substantive policy issues. Hence, one-party systems, such as New York's Democratic organization, are notoriously unsuitable institutions for launching and sustaining reform movements. It is no wonder, then, African-American and Afro-Caribbean leaders have been unable to form an insurgent coalition from within New York's dominant Democratic Party. Their relations within the party show all the symptoms of Key's diagnosis: squabbles over turf between individual politicians and disagreements over descriptive representation that deteriorate into interethnic schisms. Congruent with Key's predictions, tensions between Afro-Caribbean and African-American political leaders in the party tend to obscure the substantive issues in which they may share a common racial interest or mutual understanding.

Despite the dominance of the Democratic Party in New York City politics, there is a modest Republican organization that conceivably could serve as site for establishing a reformist coalition. Mollenkopf (1992b, 89) reminds us the Republican Party played this role in New York politics for many decades, uniting "discontented elements of the city electorate into potent, if short-lived, fusion movements." But it no longer does so today. The Republican Party has lost much of its organizational muscle and transformed into a more politically conservative institution.[13] As Mollenkopf (1997, 105) notes, "the Republican Party has forsaken its traditional role as the organizational kernel of reform." Even more significantly, the party has made virtually no effort to court African-American and Afro-Caribbean voters. Consequently, the two groups continue to ignore the Republican line in elections. There is thus little chance African Americans and Afro-Caribbeans will mount a race-based movement for reform from either the Republican or Democratic Party.

Parties, however, hardly exhaust the list of potential institutional sites from which Afro-Caribbean and African-American New Yorkers could cultivate and sustain a reformist alliance. In fact, minority group scholars note insurgent movements for greater racial inclusion typically begin in bases outside the conventional party system. For example, movements for African-American political empowerment and racial reform historically have begun in churches, civic groups, and neighborhood-based service organizations. These institutions provide a critical site for African Americans to delineate their interests, clarify ideology, groom leaders, and strike alliances with other groups (Dawson 1994a).[14] In such cities as Chicago and Atlanta, African Americans used these sites to forge reformist alliances with liberal whites (Grimshaw 1992; Stone 1989; Kleppner 1985).

In New York, African Americans attempted to launch and extend reform movements from a network of community-based organizations in the 1970s and early 1980s. The short-lived insurgent movement led

---

[13] The decline of the Republican Party in New York City politics contrasts starkly with its relative strength at the statewide level. Indeed, upstate New York has become a Republican stronghold in recent decades. But in New York City, most of the borough organizations have yet to be reinvigorated. Giuliani's mayoral success offers a signal of hope for the city-level Republican organizations, but with one important caveat: he often distances himself from the mainstream of the party to make political points. His success has often hinged on his assertions of independence from the Republican Party.

[14] Taken together, these institutions compose what Dawson (1994b) calls the African-American counterpublic.

by Al Vann in the 1970s took root in this institutional network (Green and Wilson 1989). Vann's race-based alliance, the Coalition for Community Empowerment (CCE), brought together African-American politicians with ties to Brooklyn's black churches and the community action programs spawned by President Johnson's War on Poverty and Mayor John Lindsay's liberal neighborhood government policies. The alliance included figures such as Congressman Owens and Assemblyman Norman, who traced their political beginnings to this network of community-based institutions. A handful of Afro-Caribbeans were also involved in the coalition, although none in leadership positions. Most of them had ties to community-based institutions, particularly school and community boards.

In the context of this institutional network, alliance members united around a shared vision for greater black political empowerment, community control, and racial reform. As members were elected to the state and city legislatures, the alliance became a virtual party within Brooklyn's Democratic Party. The movement collapsed in the early 1980s, however, as its institutional base began to decay. The network of community-based agencies that had furnished an organizational framework for the movement was absorbed by the local city government and lost much of its political independence. Many of these agencies fell into disarray in the face of fiscal retrenchment and federal funding cutbacks. The African-American churches that also had supplied leaders for the movement remained an important part of some Brooklyn neighborhoods, but they struggled to attract younger parishioners. Consequently, they were no longer a leading source of leadership for black politics in Brooklyn. Bereft of its independent institutional base, CCE began to lose its way. Internal divisions surfaced, former insurgents were absorbed into the regular party organizations, and the push for reform ebbed.

Just as the movement was deteriorating in the 1980s, the CCE came into conflict with Afro-Caribbean elites who were seeking to win seats on the state assembly. Most of these Afro-Caribbean candidates had no ties to the institutional network that had spawned the African-American-led CCE movement. They were largely entrepreneurial lone wolves, such as the Trinidadian-born Anthony Agard, or endorsees of immigrant organizations, such as the Panamanian-born Stewart of the CAL. In short, they had no institutional ties to the African-American politicians involved in the CCE. The organization fiercely opposed the Afro-Caribbean candidates in their races for the state legislature. Without a shared institutional framework to build trust and dialogue, African-American politicians in the CCE and Afro-Caribbean elites were unable to resolve their differences in the interest of their shared racial goals.

VI. THE FUTURE OF RACE-BASED COALITIONS

Not much has changed since then. The absence of an institutional mechanism for uniting and building trust between Afro-Caribbean and African-American elites diminishes the prospects of race-based mobilization. Of course, there have been small pockets of mutual cooperation and attempts at shared institution building in parts of Brooklyn and Queens – in political clubs and elsewhere. Recently, for example, native- and foreign-born black New Yorkers established a citywide organization to ensure their numbers in the population are accurately reflected in the decennial census (John Flateau, personal communication, June 16, 2000). The organizers have embraced pan-Africanist rhetoric and have their sights set on institutional longevity. It is too early, however, to tell whether the organization will last, especially since it has yet to face the difficult challenges posed by the city's electoral politics; reapportionment, for instance, could easily trigger many of the same conflicts over descriptive representation that have long plagued relations between Afro-Caribbean and African-American elites. All in all then, none of these recent organizational efforts have quite taken firm root; most have been ad hoc and short lived.

One potential institutional network that already has the benefit of longevity is New York's constellation of public unions. Emerging research on labor union activity in cities such as New York and Los Angeles over the last decade suggests these institutions are beginning to serve a key role in the political adjustment of new immigrants to the United States (Wong 2006). This marks a radical break with a long, notorious history of anti-immigrant activity among American labor unions. Scholars speculate changing demographic and economic realities have precipitated this shift. The growing numbers of non-white immigrants in American manufacturing and service sector jobs, coupled with the overall decline in union membership, have compelled labor leaders to target their recruitment efforts on these newcomers (Greenhouse 2000).

What is more, the new generation of labor union leaders are drawn largely from the ranks of native-born racial minority groups. African Americans, for example, are at the helm of several active unions in New York. These native-born blacks and their Caribbean-born counterparts, in fact, constitute a significant share of the membership of two of the city's most powerful public employee unions, Local 1199 of hospital workers and District Council 37 of city workers. By sharing these institutional vehicles, the two groups can engage in the kind of social learning and mutual search for shared interests that make coalition building easier. These unions may prove to be the most promising institutional site for identifying leaders skilled in bridging the intergroup divisions among Afro-Caribbeans, African Americans, and other racial minority groups. Still, there is an important caution to bear in mind. Much as local party machines have, unions historically have been prone to internal wars of ethnic and racial succession (Mink 1986). Whether these union organizations can navigate those potential pitfalls well enough to become a stable site for a race-based alliance remains to be seen.

Some observers speculate the ideological fervor for race-based mobilization has diminished, with the successes of the civil rights movement and the measurable minority progress of the last few decades (Sleeper 1993). Simply put, the claim is that race-based movements are politically passe. Post–civil rights concerns, the argument goes, do not generate the same sense of urgency and consensus among minorities that fueled the civil rights movement. The conclusion is that race-based mobilization will be unlikely or difficult to foster in the current ideological climate. Yet, Afro-Caribbean and African-American outrage over issues such as police brutality suggests there are still grounds for race-based mobilization.

This chapter, however, shows racial commonalities are not enough to generate an alliance of minority groups; indeed, appeals to racial unity actually may privilege some interests over others and thus increase divisions among non-white groups. What is more, the institutional design of a city's electoral system may exacerbate these differences. To prevent these perverse effects, political leaders looking to foster race-based alliances must turn to neighborhood and community institutions. Without an institutional framework to identify shared issue concerns, acknowledge distinct interests, and generate dialogue, fashioning stable coalitions between African Americans and Afro-Caribbeans or other racial minority newcomers will be difficult.

5

Afro-Caribbean Sojourners

Home Country Ties and the Hope of Return

Chapter 3 noted Afro-Caribbean elites complain their constituents are akin to a sleeping giant, because so many have been slow to become citizens and participate in formal politics. But the immigrants were jarringly awakened from their slumber in 1996. New York's Afro-Caribbean neighborhoods were suddenly abuzz with frenzied talk of American citizenship. Afro-Caribbean politicians urged eligible constituents to file naturalization papers. Community newspapers, such as the *Carib News*, featured articles on the imperatives of becoming an American citizen. Alongside these were the daily print ads for advocacy groups established to help immigrants acquire citizenship. Finally, there were also weekly stories tallying the scores of Caribbean immigrants flooding to Immigration and Naturalization Service (INS) centers and legal offices to file their petitions.

As I sat in the cramped Queens office of Caribbean Immigrant Services (CIS) on a brisk autumn afternoon, a steady stream of immigrants arrived in search of help with their applications. All around Brooklyn and Queens, the word was on the street: "Did you file your naturalization papers yet?" In small circles of friends, Afro-Caribbeans called each other to find out who had filed, who had not, and where to find legal help with their applications. There were ready remonstrations for those who had not, and relieved commendations for those who had. It is no exaggeration to say New York's Afro-Caribbean community was consumed with the idea of American citizenship in the summer and fall of 1996.

The spark for all this frenzy was a pair of laws enacted by Congress in the early part of that year. The first, a provision included in the much discussed welfare reform bill, stripped unnaturalized legal immigrants of social service benefits. The second, part of a new antiterrorism law, ordered deportation for non-citizen immigrants convicted of certain crimes or felonies. Afro-Caribbean political leaders fulminated at the enactment of both these laws, decrying them as draconian and unfair. But even as they did so, they urged and pleaded with their constituents to petition for citizenship to protect themselves. As the alarm spread, hundreds of anxious Afro-Caribbean immigrants were galvanized to become citizens.

The same scenario was playing out in other immigrant communities throughout New York and around the country (*New York Carib News*, March 4, 1996; Dugger 1996). Record keepers reported an unprecedented fivefold increase in petitions for citizenship across the United States between 1992 and 1997 (Mollenkopf et al. 2001). The Afro-Caribbeans I saw waiting patiently for help at the CIS offices were part of this larger national wave of new applications for American citizenship.

Most interesting about these new petitioners for naturalization is how many of them were longtime residents of the United States. Many of the Afro-Caribbean immigrants flocking to INS centers and courtrooms in the late 1990s had been eligible for citizenship for many years and yet had decided not to pursue naturalization. Now faced with the unpalatable prospect of losing access to social services and a safety net – which they might never have used but certainly helped to subsidize with their tax dollars – these immigrants were finally deciding to become citizens. Other Afro-Caribbean petitioners for citizenship were perhaps responding to widespread perceptions of growing anti-immigrant sentiment throughout the country. Whatever the motivation, many immigrants finally were opting to file for citizenship after many years of residence in the United States – albeit under some duress.

Why do Afro-Caribbean immigrants put off the decision to become citizens and participate in formal politics? Chapters 3 and 4 showed how New York's political parties and entrenched African-American elites have often tried to block or discourage Afro-Caribbean participation in politics. Yet the lingering question is why the immigrants themselves have been so slow to file for citizenship and engage in the formal political process. Recall from Chapter 3 even upwardly mobile, middle-class Afro-Caribbean immigrants put off the decision to become citizens for many years. Many of the petitioners for citizenship streaming into the CIS office in the early fall of 1996 were well-off Afro-Caribbeans with long years spent in the United States. Their reluctance runs counter to the standard pluralist account of political incorporation. Dahl (1961) was confident upwardly mobile immigrants inevitably would become citizens, registered voters, and active participants in the political process, each in turn. The fact so many first-generation Caribbean immigrants choose instead to remain permanent residents – occupying the political margins for much of their lives – suggests incorporation is hardly the matter of course described by Dahl.

Indeed, were it not for the imminent loss of legal privileges in 1996, many Afro-Caribbeans might not have bothered to change their status from permanent residents to naturalized citizens. These immigrants arguably chose citizenship not for reasons of civic duty but, rather, as a safeguard against the loss of these privileges. Their decision to become citizens therefore may not have been motivated by "assimilationist" aspirations. Rather, it simply may have been a practical concession to new legal imperatives. By this light, naturalization is not necessarily a first step or gateway into mainstream political life for these immigrants, as traditional pluralists might have expected. Rather, it simply may be a means of retaining certain basic social service privileges and legal protections. Even more significantly, naturalization is not a gateway Afro-Caribbean immigrants seem eager to enter. What accounts for their reluctance?

This chapter finds the immigrants' disinclination to become citizens and participate in formal politics is the result of their strong ties to their home countries and their view of themselves as sojourners to the United States. Most first-generation Caribbean immigrants maintain active attachments to the island nations from which they emigrated. Almost as many also hold on to the idea of returning to their home countries. They consider their stay in the United States a temporary enterprise. Scholars have called this idea of return a myth, because only a very small proportion of immigrants actually move back to their home countries. But whether it is a myth or simply a dream deferred, it nonetheless has a powerful hold on the immigrants' political attitudes, behavior, and view of themselves.

The hope of return and emotional ties to their home countries appear to dampen Afro-Caribbeans' interest in becoming American citizens and participating in formal political life in the United States. Yet the chapter does not end with the simple conclusion that transnational attachments depress Afro-Caribbean engagement with the political process. In fact, I find my Afro-Caribbean respondents who had become American citizens and maintained their involvement with home country organizations and causes tended to participate in American political life as well. I conclude that immigrants' home country attachments discourage naturalization and engagement with American politics when they are expressed simply as an emotional longing for their home countries. But when these ties translate to involvement in home country civic activities, they actually may promote participation in American politics. Still, these attachments do make political incorporation far less inevitable for this group of foreign-born blacks than the pluralist perspective would predict. I show, in fact, pluralism has been wrong about the inevitability of incorporation for immigrants throughout the course of American history.

I. HOME COUNTRY TIES AND THE HOPE OF RETURN:
A HISTORICAL OVERVIEW

The classic pluralist view is undergirded by the assumption that immigrants enter the United States prepared to stay and melt into the American mainstream. The preeminent pluralist, Dahl (1961, 33), concluded European immigrants to New Haven "yearn[ed] for assimilation and acceptance." He reasoned the immigrants were eager to participate in politics and have their own share of power. This is, in fact, the long-standing popular view of immigrants. Indeed, when newcomers show any signs they are not prepared to stay and commit to their new host country they are criticized for not living up to American tradition (e.g., Huntington 2004; Schlesinger 1992). As Jones-Correa (1998, 93) points out, "Americans like to say the United States is a land of immigrants. That pronouncement assumes that immigrants always come to the United States to stay." In short, it ascribes "assimilationist" aspirations to most immigrants.

But this broad characterization of immigrants' motives and desires does not square with the actual historical record. Many European immigrants were quite ambivalent about the United States and lukewarm about the prospect of assimilation. Historians have shown many early European immigrants viewed their stay in America as a limited sojourn from the home country (Wyman 1993). They wished simply to work, save money, and return home with their newly acquired wealth, ready to purchase a better quality of life for themselves and their families. These migrants maintained ties to family and friends in their home countries through letters and remittances. Some made seasonal trips to America's industrial cities to find well-paid work, "always trying to get enough for that additional plot, to pay off previous purchases, or to remove the load of debt from their backs" (ibid., 131). Others shuttled between the United States and their home countries every few years. These immigrants had no intention to stay. Even those who initially had designs on permanent residence sometimes found life in America disappointing, even alienating, and soon resolved to return home.

The Impact on Naturalization

This sojourner disposition tended to slow political incorporation among early European immigrants. Naturalization rates for some of these groups were quite low. One study found that as late as the 1920s less than one-third of the immigrants from countries such as Poland, Hungary, Italy, and Portugal had become citizens (Ueda 1980). Many of these immigrants had little interest in American citizenship because their intention was to return to their home countries. Quite a few actually did go home. Researchers have determined return migration rates were actually higher during the early part of the twentieth century than they are today. Although the evidence is scant and figures are imprecise, historians and demographers estimate as many as one-third of the 34 million immigrants to the United States between 1890 and 1930 repatriated. One study (Foner 1997) concludes for every one hundred immigrants who entered the country between 1901 and 1920, thirty-six left. In contrast, only twenty-four of every one hundred immigrants who arrived between 1971 and 1990 made the return voyage home.

Home Country Ties Then and Now

This brief historical overview demonstrates immigrants are not always as wedded to the idea of incorporation or assimilation as the traditional pluralist view implies. The same early European immigrants who served as the mold for America's pluralist melting pot ideology were often ambivalent about assimilation. Many tried to keep one foot planted in their home countries, and a significant proportion eventually repatriated.

Afro-Caribbeans and other recent newcomers to the United Sates also often keep one foot firmly planted in the countries from which they emigrated. Scholars of contemporary immigration have noted the salience of home country ties among this latest wave (e.g., Jones-Correa 1998; Portes 1996b; Pessar 1995; Basch et al. 1994; Schiller et al. 1992). Although some have written about this form of transnationalism as if it were an entirely new phenomenon, the historical research I have summarized makes it clear early European immigrants also tried to maintain ties to their home countries.

Critics of contemporary immigration often miss this historical continuity. Recent immigrants, they have argued, are less willing to give up their attachments to home country cultures, languages, and customs than their European predecessors (e.g., Huntington 2004; Beck 1997;

Schlesinger 1992; Glazer 1983). In their view, early European immigrants were much more inclined to assimilate into the American melting pot than today's intransigent newcomers from Latin America, Asia, and the Caribbean. But careful historical research has indicated today's immigrants are no more emotionally attached to their home countries or ambivalent about committing to this one than their European predecessors.

There are, however, important differences between the home country ties of today's newcomers and those of earlier European immigrants. Technological advances in travel and communication and greater social tolerance for multiculturalism have made it easier for recent immigrants to sustain deep home country ties. Without easy travel or speedy communication to their home countries, earlier European immigrants had a more difficult time maintaining home country attachments. What is more, continuing ties to foreign cultures and customs were viewed with much greater suspicion and hostility than they are today. Early European immigrants were often forced to relinquish their home country attachments to avoid prejudice. Or their ties to their home countries gradually diminished as they moved into the American mainstream.[1] Short of that, they could choose simply to return home.

Today's immigrants need not make the same mutually exclusive choice and can live more easily "between two nations," in the words of Jones-Correa (1998). It is perhaps not surprising, then, return migration rates are significantly lower for today's newcomers than they were for their European predecessors. Contemporary immigrants can keep one foot firmly planted in their home countries without necessarily making the permanent trip back. They can sustain ties to family and community back home and hold on to their hopes of eventual return, all the while living in the United States.

II. AFRO-CARIBBEAN SOJOURNERS

New York's Afro-Caribbean immigrants are an instructive case. Among the fifty-nine Afro-Caribbean respondents interviewed for this study, transnational ties and hopes of return to the home country were quite salient. The interview data suggest many of these immigrants see their lives in the United States as an extended sojourn from their home countries. Recall the respondents were all middle- and working-class immigrants

---

[1] See Chapter 6 for further discussion.

with an average of twenty-three years of residence in this country. The traditional pluralist view would expect diminishing ties to their home countries and deepening attachment to the United States among these upwardly mobile immigrants. But the majority of these respondents defy the assimilationist logic of the pluralist perspective.

To be sure, many were homeowners, parents, successful professionals, and the like. Their lives showed many of the signs pluralists might take as evidence of deepening commitment to the United States. Yet most of the respondents have maintained active ties to their home countries and retain the idea of returning eventually. Although they have planted roots and enjoy some measure of success in this country, they nonetheless continue to see themselves as sojourners.

Home Country Attachments and Obligations

Newcomers to this country typically leave immediate family members and other relatives behind. Often these immigrants plan to stay in the United States only for a limited time and then return to their home countries to reunite with their families. In other instances, they may expect family members to join them in this country once they have settled (Foner 1997). Whatever the case, these immigrants often maintain close personal and familial linkages to their home countries.

There is often an economic impetus behind the decision to immigrate. Many Caribbean immigrants enter this country in search of economic security for themselves and their families back home. As Patricia Pessar (1987, 104) has pointed out, the income immigrants earn in the United States may be enough to bolster or improve the socioeconomic situation of their families at home. Accordingly, they often send remittances back home to help support their families and friends. All in all, immigrants typically sustain a transnational web of personal, familial, and economic linkages to their home countries even as they pursue lives here in the United States.

Most of the first-generation Afro-Caribbean immigrants interviewed for this study fit this transnational mold. Of the fifty-nine respondents, forty-three reported they sustain regular contact with family and close relatives back home. A few others, although they no longer have immediate family on the island, claimed they nonetheless maintain ties to friends and extended kin. Many of the respondents also reported they routinely send remittances to their home countries to help support family members and close friends there. Their emotional attachments to their home countries thus are reinforced often by economic commitments. Consider how this fifty-year-old businessman (interview, April 17, 1997) explains his ties to his home country of Trinidad.

Q: Do you have relatives and friends on the island?
A: Oh boy! Do I! Thirteen brothers and sisters, thirty-seven nieces and nephews, grand-nieces . . . Should I go on (laughing)?
Q: Do you send money or material goods back to Trinidad?
A: Yes. Three or four times a year, or more. I have thirteen brothers and sisters, so I get called all the time. Whatever they need I send. Whatever my parents need I send. And when I go down there once a year, I make sure the needs are taken care of until I come again.

These emotional and economic commitments typically continue for many years. Another almost retired seventy-three-year-old immigrant from Trinidad (interview, April 8, 1997) has lived in the United States for thirty-two years but still supports his aging mother on the island.

Q: Do you have relatives and friends on the island?
A: I have many friends and one relative, my mother. Only I came over here. There were only three of us, Mother, my brother, and myself. Both of them remained, and my brother died in January of this year. But I still support my mother. I send her a little something every month. I've been doing that since I moved here.

The immigrants typically remit money. Many also send "barrels," the colloquial term for packages of goods purchased here in the United States. Thirty-seven of my respondents reported they regularly send money or material goods to their home countries. Of the remaining twenty-two respondents, fourteen claimed they send remittances only occasionally – when family and friends back home make specific requests for support, or when they return to the islands for short vacations or business.

The economies of many Caribbean and Latin American countries depend heavily on remittances from immigrants abroad. In the deeply impoverished Dominican Republic, for example, immigrant remittances rank as the most important source of foreign exchange (Foner 1997, 367). Remittances constitute a similarly vital part of economic life in such Caribbean countries as Jamaica, Guyana, and Barbados. Even as Afro-Caribbean immigrants are working, paying taxes, and participating in the American economy, then, they also continue to play a role in the economic life of their home countries in the Caribbean.

In fact, a sizable minority of the respondents also reported they main-tain bank accounts or property holdings in their home countries. Seven have bank accounts, and another ten have property they hold individually or jointly with relatives or business partners back home. Even two of the respondents (interview, April 1, 1997) who have almost no close relatives remaining in their home countries nonetheless maintain financial holdings there.

Q: Do most of your relatives still live in Jamaica, or do they live here in the United States?

A: Only a few extended relatives there live back home. Most of my family are scattered. They are here, there, and everywhere. I have some in Switzerland, Canada, and I have in the United Kingdom and Canada. My father is deceased. And my mother is here. She is retired and lives in Florida.

Q: So I suppose you don't maintain any business, bank accounts, real estate holdings, or anything like that on Jamaica, then?

A: That I do, in fact. My mother and I have some real estate. And I have a bank account related to that property.

Similarly, another respondent reported he owns a store and a restaurant on the island of Saint Kitts. He has enlisted relatives to oversee the day-to-day operations of these two businesses and thus maintains close contact with them to stay abreast of developments.

Many respondents also maintain their transnational attachments with frequent trips back home. Forty-eight reported they make regular visits. Twenty-three go once a year, and the remaining twenty-six make the trip every few years. Of course, a handful of well-off respondents also reported they visit their home countries several times a year. The Trinidadian immigrant with thirteen brothers and sisters on the island visits three of four times a year. As he explained, the trips are typically for pleasure, but he also flies back to help address the occasional family emergency. A handful of respondents (interview, July 2, 1997) also send their children to spend their vacations on the islands.

Q: Do your teenage children visit Guyana, too?

A: I used to send the kids home every summer when they were younger. My oldest sister, who still lives in Guyana, would look after them. They would enjoy it, too. They couldn't wait for school to let out for the summer, so that they could go. I guess they liked getting away from me so they could run wild in Guyana (laughing). But now they big, they don't really go anymore. Sometimes I offer to send them, but they make all kinds of excuses. They like to work for their own money during the summer. You see, they into their own thing now. But I still try to go back home when I can.

The contrast between this woman's continuing attachment to her home country and her children's clear commitment to the United States was a recurrent theme in my conversations with the parents in my sample. Waters (1994a) concluded middle-class Afro-Caribbean parents consciously endeavor to pass on their ties to the Caribbean to their children. These immigrant parents, she reports, often express frustration at the growing "Americanization" of their children, which often overwhelms the parents' attempts to "Caribbeanize" the second generation. My respondents reacted to the Americanization of their children with more resignation than frustration. Many saw the process as inevitable for their children (interview, April 3, 1997).

Q: How often do your children visit Jamaica?
A: I used to take them every year. But now they're in high school, they don't really go back much. You see, they Americans now. They can't be bothered with Jamaica (laughing). But you know how it is: America is what they know.

Still, most of the adult respondents keep their own ties to the Caribbean intact. Regular trips back home coupled with frequent telephone calls and other modern forms of communication help the immigrants keep one foot squarely planted in their home countries. As Nancy Foner (1997, 362–363) observes, "In the jet plane age, inexpensive air fares mean that immigrants, especially those from nearby places in the Caribbean and Central America can fly home for emergencies, such as funerals, or celebrations, such as weddings; go back to visit their friends and relatives; and sometimes move back and forth, in the manner of commuters." Although only two of my respondents would qualify as monthly or seasonal commuters, the majority of them traveled back to their home countries often enough to maintain their transnational ties.

Reinforcing Home Country Ties in New York

Afro-Caribbean immigrants who forgo the yearly trip to the Caribbean still can maintain their emotional and social ties to their home countries. First, New York City boasts a vibrant Caribbean ethnic press that focuses heavily, if not predominantly, on news and developments in the sending countries. Most of the respondents reported they read weeklies and periodicals, such as *New York Carib News, Caribbean Life*, and *Everybody's Magazine*, to keep abreast of the goings-on back home. A substantial minority of the respondents noted they have more than a passing interest in the politics of their home countries. Second, most Afro-Caribbean organizations and voluntary associations in New York have a strong, and sometimes even exclusive, transnational emphasis. These organizations routinely sponsor cultural events and support political and social causes centered on the Caribbean. For example, it is not unusual for these organizations to host candidates running for political office in the Caribbean. Well aware of the considerable numbers and resources of the city's Caribbean population, candidates make trips to New York to seek financial support for their campaigns.

At the invitation of a few of my respondents, I attended several Caribbean social events in the summer of 1997. I was struck by the number of dignitaries from the Caribbean who were on hand to receive awards and plaudits for their work on the island or raise money for some cause back home. Several of these events, in fact, were held expressly for the purpose of generating funds for home country campaigns or activities. These transnational social events are part of the fabric of many Afro-Caribbeans' lives.

Most of my respondents reported the majority of their social and civic activities either put them in contact with others from the Caribbean or were somehow focused on their home countries. Consider this account (interview, April 2, 1997) of civic life from one of my more socially active respondents.

Q: What community, civic, and political organizations are you involved in?
A: I'm a member of the New Era Community Democratic Club. I'm a member of Planning Board 17. I'm active in the Jamaica Progressive League. And I've been involved in the planning for the West Indian Labor Day Carnival.
Q: Are most of the organizations you listed composed mostly of Caribbean Americans and African Americans?
A: It's mostly other people from the Caribbean like me.

This Grenadian man (interview, December 2, 1996) reports similar engagement with civic activities focused on the Caribbean.

I'm a member of the Caribbean American Chamber of Commerce and Industry. I've worked on fund-raising events with Herman Hall for *Everybody's Magazine*. I helped to organize Caribe Fete. I'm also an active member of Community Board 17 . . . Most of these events I do are with other Grenadians or other people from the Caribbean. You know we need to stick together and do something for people back home.

Civic life for some Afro-Caribbean immigrants clearly has a strong transnational emphasis.

Finally, with the steady influx of new immigrant arrivals and their high rate of residential concentration, many Afro-Caribbeans have daily contact with coethnics from their home countries. Even the most upwardly mobile Afro-Caribbean immigrants continue to live in these residential enclaves and sustain social bonds with friends and acquaintances from home. Most of my respondents lived in such neighborhoods and claimed the majority of their social and associational contacts are with other immigrants from the Caribbean. In short, Afro-Caribbeans can retain and perhaps even reinforce ties with others from the Caribbean without ever leaving New York.

This point bears some elaboration, because it highlights a key difference between Afro-Caribbeans and other immigrants. Earlier European immigrants often saw their ties to coethnics weaken as they achieved upward mobility and moved into more integrated neighborhoods. The same trajectory has been observed among some of today's Asian and Latino immigrants (e.g., Zubrinsky and Bobo 1996). Upwardly mobile Afro-Caribbeans, in contrast, often remain confined to ethnic residential enclaves and predominantly black neighborhoods, as a result of continuing racial segregation in the housing market. The irony, of course, is this high level of residential segregation allows them to sustain their ties with other immigrants from the Caribbean.

Sustaining the Hope of Return: Myth or Dream Deferred

The question, of course, is whether these continuing transnational attachments are the prelude to a permanent return to the home country. How many Afro-Caribbean immigrants plan to make the dream of return a reality? My interviews reveal many Caribbean immigrants hold on to the hope of returning to their home countries, even after they have lived in the United States for many years. The fact that so many of the respondents were middle-class immigrants who ostensibly have had some measure of success in this country makes their attachment to the idea of return all the more striking.

Of the fifty-nine respondents, thirty-six evinced some desire to return to their home countries. Of course, this desire was not equally strong among all the respondents. Some were emphatic about their plans to return; others were less sure. But a majority had given serious consideration to the idea. Here is a sampling of the attitudes registered by these Afro-Caribbean respondents. Consider first those who were unequivocal about their desire to return to their home countries. One sixty-eight-year-old immigrant from Jamaica (interview, April 16, 1997) has lived in the United

States for thirty-one years but still sees the island as his home. He plans to return there to live.

Q: Do you consider New York to be your permanent home?
A: No.
Q: Are you a naturalized U.S. citizen?
A: Yes, but I am still a citizen of Jamaica. I'll always be.
Q: Do you plan eventually to return to Jamaica?
A: Yes, most definitely. We are planning that now. Our last daughter is going to graduate next month – I promised my kids to help them up to their bachelor's [degrees], then I'm done. If God spare life, between three to five years' time, I'll move back.

This Jamaican immigrant hardly looks like the typical sojourner. Indeed, his life in New York shows all the signs of permanent settlement. He has lived here for more than three decades, has raised children, owns a house, and runs a small business. Yet despite his many years and apparent success in this country, he has held on to the idea of returning to Jamaica. In his mind, it seems, he has never ceased to be a sojourner to the United States.

Other respondents showed similarly strong commitment to the idea of returning to their home countries. One immigrant from Grenada (interview, July 3, 1997) went to New York with the intention to stay for only a few years. He now has lived here for thirty years but still has designs on moving back to Grenada.

Q: What was your primary reason for moving to the United States?
A: Well, I was supposed to come, hopefully to get an education, spend no more than four years, and go back to Grenada to participate in what you could call nation building. When I left Grenada had just got "associated statehood." Independence didn't come yet, but everyone knew it was just a matter of time. I think, for people like me who witnessed "associated statehood," the whole objective was to come, get some sort of degree, and go back to Grenada. Of course, it hasn't happened that way.
Q: So have you completely abandoned the idea of returning?
A: No, no, no! I'd still like to go back and get involved in politics there. I still stay on top of what's going on. But I'll be frank with you; I'm very frustrated with politics in Grenada. They need some changes there.

This man's intended short stay has turned into a lifetime in the United States. Nevertheless, he has sustained both his dream of return and his political ambitions for his home country. He confessed he often pays more attention to the political affairs of his home country than the local politics of New York. Whether he ultimately makes the permanent trip back or not, much of his thinking continues to be informed by the hope of return.

Some respondents, however, were more ambivalent about their prospects for a return to the home country. Although many signaled the desire to return, they also conceded the decision would be complicated by the ties they have established to this country. These respondents, though attracted to the notion of return, expressed misgivings about the practicalities of the idea. Take, for instance, this sixty-three-year old Jamaican immigrant (interview, April 2, 1997). He immigrated to the United States in 1962 with plans to secure an education and return home. In the intervening years he has developed attachments in the United States that make return more difficult to negotiate. Still, he continues to hold on to the idea, however unlikely it now seems. His comments typify the concerns of several immigrants in the sample.

Q: What was your primary reason for moving to the United States?
A: To get an education and return home. But I ended up staying (laughing).
Q: Do you ever consider going back to Jamaica to live?
A: I'd very much like to. I actually visit every year for a couple weeks. But I don't know if I go back for good. You see, my wife is not Jamaican. She's from Panama. I'm not sure if we can work that out.

Another immigrant from Jamaica (interview, April 4, 1997) declared that she was attracted to the idea of return and still saw the island as home but concluded that her ties to the United States would be difficult to sever.

Q: Do you ever plan to return to Jamaica and live there permanently?
A: I've considered it from time to time. And going home does appeal to me. But I don't think I could, quite honestly.
Q: Why?
A: Because I've become spoiled, accustomed to a lot of the conveniences here. I may be able to get them there; I don't know. But because, I guess, most of my adult years have been here, and because I have very strong ties here, mainly because who I consider my immediate family circle, they're really all here somewhere, I don't see myself [going back].

This respondent highlights an important distinction among immigrants. The idea of return may be more viable for immigrants who moved to the United States during their adult years than those who did as youths. The four other immigrants in my sample who entered this country as teenagers or young children either rejected the idea of return or viewed it as improbable. One of these respondents (interview, August 7, 1997) was unequivocal about the impossibility of return.

Q: Do you ever plan to return to Guyana and live there permanently?

A: No. My mom always talks about that. But me, this is where my life is. I'll visit Guyana. But I really couldn't live there now. My boyfriend is American. He's from the South. If we stay together, I don't think he would go for that. Plus, all my real ties are here. Now, don't get me wrong, I love me some Guyana. But I couldn't go back there to live.

More generally, though, the majority of the respondents had given some thought to the idea of returning to their home countries. Whether they plan to return home or not, most have maintained ties. These findings confirm what many scholars of immigration have long contended: immigrants continue to see themselves as sojourners for many years and sustain strong emotional ties to their home countries (e.g., Piore 1979). This pattern of persisting home country attachments is a clear contravention of the standard pluralist account of immigrant adjustment to American life, especially in the case of the middle class. The pluralist view would expect this particular cross section of the immigrant population – those who have lived here for many years and done relatively well – to be more committed to remaining in this country and participating in the mainstream of American life. My findings, however, run counter to this prediction.

This counterintuitive conclusion is somewhat analogous to the paradox Jennifer Hochschild (1995) has identified among middle-class African Americans. She found even as the African-American middle class has grown larger and more stable, its members have become more ambivalent about and even disillusioned with the American dream.[2] Similarly, many middle-class Afro-Caribbean immigrants in this sample were ambivalent about staying in United States and held on to the idea of returning to their home countries, despite their apparent success here.[3]

III. POLITICAL CONSEQUENCES OF THE SOJOURNER OUTLOOK

What are the political consequences of this sojourner disposition and these home country attachments? As I noted previously, the sojourner mentality slowed political incorporation among earlier European immigrants. Likewise, there is reason to believe a similar sojourner outlook, coupled

---

[2] Also see Patterson 1997.

[3] Of course, this shared ambivalence about American life does not necessarily mean Afro-Caribbeans and African Americans will have identical political outlooks or responses. I show in Chapters 6 and 7 that they do not. Nonetheless, I demonstrate both groups, despite their seeming success, are dubious about their prospects for full inclusion in American society.

with emotional ties to their home countries, dampens Afro-Caribbeans' interest in naturalization and sometimes in American politics more generally. In fact, the impact of home country attachments on the political behavior of today's immigrants is arguably much greater than it was for earlier European immigrants, largely because these ties are much easier to sustain in contemporary American life.[4] Jones-Correa (1998), for example, finds the myth of return has such a powerful hold on the thinking of New York's Latino immigrants they often put off or completely reject the idea of becoming United States citizens. The sojourner outlook has had a similar impact on the city's Afro-Caribbean immigrants.

Putting Off Citizenship

Recall from Chapter 3 Afro-Caribbean elites believe New York's party organizations have done little to encourage immigrant constituents to become politically active American citizens. But they also agree Afro-Caribbeans themselves have not shown a strong interest in becoming American citizens. Much of this lack of interest, elites insist, stems from the salience of the sojourner or transnational outlook among their immigrant constituents. The consensus among the leaders interviewed for this study is the immigrants' attachment to the idea of return and the emotional pull of their home country loyalties make them reluctant to become citizens and slow to engage in American political life more generally.

The former city councilwoman Una Clarke (interview, December 13, 1996) carefully laid out this insight.

Q: What do you think explains the reluctance of Caribbean immigrants to become American citizens and participate in the political process?

A: Well, the reluctance has to do with, one, people's pride. Again their emotional ties to their home country. The fact that many people saw themselves as coming to live in America for a discrete number of years, and after which time they would return. Other people not recognizing that if they are citizens here, when they return to their hometown, or home country, that they remain citizens of those nations. So where there is dual citizenship, there is no reason for people not to become citizens. Some people didn't want to go home and then have to live for another five years to reclaim the citizenship of the nation in which they were born. So there's this emotional tie to where people come from, and so they aren't inclined to become citizens. Because everybody was gonna earn some money and return home. That's usually the plan they come with.

---

[4] In the next chapter, I also argue home country attachments have greater cognitive utility for Afro-Caribbeans than for other immigrants, largely because of their greater vulnerability to racial discrimination and exclusion.

Hence, Afro-Caribbean immigrants typically put off the decision to become United States citizens for two reasons. First, many see themselves as sojourners and expect to return to their home countries after a limited period of residence in this country. Before the passage of the 1996 legislation, these immigrants perhaps regarded naturalization as a superfluous option, because many of them have no intention of staying in the United States. Second, these foreign-born blacks often maintain strong emotional ties to their home countries and deeply prize their native citizenship. Although all Caribbean countries except Trinidad allow dual citizenship, immigrants are sometimes unaware of the privilege.[5] They mistakenly assume naturalization in the United States will result in the forfeiture of their native citizenship, a prospect most find unpalatable.

Interestingly enough, one immigrant advocate (interview, June 8, 1997) noted some Afro-Caribbeans are still reluctant to pursue naturalization, even after they learn about dual-citizenship privileges. He speculated their unwillingness was a matter of their strong emotional ties to their home countries.

Q: Why do you think the immigrants are still reluctant to become citizens?
A: It's the emotional and psychological attachment, man. Folks just have a hard time thinking of themselves as citizens of any place other than their nation of birth. You know, Jamaicans, Trinidadians, we West Indians are very patriotic about the Caribbean.

Other elites echoed this line of reasoning. Nick Perry, a Caribbean-born assemblyman for the Fifty-eighth District (interview, December 13, 1996), agreed his Afro-Caribbean constituents have strong, patriotic ties to their home countries. Indeed, he speculates the immigrants' patriotic sentiments for their home countries run especially deep, because so many of the islands in the Caribbean are relatively new, fledgling nations.

Q: Why do you think naturalization rates among Caribbean Americans have been so low? What explains their disinclination to become American citizens?
A: I am trying to remember the name of the poem that goes something like, "Breathes there a man who never to himself has said, 'This is my home,

---

[5] Scholars of Caribbean immigration have noted the governments of this region find it in their economic and political interest to extend full citizenship rights to their subjects abroad. Recall Caribbean immigrants in the United States are an important source of remittances, social capital, and even political clout – all of which these countries are eager to retain. By allowing dual citizenship, Caribbean nations can continue to draw on the loyalties and resources of their subjects living in the United States. Some Caribbean countries even extend citizenship rights to the American-born children of these immigrants. See Foner 1997; Basch et al. 1994.

my native land.'" Just like blacks around the world feel some attachment or identification with Africa, blacks who were transplanted from Africa and taken to the Caribbean and [those who were] born there, that became their native land. They developed a native culture, a mixture of European and African, as their way of life. It is sort of natural that they feel identity to that native land and that native culture, some to more degree than others, and might accommodate or harbor intense nationalistic feelings. In the Caribbean, my generation grew up as subjects, a colony of European powers, and fought for independence for sovereignty as nations. That was something that was a significant part of our lives... something significant to fight for... Caribbean people developed pride in the sovereignty and nationhood they were granted. So, it's a hard decision for you to give up your allegiance to that nation, that native soil; that land is yours... Even though you transfer yourself to another land, your identity and allegiance to the place of your birth make it difficult to cut off that allegiance and swear allegiance to a foreign land, a foreign government.

Perry also elaborated on how the sojourner outlook leads the immigrants to put off petitioning for citizenship and thus keeps them out of the formal political process in the United States:

The barriers [to mobilization] exist to the extent that as individuals, and then as a group, they will exercise the entitlement of citizenship. You can't vote without citizenship, and for a lot of Caribbean Americans that's a big decision to make. Previously, there were obstacles to becoming U.S. citizens because some... Caribbean countries would not recognize dual citizenship, or would force you to give up your citizenship in order to become an American and get the right to vote. But that's changed now. Most countries allow dual citizenship. Even so, traditionally, Caribbeans traveling to the United States always had the intention to return home. They very seldom travel with an abandonment in their mind – I'm leaving, I will never be coming back! They usually leave with a dream, "I'm gonna make good. I'm gonna either get an education, or I'm gonna find a fortune, and I'm coming back to my home."

My Afro-Caribbean respondents certainly confirmed Perry's insight. Recall many of them reported they immigrated to the United States with plans to pursue an education or earn money, and then return home. Although all the immigrants interviewed for this study were naturalized American citizens, most reported they had put off the decision for many years. The respondents had an average of twenty-three years of residence in the country, but most had not been citizens for more than ten years. In fact, the average number of years of citizenship among the fifty-nine respondents was nine. This figure is roughly in keeping with the overall naturalization trends for Afro-Caribbean immigrants. One Caribbean Immigrant Services (CIS) official (interview, November 29,

1996) explained the majority of the immigrants who have sought out the agency's help with filing for citizenship in recent years have been longtime residents of the United States. He recalls, "Most of the folks who come in here could have become citizens a long time ago, but they kept putting it off. Now they're all finally doing it. And now they're saying, 'You know how long I've been here?!?! If I did know.'"

This CIS official, like other elites interviewed for this study, attributed the tendency of Afro-Caribbeans to postpone or reject the idea of becoming American citizens to three factors.

Q: What accounts for the reluctance of Caribbean Americans to become citizens?
A: Number one, many of us come here as transients. We plan to be here only for five to seven years. Number two, patriotism. We don't want to give up our native citizenship. But you're really not. Actually, you're acquiring U.S. citizenship and losing nothing.
Q: So immigrants worry they might lose their home country citizenship?
A: Yes, yes. Many of them don't know that they can have dual citizenship. So the whole situation is that you don't want to change your nationality. But you're not really changing; you're only acquiring U.S. citizenship.

Home Country Ties and Political Participation

Although Afro-Caribbean elites are correct that their constituents' ties to their home countries appear to dampen their interest in naturalization, these attachments do not necessarily diminish their propensity to participate in American politics once they have become citizens. Some researchers have argued home country linkages tend to depress political participation among first-generation immigrants (e.g., Cain and Doherty 2003; Desipio 2003; Portes and Rumbaut 1996). These ties, they reason, focus the immigrants' attention on home country affairs while distracting them from the politics of their host country.

Yet my interview data reveal a more complicated pattern. True enough, respondents whose home country engagements consisted mostly of personal and social ties tended to have postponed naturalization for many years and did not participate in American politics much after they finally became citizens. But those whose home country ties also entailed civic activity targeted at their home countries often participated in politics in the United States as well. Eighteen of my fifty-nine respondents reported moderate to high levels of involvement in home country civic affairs. Their activities ranged from membership in home country associations to campaigning for political candidates in races back home. One respondent (interview, April 2, 1997), for example, was an active member of the Jamaica Progressive League and helped organize fund-raisers in New York for candidates in his home country.

These respondents with high levels of involvement in home country civic activities showed higher levels of voting than others in the sample. All eighteen reported they vote in both local and national elections. In contrast, only about one-third of the remaining respondents in the sample go to the polls regularly. Even more significantly, those who were involved in home country civic activities also were more likely to engage in other forms of political participation beyond voting. The Jamaican respondent (interview, April 2, 1997) who helped raise money for political candidates back home also had helped fill the campaign coffers for a handful of New York politicians. He also was an active member of his local community board and a Democratic political club. Although he was more civically engaged than most other respondents in the sample, he was hardly atypical of others in the sample with strong attachments to transnational organizations and causes.

Uncovering this pattern in a small sample of respondents is not enough to conclude home country civic activities actually promote participation in American politics. Yet the correlation between the two forms of civic engagement suggests immigrants' home country attachments do not necessarily dampen their propensity to participate in politics in this country. Other researchers are uncovering similar patterns among other immigrant groups (i.e., Wong, Lien, and Conway 2005). In short, strong home country ties do not automatically inhibit participation in American politics, as some researchers have argued. Indeed, the data imply the skills, aptitude, and appetite for civic engagement immigrants develop in the transnational arena may translate to American politics. Still, the correlation applies only to those who express their transnational ties through civic outlets. Immigrants whose home country attachments consist solely of personal or social ties and an emotional longing to return are slow to become citizens and participate in American politics.

Will Participation Follow Naturalization?

CIS and other immigrant advocacy groups spent much of the late 1990s trying to convince Afro-Caribbeans that filing for American citizenship did not mean giving up their ties to their home countries. This typically meant informing them of their dual-citizenship privileges and helping them to navigate the legal and administrative niceties of the naturalization process. Recall unprecedented numbers of Afro-Caribbeans applied to become citizens in the wake of the new policies enacted by Congress. With these legislative changes, postponing or rejecting the decision to file for United States citizenship has suddenly become a far more costly choice for Afro-Caribbeans and other immigrants. Not surprisingly, more and more of these foreign-born blacks are finally opting for naturalization.

Many Afro-Caribbean elites are predicting – or perhaps hoping – this increase in naturalization rates will precipitate a major sea change in Afro-Caribbean political behavior. The expectation is higher naturalization rates will lead inevitably to greater political participation among these black ethnics. Community leaders note the 1996 legislation ignited anger and concern among their immigrant constituents. They believed the same outrage and anxiety that led Afro-Caribbeans to apply for citizenship at record rates also would spur them to vote in greater numbers and become more involved in the political process. Consider this sampling of elite opinion (interview, December 18, 1996):

Q: Are you satisfied with the level of Caribbean American representation in New York City politics?

A: I think we can do much more; we should do more. I think we can do better; we must do better. I think this current wave of citizenship and citizenship drives will also lead to greater aspirations across the board of being in elective office. I think our people's mind-set was always that we carry a briefcase. We take a profession, buy a house, have children, earn money to go back home, and leave politics to somebody else. But I think once the antiterrorist act came in, and the welfare reform bill, people now understand that they gotta play a more intricate role in terms of making sure that they act upon the politics of the nation, of the state, and of the city.

Another community leader (interview, April 18, 1997) predicted waves of newly naturalized Afro-Caribbean immigrants would be flocking to the polls in future elections.

I think more Caribbean Americans will vote now. It's just that, now they are naturalized, and you've walked them through the process and shown them their effectiveness, they will exercise it. And I think they have in the last election. You'll probably see more of it in the local elections, which will be held next year. Now because of the anti-immigrant sentiment, they're forced to get involved.

Similarly, Assemblyman Perry (interview, December 13, 1996) declared Afro-Caribbeans' outrage over the congressional legislation would likely turn to political action.

[T]he recent immigrant policies of the federal government certainly got a lot of emotion from Caribbean Americans, not just Caribbean Americans, but the whole immigrant population of the United States. Look at the voter registration throughout the United States. Look at those who sought to become naturalized. The impact of that in such a positive way, as far as getting people into the process of registering to vote, acquiring citizenship, that is something that has been phenomenal.

These predictions follow standard pluralist logic. Dahl (1961) argued immigrants could be expected to naturalize, register to vote, and inevitably become active participants in the political process. In their neopluralist account of Miami politics, Portes and Stepick (1993) chronicle a similar trajectory for the city's Cuban population. Cuban immigrants rallied together in the face of prejudice, became citizens, practiced self-conscious ethnic group politics, and ultimately seized electoral power in Miami.[6]

Some Afro-Caribbean elites predicted their constituents' outrage over the 1996 congressional legislation would galvanize the group to pursue a similar course. In their estimation, the upsurge in Afro-Caribbean naturalization rates would be the prelude to a new and unprecedented wave of mobilization. It is not at all clear, however, that naturalization is followed closely or inevitably by active participation in the political process. In light of the patterns uncovered in my interviews, engagement in American politics is likely for those immigrants already immersed in civic activity, even if their focus has mostly been home country affairs. Beyond this subset of the population, then, there was no guarantee new Afro-Caribbean citizens would flock to the ballot box to express their outrage over the congressional legislation and become active voters.

In fact, existing evidence suggests the upsurge in Afro-Caribbean naturalization trends was not accompanied by a sustained increase in voting rates. Table 5.1 shows voting participation data for first-generation Afro-Caribbeans in recent elections. Between 1994 and 1998 – the period

---

[6] This trajectory may appear, at first blush, to conform to the minority group view, rather than the pluralist model. But Miami's Cuban immigrants have not made the demands for redistribution or systemic reform predicted by the minority group perspective. Recall from Chapter 1 Portes and Stepick explicitly liken the Cuban experience in Miami to the classic pluralist trajectory described by Dahl.

TABLE 5.1. *Length of Residence and Voting Participation among First-Generation Afro-Caribbeans in New York (Relative odds with thirty or more years as baseline – no controls for other variables)*

Residence	1994	1996	1998	All Years	Midterm Elections
Less than 15 years	0.249**	0.270	0.195***	1.073***	0.213***
15 to 29 years	1.054	0.732	1.052	2.389	1.032
30 or more years	1.00	1.00	1.00	1.00	1.00

***$p < .05$, **$p < .10$.

Source: Karthick Ramakrishnan from Current Population Survey.

when naturalization rates for the group were on the upswing – voting turnout actually declined. Although more Afro-Caribbeans were choosing to become citizens, there was no parallel increase in voting rates. Many of the Afro-Caribbean immigrants who filed for citizenship in the wake of the 1996 congressional legislation were probably not motivated by the kind of civic duty or assimilationist aspirations that might lead to more political involvement. As I noted at the outset of the chapter, most probably were choosing citizenship to safeguard against the loss of social service entitlements and key legal protections.

Why Afro-Caribbeans Finally Choose Citizenship

Anecdotal evidence suggests when Afro-Caribbean immigrants do choose to become citizens, civic obligation or assimilationist aspirations are rarely the chief motivation. Kasinitz (1992, 31–32), for instance, concludes most Afro-Caribbeans who opt to become citizens do so out of a desire to sponsor relatives in their home countries wishing to immigrate to the United States. Federal immigration law encourages family reunion by granting entry preference to the relatives of immigrants already living in this country.[7] Kasinitz speculates many Afro-Caribbean immigrants become citizens to capitalize on this privilege.

The respondents in this study confirm this conjecture. Many of them reported they filed for citizenship to secure these kinds of benefits for

---

[7] The Hart-Cellar Immigration Reform Act of 1965 established this policy. The family preference provision was included in the law to placate nativist opposition and ensure that new immigrant populations would reflect the majority-white, European racial composition of the United States. Of course, the predominantly non-white, non-European immigrants who have flocked to this country since the 1970s have turned the original racist design of the law on its head.

family members or relatives in their home countries. This Guyanese immigrant's explanation (interview, April 7, 1997) for his decision to become a United States citizen is typical.

Q: Why did you decide to become an American citizen?
A: I wanted to help out my mother and younger brother back home. You know, if they wanted to come here and live for a while, I could sponsor them. Only one brother came, though. But I was able to help him with his papers.

Twenty-four of the respondents cited similar reasons for their decision to naturalize.

Others reported they filed for citizenship when they realized their sojourn away from their home countries might be longer than they originally planned. As one Jamaican woman (interview, April 1, 1997) concisely explained, "I didn't do it [file for citizenship] right away. But when I realized that I would be here for a while and wouldn't lose my Jamaican citizenship, I decided to go ahead and file the papers." Length of stay and the desire to sponsor relatives were thus the most common motivations. In contrast, very few mentioned purely civic or assimilationist objectives, such as the right to vote or the desire to be accepted by native-born Americans.

With the passage of the 1996 legislation, many Afro-Caribbean immigrants now appear to be choosing citizenship to safeguard against the loss of social service benefits and important legal protections. None of my respondents were among these new petitioners for American citizenship. My conclusions about the latter group therefore are speculative. Still, most of the media coverage and conversations about the new wave of citizenship applications by Afro-Caribbeans emphasized these instrumental factors as the driving force behind the immigrants' decisions. One of my respondents (interview, May 7, 1997) observed:

Folks feel like they work hard all these years and put their money into this country. And now they gonna try to take away some of our basic rights. So now people have a real incentive to become citizens. So they can hold on to these rights for themselves and their children.

It would be a mistake, then, to assume Afro-Caribbeans who decide to become citizens are doing so out of a firm commitment to remain in the United States, a desire to participate in the political process, or weakening attachments to their home countries.

IV. CONCLUSION

On the contrary, this chapter has shown Afro-Caribbean immigrants maintain strong transnational ties and hopes of return to their home countries, even after they become United States citizens. All the Afro-Caribbean respondents interviewed for this study were American citizens. Yet most boasted strong continuing attachments to their home countries, and a significant proportion also evinced a desire to return. This sustained sojourner outlook and transnational orientation explain why Afro-Caribbeans have tended to defer the decision to become American citizens and why they have been slow to engage in the political process. But the immigrants' transnational ties do not inevitably inhibit their participation in politics in this country. When these attachments are expressed through civic outlets, they actually may promote engagement in American politics.

But the lingering question is why these immigrants continue to maintain home country ties and the idea of return, even after they have become citizens and established what appear to be permanent roots in the United States. Many of the respondents in this study were citizens. Some were active voters, parents, and homeowners, and a few were even business owners. In short, they all showed signs of permanent settlement in New York City. Yet they continue to hold on to their home country loyalties and the possibility of return however dim.

It turns out the significance of these ties for Afro-Caribbean immigrants goes beyond emotional investments or patriotic fervor for their home countries. As the next two chapters show, home country attachments and the sojourner outlook have deep cognitive utility and instrumental significance for these foreign-born blacks. A home country frame of reference is integral to how Afro-Caribbean immigrants view themselves, respond to racial barriers, and make sense of the political world. In fact, it is what most distinguishes these black ethnics from their African-American counterparts in their bid for political inclusion.

6

Black Like Who?

Afro-Caribbean Immigrants, African Americans, and the Politics of Group Identity

Group identity has been a key concept for understanding how racial minorities and newcomers to the United States have achieved political incorporation. The classic literature on early European immigrants, for example, emphasized group identity as a resource for political engagement (Wolfinger 1965; Dahl 1961). Researchers believed feelings of group identity motivated European newcomers to naturalize, register, and go to the polls to support their coethnics running for political office. Identity thus was seen as a powerful fuel for immigrant political incorporation. The concept holds an even more important place in accounts of African Americans' bid for inclusion in the American polity. Studies of the civil rights movement, for example, suggest group identity served as a key rallying device for African Americans in their efforts to overcome discriminatory barriers. It helped galvanize thousands to engage in collective action to demand equal rights to participate fully in all arenas of American society (Chong 1991; Morris 1984; McAdam 1982).

It is no surprise, then, that scholars of contemporary immigration are also turning their attention to the concept of group identity (e.g., Lien, Conway, and Wong 2004; Lien 2001; Marschall 2001; Jones-Correa and Leal 1996). Insofar as previous studies give political weight to group identity among African Americans and early European immigrants, there is reason to wonder whether it will have similar significance for today's mostly non-white newcomers. The question is whether racial or ethnic group identity becomes politically salient for recent immigrants as they adjust to life in the United States.

Afro-Caribbeans are an intriguing case for exploring this question. As the Introduction noted, these black newcomers share a number of racial commonalities with African Americans. Most obviously, the two groups share physical attributes – skin color, hair texture, and facial features – that define them as black in American society. This shared designation provides a clear basis for racial group identification between Afro-Caribbeans and African Americans. Yet the immigrants also have claim to a distinct ethnic identity, a cultural background based on their ties to the Caribbean and separate from the racial minority status they have in common with African Americans. In short, these black ethnics have access to a racial identity they share with their native-born counterparts and an ethnic identity all their own.

Which identity do Afro-Caribbeans embrace as they adjust to life in the United States? Do they subscribe to the same politically significant feelings of racial group identity as African Americans? Or do they instead embrace a distinctive ethnic identity that sets them apart from their native-born black counterparts? Insofar as they are likely to be viewed simply as black and stigmatized for it by many in American society, how much latitude do Afro-Caribbeans even have to signal a distinct ethnic identity? After all, "what [others] think your ethnicity is influences what you think your ethnicity is" (Portes and MacLeod 1996). Do these black immigrants have meaningful ethnic options?[1] Or is race such a master status in American society it overwhelms and forecloses these other options for group identification (Dawson and Cohen 2002; Waters 1999)?

This chapter takes up these questions with an analysis of the dynamics of group identity among Afro-Caribbean immigrants. Scholarly interest in group identity among blacks in this country has exploded over the last two decades, as the population has become more diverse. Political scientists have wondered whether emerging divisions within the African-American population have undermined individual feelings of group solidarity and diminished the influence of group identity on political behavior (e.g., Gay 2004; Gay and Tate 1998; Dawson 1994a; Tate 1993). But the literature has focused mostly on the effects of class differences on racial identity, with comparatively little attention directed to other cleavages. There has been, for instance, virtually no focus on divisions between native- and Caribbean-born blacks.

There is, however, a lively body of research in other disciplines on the question of how Afro-Caribbean immigrants conceive of their group identity – that is, whether they tend to identify ethnically or racially. Some

---

[1] I borrow the term "ethnic options" from Waters 1990. Waters contends non-whites have limited ethnic options.

researchers have argued Afro-Caribbeans tend to emphasize their ethnic identities as voluntary immigrants, often with the aim of distancing
themselves from African Americans and avoiding racial stigmatization as
blacks in the United States (Waters 1999; Bryce-Laporte 1972; Ried 1939).
Waters has argued this tendency is most pronounced among middle-class
Afro-Caribbeans eager to shore up their status and guard themselves and
their children against socioeconomic backsliding (Waters 1999). In its
least blunt and perhaps most common formulation, this view suggests
ethnic group identification among Afro-Caribbeans militates against any
strong sense of shared racial identity between the immigrants and their
African-American counterparts (e.g., Foner 1985).

Other researchers, however, take a view more in keeping with the
minority group perspective. They maintain prevailing racial inequalities
in American life ultimately compel the immigrants to identify with African
Americans around a shared racial group identity (Vickerman 1999;
Kasinitz 1992; Sutton and Makiesky 1975). Most of these researchers
acknowledge the strong pull of ethnic group loyalties among Afro-
Caribbeans. Yet they contend these foreign-born blacks gradually begin
to emphasize their racial identity as they adjust to life in the United States
and the reality of discrimination.

This argument recalls the theory of reactive ethnicity in the sociological literature. It predicts racial threat and discrimination will engender
racial group identification among immigrants (e.g., Portes and Rumbaut
1996; Portes and Stepick 1993). By this formulation, becoming American for Afro-Caribbeans means most of all confronting the grim reality
of racism in this country, which in turn leads the immigrants to think of
themselves primarily as blacks and identify with African Americans. The
shared experience of discrimination and the racial awareness it fosters
inevitably trump the ethnic differences between the immigrants and their
native-born counterparts.[2]

---

[2] This view echoes recent findings on the effects of class divisions on racial group identity
among African Americans. Researchers have discovered racial identity has remained surprisingly salient and politically significant for African Americans despite deepening class
cleavages within the population (Hochschild 1995; Dawson 1994a; Tate 1993). Contrary
to the predictions of the pluralist model, middle-class African Americans, in particular,
continue to emphasize their racial identity even as they move up the socioeconomic ladder. Researchers believe the prejudice middle-class African Americans face even as they
rise in status leads them to retain their racial identity. The vulnerability to discrimination they share with their lower-income counterparts engenders strong feelings of mutual
identification and common fate and thus eclipses the class divisions between the two
groups.

To put all this axiomatically, there are two leading hypotheses on how Afro-Caribbeans conceive of their group identity. One predicts a greater emphasis on racial identity, whereas the other anticipates more attachment to ethnic identity:

H1:   Concerns about racial stigmatization lead Afro-Caribbeans to high-light their ethnic identity, downplay their racial identity, and distance themselves from African Americans.

H2:   Encounters with discrimination ultimately lead Afro-Caribbeans to emphasize their racial group identity much as African Americans have.

There are also two corresponding corollaries. Each pinpoints discrete causal factors in the social environment that predispose Afro-Caribbeans to identify either ethnically or racially.

H3:   Afro-Caribbeans embrace their ethnic identity but feel less attachment to their racial identity as they achieve upward socioeconomic mobility and move into better-quality neighborhoods.

H3:   Afro-Caribbeans living alongside African Americans in highly segregated, predominantly black neighborhoods are disposed to emphasize their racial identity.

The first corollary is a modification of the pluralist argument that an individual's attachment to racial or ethnic group identity weakens as he or she moves up the socioeconomic ladder. In this case, however, Afro-Caribbeans hold on to their ethnic identity but feel less attachment to their racial identity as they achieve economic success – especially residential mobility into higher-quality neighborhoods.[3] The second corollary, in contrast, suggests casual neighborhood exposure to African Americans prompts Afro-Caribbeans to embrace their shared racial identity with their native-born counterparts. This hypothesis is simply a reformulation of the social contact thesis: interaction breeds mutual identification.[4] All told, each of these hypotheses predicts that as Afro-Caribbeans adjust to a particular facet of American life – whether it be the reality of discrimination, the threat of racial stigmatization, segregation, or the chance

[3] For a similar argument about upwardly mobile African Americans, see Gay 2004.

[4] The same thesis has been advanced to explain the strong feelings of racial solidarity among middle- and lower-class African Americans (Dawson 1994a; McAdam 1982). Residential segregation promotes greater social contact among African Americans across class lines. This contact in turn fosters feelings of racial solidarity within the population.

for socioeconomic success – they will be inclined to embrace either their ethnic or racial identity.

But the question is not so much whether Afro-Caribbeans embrace or reject one identity or the other. Rather, it is whether the immigrants' racial or ethnic identity becomes relatively more or less salient as they adjust to life in the United States. Identities are not dichotomous or zero-sum: embracing of one identity is not an automatic negation of the other. Racial and ethnic identities are complex, fluid categories. Individuals have multiple identities they hold simultaneously, although one may be more salient than another in a particular context. Afro-Caribbean immigrants thus may feel an attachment to both their ethnic and racial identities without contradiction.

Indeed, I find only limited support for the dominant hypotheses in the literature on Afro-Caribbean group identity. My interviews suggest these hypotheses are mistaken in emphasizing either ethnic or racial identity. Most first-generation Afro-Caribbeans place considerable emphasis on their ethnic or home country identity. But the immigrants also identify readily as blacks and see no contradiction between their ethnic attachments and their racial identity.

Nevertheless, I also find Afro-Caribbeans' conception of their racial identity often is not consistent with African-American understandings of this identity. Contrary to the leading hypotheses in the literature, then, the difference between Afro-Caribbean and African-American group identification is not a matter of the immigrants' emphasizing their ethnicity over their race. Rather, the difference is due largely to the fact that these Caribbean-born blacks do not subscribe to the same form of racial identity as their native-born counterparts.

More specifically, Afro-Caribbeans do not evince the high levels of racial group consciousness African Americans tend to express. Group consciousness among African Americans has served as a cognitive device for diagnosing and responding to racism. The Afro-Caribbeans interviewed for this study showed less familiarity with the antiracist, collectivist belief system associated with group consciousness. In fact, the immigrants usually turn to their own distinctive ethnic identity to navigate racial barriers in the United States. The interviews reveal Afro-Caribbeans' ethnic ties to their home countries give them an exit option for responding to American racism.

I conclude that these critical distinctions in how the two groups of blacks conceive of their racial identity and react to discrimination stem from differences in their cognitive frames of reference and their socialization patterns. The findings ultimately show how variations in background and everyday life can lead to differences in how blacks understand and experience their racial identity. My interviews with Afro-Caribbean respondents included a series of questions about group identification. Many of these questions were replicated from the National Black Election Study. But the interview format allowed me to expand on them and prod respondents to elaborate on the more deeply subjective dimensions of group identity.

For the sake of analytical comparison and symmetry, the chapter begins with a consideration of the dynamics of racial group identity among African Americans. The discussion then turns to the main analysis of Afro-Caribbean group identity and its political implications. I conclude with some tentative predictions about how patterns of group identity among Afro-Caribbean immigrants and their second-generation children might evolve over time.

I. THE POLITICS OF AFRICAN-AMERICAN RACIAL GROUP IDENTITY

Group identity has had varying degrees of political influence for blacks and whites in the United States. Ethnic group loyalties provided cues for party allegiance and candidate choice for whites, especially the immigrant generation. Early European immigrants backed coethnic candidates or a particular political party as a means of expressing their group identity and garnering symbolic recognition for their group in the broader society (Wolfinger 1965; Dahl 1961). Yet these feelings of group solidarity almost never crystallized into sustained political identities with distinct ideological implications.[5] In fact, their salience tended to diminish once individuals attained middle-class status, in keeping with the predictions of the traditional pluralist model. Most scholars agree ethnic identity is usually a matter of cultural symbolism or nostalgic fancy – and hence of little practical political significance – for middle-class whites (e.g., Waters 1990).

Racial group identity among black Americans, however, has had much deeper and more sustained political significance. It has served as a rallying point for African-American mobilization, fuel in their bids for political incorporation, and a device to help them make sense of the political

---

[5] Jews may be the notable exception, although ethnic identity no longer seems to have the same strong ideological significance for group members today that it had for them early in the last century (Mollenkopf 1992).

world. The strong influence of racial group identity among African Americans can be traced as far back as the emancipationist struggles of the antebellum era. But this identity took on heightened political salience for African Americans during the civil rights movement, when it became a flashpoint for this epic instance of collective action (e.g., Morris et al. 1989; Chong 1985; McAdam 1984). Today, racial identity continues to affect voting patterns, policy preferences, and even attitudes about the American Dream among African Americans (e.g., Gay and Tate 1998; Hochshild 1995; Dawson 1994a; Tate 1993). The enduring political significance this identity has had among middle-class and poor African Americans is a clear contravention of the pluralist model.

Racial Group Identification and Consciousness

But how exactly does group identity influence African-American political behavior? Group identity is a complex social category. By the standard definition, it consists of two integral components: group identification and group consciousness.[6] Political scientists, however, have not always differentiated between these two forms of group identity (Chong and Rogers 2005).[7] Group identification is a self-awareness of membership in a group and a psychological sense of attachment to the group. Group consciousness, on the other hand, is a belief system or ideology about the group's relative status in society and a prescription for what should be done to improve it. These two forms of group identity have both had considerable political import for African Americans (e.g., Conover 1984).

First, group identification among African Americans – that is, their sense of racial group attachment and awareness – has had more political significance than have comparable ethnic group ties among whites, Latinos, or Asians.[8] Indeed, feelings of racial group attachment are so

---

[6] Social psychologists and sociologists have developed most of the literature on group identity. For some important works on group identity that also devote attention to political behavior, see Tajfel 1981; Brown 1986; Conover 1984; Shingles 1981; Miller et al. 1981.

[7] I use the term "group identity" to refer to the combination of "identification" and "consciousness" and as a generic label for both. But I maintain the distinction between identification and consciousness throughout the chapter.

[8] The political significance of group identification among Latinos and Asians is still an open question; however, research to date has turned up almost no consistent evidence that it has the same deep political meaning among Latinos or Asians as racial identity among African Americans (e.g., Lien 2001; Marschall 2001; Leighley and Vedlitz 1999; Jones-Correa and Leal 1996). For an exception to this trend, see Wong et al. 2005.

pronounced among African Americans many of them routinely subscribe to what researchers describe as a linked racial fate outlook. Their group identification is not simply a matter of racial in-group awareness or affinity. Rather, many African Americans perceive a determinative link between their own individual well-being and the status of African Americans as a whole. They "believe that their lives are to a large degree determined by what happens to the group" (Dawson 1994a, 57).

This linked racial fate outlook has deep instrumental significance for political decision making. It essentially makes the racial group a central analytical category in African Americans' political judgments and policy choices. In Dawson's (ibid., 61) formulation, as long as "African Americans' life chances are powerfully shaped by race, it is efficient [and rational] for individual African Americans to use their perceptions of [African Americans' group interests] as a proxy for their own interests." Hence, the voting behavior, partisan allegiances, and policy preferences of many African Americans are not governed strictly by their individual interests. Rather, these choices often are determined by their ideas of what is good for the racial group as a whole. Group identification never assumed this high level of instrumental political significance for whites, even among the early European immigrants who used their ethnic ties as a cue for many of their electoral choices.

Likewise group consciousness has been largely non-existent or negligible among whites but has been highly developed among African Americans. Group consciousness is the component of racial identity that gives distinctive ideological thrust to African Americans' political attitudes and behavior. If strong group identification disposes African Americans to elevate the interests of the racial group in their political thinking, group consciousness supplies the interpretive framework for actually making political decisions. It furnishes ideological cues for making such judgments and motivation for taking actions on behalf of the group.

Group consciousness among African Americans has had a distinctive ideological makeup over the last half-century or so. African Americans who have high levels of racial group consciousness are often dissatisfied with their group's share of social, political, and economic resources (Gurin et al. 1989). They tend to take stock of the group's relative position in society by drawing comparisons between themselves and whites. Highly group-conscious African Americans, then, reject the persisting group disparities as the unjust result of racism and other structural barriers beyond their individual control (Shingles 1981). They seek redress for these inequalities through collective strategies.[9]

It is worth noting the ideological beliefs or dictates associated with group consciousness are not fixed. There are often within a population ongoing debates and attempts to build consensus over which beliefs should constitute group consciousness. For instance, there might be disagreements about whether consciousness and solidarity require turning to government to solve group problems or instead relying on self-help strategies, as in the famous debates between W. E. B. DuBois and Booker T. Washington. Whatever the case, group consciousness is a cultivated belief system with the potential to guide individual actions in the social, economic, and political arenas.

Taken together, then, group identification and consciousness can exert a powerful cognitive influence on African-American political behavior. In fact, survey findings suggest much of what is distinctive about African-American political choices is influenced by heightened racial group identification and consciousness. African Americans' political participation patterns (e.g., Guterbock and London 1983; Shingles 1981) their reliance on extrasystemic forms of collective action (e.g., Chong and Rogers 2005), and their liberal policy preferences (e.g., Dawson 1994a; Tate 1993) all appear to be shaped to some degree by the high levels of group identification and consciousness within the population. In sum, group identification and consciousness are potent psychological resources for African Americans in their political decision making. These native-born blacks have turned what was once and often still is a stigmatized social identity into a political resource for improving their status in this country.

African-American Institutional Networks and Racial Group Consciousness

Why have racial group identification and consciousness had such deep and abiding political significance for the group? Many researchers believe the high levels of group consciousness among African Americans are the result of their experiences with discrimination and the sharp racial

---

[9] Many researchers believe race-conscious African Americans are inclined to turn to government for solutions to these inequalities (e.g., Verba et al. 1995; Gurin et al. 1989). It is not clear, however, that group consciousness always entails seeking government relief. It may just as easily direct individuals away from government to other kinds of solutions (see Chong and Rogers 2005). But consciousness does orient individuals to collectivist interpretations and strategies for group problems.

divisions in American life. Race, the argument goes, casts such an inescapable shadow on African Americans' life prospects that racial identity, in turn, takes on greater meaning within the population. But the absence of heightened or sustained group consciousness among white ethnics, Latinos, and Asians, all of whom have encountered some forms of prejudice, suggests discrimination alone cannot account for the intensity of this form of identity among African Americans. If group consciousness were an inevitable result of discrimination, we might have seen it among white ethnics in the early twentieth century and certainly should expect it among Latinos, Asians, Afro-Caribbeans, and other recent non-white immigrants today.

African-American racial group consciousness, however, is not just a reaction to discrimination. Rather, it is the result of a complex socialization process that unfolds within a particular social context. The interpretive and prescriptive beliefs that compose group consciousness typically are transmitted through elite messages, exposure to a common culture or history, and contact with in-group members (Herring et al. 1999; Turner 1999; Laitin 1998; Hardin 1995; Smith 1986; Horowitz 1985). These social experiences all contribute to consciousness raising. Individuals immersed in a social context where such influences exist are likely to develop group consciousness and subscribe to the accompanying group-based beliefs. On the other hand, individuals at a remove from such a social context will be less privy to such beliefs and thus less likely to cultivate strong feelings of group consciousness. Whether one develops group consciousness or not is therefore largely a matter of socialization.

This socialization process among African Americans typically occurs in a network of all-black institutions – churches, colleges, social clubs, community organizations, and so on – that first developed during the segregationist Jim Crow era and continues today, albeit in attenuated form. Dawson has labeled this network a "black counterpublic"; Harris refers to it when he writes of an "oppositional civic culture" among African Americans; and Harris-Lacewell has deemed it a "black dialogic space" (Harris-Lacewell 2004; Harris 1998; Dawson 1994b). What these writers have in mind is the network of institutions in which African Americans historically have undergone much of their political socialization.

In addition to serving as a staging ground for episodes of collective mobilization such as the civil rights movement, these institutions have functioned as socializing agents that instill in African Americans a heightened sense of racial group identification and consciousness. They reinforce African-American group identity, sustain a historical memory about the group's racial suffering, and convey values and lessons for how to make sense of the political world, respond to discrimination, and improve group conditions.[10] In short, these networks are sites of political learning. African Americans immersed in them learn to think of themselves as blacks first and to consider the extent to which this racial designation influences their standing in American society.

The salience of racial group consciousness for an individual therefore varies with the extent of his or her socialization within this network of institutions, as well as his or her experiences with discrimination. Although group consciousness can be transmitted from generation to generation, some African Americans subscribe to this form of identity quite intensely whereas others do so only tenuously if at all. For example, researchers have found middle-class African Americans tend to express a greater sense of racial group consciousness than their poor and working-class counterparts (e.g., Hochschild 1995; Dawson 1994a; Gurin et al. 1989; Dillingham 1981). Although this finding may run counter to the predictions of pluralist theory, it is consistent with the socialization thesis on group consciousness I have outlined here.

Middle-income African Americans are more likely than their lower-income counterparts to encounter whites, especially in situations in which they expect to be treated as equals but instead find antiblack prejudice and discrimination.[11] Such experiences seem likely to heighten racial self-awareness and in turn potentially strengthen group identification among middle-class African Americans. But discrimination by itself hardly would deepen their attachment to group consciousness and the attendant collectivist belief system. Rather, heightened consciousness would require exposure to these beliefs. It turns out middle-class African Americans are more likely than their lower-class counterparts to participate in the institutional networks that foster a deeper and more assertive racial group consciousness.

Black institutional sites historically have brought together African Americans of divergent socioeconomic backgrounds and have cultivated

---

[10] As Dawson (1994a, 58) explains, these institutions "transmit the lessons of how to respond to shifts in race relations, economic climate, and political environment across generations." Similarly, Marable (1994) notes they serve as a reservoir for "collective experiences, survival tales, and grievances [that] form the basis of a historical consciousness, [the] group's recognition of what it has witnessed, and what it can anticipate in the near future."

[11] For a useful discussion of status inconsistency among middle-class African Americans, see Hochschild 1995.

and reinforced racial group consciousness across class lines. But the middle class always have participated in such organizational networks to a greater degree than the poor. In fact, participation by the poor in black associational and civic life generally has declined over the last two decades (Harris 1998; Dawson 1994b; Cohen and Dawson 1993).[12] It is no wonder, then, middle-class blacks tend to evince higher levels of racial group consciousness than their lower-class counterparts. They spend more time in the institutional networks where consciousness raising happens. More generally, though, African-American institutional sites have been on the wane; likewise, some researchers believe group consciousness has lost some of its hold on the population. Nevertheless, racial group identification and consciousness remain salient among African Americans, even in the face of growing class divisions.

II. GROUP IDENTITY AMONG AFRO-CARIBBEAN IMMIGRANTS

Divisions of nationality, however, are another matter. There are obvious grounds for racial solidarity and identification among Afro-Caribbeans and African Americans: a shared ascriptive category, vulnerability to discrimination, residence in the same highly segregated all-black neighborhoods, and so on. But there are also ethnic differences between the two groups of blacks: nationality, culture, and even modest socioeconomic disparities favoring the immigrants.[13] The question, then, is whether racial similarities lead Afro-Caribbeans and African Americans to embrace similar forms of racial group identity or whether the immigrants emphasize their distinct ethnic identity and downplay their commonalities with African Americans.

Ethnic and Racial Identification

My interviews suggest there is some truth in the two leading hypotheses on how Afro-Caribbeans conceive of their group identity. Racial identification and ethnic identification are not dichotomous choices for Afro-Caribbean immigrants. They identify both racially and ethnically without contradiction. They do not, however, subscribe to the same form of racial

---

[12] There is also good reason to suspect the African-American counterpublic has lost its intergenerational diversity. Organizations like the National Association for the Advancement of Colored People (NAACP) lately have lamented their lack of younger members.

[13] For a discussion of conflicts between the two groups, see Chapter 4.

identity as African Americans. African Americans' conception of their racial identity is often a powerful combination of group identification and group consciousness. Afro-Caribbeans, on the other hand, express clear feelings of racial group identification but do not exhibit the kind of racial group consciousness associated with African Americans.

This distinction between group identification and group consciousness has been overlooked in the literature on identity among Afro-Caribbean immigrants. But it is critical to understanding differences in how they and their African-American counterparts conceive of their racial identity. It is not a matter of the immigrants' emphasizing their ethnic identity and minimizing their racial ties to blacks born in this country. Rather, Afro-Caribbeans have a different conception of their racial identity than African Americans.

Afro-Caribbean immigrants place considerable emphasis on their ethnic identity, to be sure. Most of the immigrants interviewed for this study chose their ethnic or home country identity as their primary group identification. Of the fifty-nine respondents, forty-eight claimed their ethnic or home country identity as their core group attachment. One respondent (interview, November 29, 1996) proudly avowed, "I have been in the United States for many [years], but I am a natural Jamaican and a naturalized American." Speaking with the same unequivocal pride, another (interview, May 6, 1997) put it this way: "I'm Jamaican. There is a mixture because I know that my racial ancestry is that of Africa ... but most immediate is that of the Caribbean. I'm from Jamaica. Jamaica is my home. Not Ethiopia, not South Africa. Those are the homes of my foreparents. I respect that, but Jamaica is from whence I came."

The respondents' strong attachment to their home country identity emerged regardless of how the question was posed. Consider this series of replies (interview, April 17, 1997).

Q: Some people describe themselves differently according to whom they are speaking. How do you describe yourself when speaking to other Caribbean Americans?
A: I'm Trinidadian.
Q: African Americans?
A: Trinidadian.
Q: Whites?
A: Same thing, Trinidadian.
Q: Do you usually let others know that you're from Trinidad or the Caribbean?
A: Well, the minute I open my mouth it is sort of self-evident. So I make it known voluntarily and involuntarily.

A sixty-three-year-old Jamaican man (interview, May 5, 1997) was similarly emphatic about his attachment to his Caribbean identity.

Q: How do you describe yourself when someone asks about your social background?

A: I'm very proud to be Jamaican. I'm proud to be an American, by citizenship, by virtue of having worked and paid a lot of dues, taxes, rendered service to the community. I have no constraints in saying that I have earned the right to be an American. But I am Jamaican first

Q: Some people describe themselves differently according to whom they are speaking. How do you describe yourself when you are speaking to others from the Caribbean?

A: Jamaican. Yes, I have the same pride in speaking to any Caribbean from any country, and hope they have the same pride in their country.

Q: What about when you're talking to African Americans?

A: I have no problems with that either.

Q: So you don't modify how you identify yourself?

A: I don't modify. However, I am cognizant of the fact that there is some animosity [between African Americans and Caribbean Americans], and I'm careful how I express that.

Q: What about when you're talking to whites?

A: I have no problem with that either.

Q: Do you usually let others know you're from the Caribbean?

A: Yes. Absolutely.

Q: What is most important to you? Being Jamaican, Caribbean, Black, American, none?

A: Jamaican, Caribbean, American, in that order.

The interview subject is a naturalized American citizen who has lived in the United States since 1962; yet he continues to view Jamaica as his home country and define himself primarily as a Jamaican ethnic. Most of the respondents echoed similar sentiments of an abiding attachment and identification with the Caribbean, and their home countries in particular.

Even with this strong commitment to their ethnic identity, most of my respondents nonetheless expressed a sense of racial group identification with African Americans. If by identification we mean strictly a sense of racial in-group awareness and attachment, then almost all of the interview subjects evinced it in some measure. Fifty-two of them reported they "felt close" to African Americans, and almost as many said they are personally affected by "what happens to African Americans" in this country. One middle-aged Afro-Caribbean man (interview, November 29, 1996) gave what proved to be a common response: "I feel close to African Americans because we have the same racial background. Our histories are

similar." Another man from Guyana made a similar observation, point-
ing specifically to a common ancestral history. He explained (interview,
April 2, 1997), "Yes. The closeness is as it relates to mother Africa."

Even those respondents who did not feel particularly close to African
Americans recognized a racial bond with their native-born counterparts.
One (interview, April 1, 1997) made this observation about his lack of
close ties to African Americans: "I'm not too close to many of them. Most
of my friends and acquaintances are from the Caribbean like me. But I
know that we're all black. Caribbean Americans and African Americans.
So we have that in common."

All in all, most respondents were quite mindful of the similarities
between Afro-Caribbeans and African Americans and expressed some
affinity for their native-born counterparts. Insofar as the majority of these
immigrants were middle class, their clearly expressed feelings of racial
identification with African Americans cast serious doubt on the hypothesis
that suggests upward mobility diminishes their racial awareness and ties to
their native-born counterparts. Indeed, many of these middle-class Afro-
Caribbean respondents articulated a vague sense of linked racial fate with
African Americans.[14] Racial self-identification among Afro-Caribbeans is
perhaps not surprising, in light of the still significant racial divide between
blacks and whites in the United States. Racial divisions in this country perhaps make racial identification among blacks, both immigrant and native
born, a virtual inevitability.[15]

Racial Group Consciousness

Although my Afro-Caribbean respondents readily acknowledged their
racial identification with African Americans, they did not register the same
highly cultivated feelings of racial group consciousness often expressed by
their native-born counterparts. They generally did not attach the same set
of political meanings or collectivist ideological beliefs to their racial identity as African Americans. In answering questions designed to tap feelings
of racial group consciousness, the respondents expressed considerable
ambivalence. Take, for instance, this fairly typical sampling of responses
(interview, April 2, 1997).

---

[14] See later discussion for elaboration.
[15] Whites, in contrast, have much greater latitude in choosing whether or not to signify
ethnic group attachments. As Waters (1990) has argued, expressions of ethnicity among
whites are voluntary and symbolic; they are fundamentally a matter of choice.

Q: Some people think it's harder for blacks to do well in this country. What
      do you think?
A: Um ... It probably is.
Q: If blacks don't do well in life, is it because they are kept back because of
      their race, or is it because they don't work hard enough?
A: Probably half and half.

Although less terse in her response, a middle-aged Afro-Caribbean woman
(interview, April 1, 1997) registered similar ambivalence.

Q: Some people think it's harder for blacks to do well in this country. What
      do you think?
A: It depends on where they are. I don't know if I would make that blanket
      statement. Maybe within some systems it is. Where they are – the part of
      the country, what skills they come with – it could be, but I wouldn't say
      across the board, nationwide, that is how it is.
Q: If blacks don't do well in life, is it because they are kept back because of
      their race, or is it because they don't work hard enough?
A: It depends on the situation. I would really have to look at it more.
Q: Is success in the United States mostly a matter of hard work, or is it more
      a matter of one's racial or socioeconomic background?
A: I think it's a combination. I really think it's a combination.

Another interview subject (interview, April 8, 1997) moved from
ambivalence to certainty during the course of his reply.

Q: Is success in the United States mostly a matter of hard work, or is it more
      a matter of one's racial or socioeconomic background?
A: I'm not so sure. It could be both. But then again, in my experience it's
      mostly been about hard work.
Q: Why do you think some people in America make it while others don't?
A: Well, I'll show you. A lot of people in America, I call them dreamers. They
      will dream of everything they want, but they would never work towards
      it. I have a way I tell my children, if you want to achieve anything – and
      I usually use a car as an example. "You want to buy a car; the car is five
      hundred dollars. You haven't got five hundred dollars. You can only afford
      fifty dollars a week. So now you have to wait ten weeks to get your car.
      Don't take it on credit, because it will not cost you five hundred dollars. It
      will cost you much more. Don't dream. Just do the hard [work], whatever
      it takes.
Q: So you think it's about hard work and frugality?
A: Yes. Let me explain something about the Caribbean, too. I don't know if
      you know it. We call it *su-su*. Now, this is trust, because we will pay one
      hundred dollars a week, might be fifty, sixty of us. And each week you get
      the amount. You understand what I mean? You are letting a man hold six
      to seven thousand dollars of yours, with no interest. And he hands it to
      you. When that man gives you the money you could run away with it and

don't pay again. But it's trust and savings. That's how we do everything in
the Caribbean.

Q: I understand. But some people think it's harder for blacks in this country
to get ahead, get loans, and so on. What do you think?

A: I don't believe that.

Q: If blacks don't do well in life, is it because they are kept back because of
their race, or is it because they don't work hard enough?

A: It is because they are not educated enough. You see, I don't really believe
in hard work. I believe in working smart, and to work smart, the first tool
in the trade is education, because that is the only thing you cannot lose. As
much as the white man might try to keep you down, he can't take education
away from you.

The respondent acknowledges the presence of racial barriers in his final
sentence. Yet he is confident they can be overcome with hard work. Of the
fifty-nine respondents, thirty-eight claimed success in the United States
turned on a combination of individual hard work and environmental
factors. Another thirteen believed success stems from hard work alone.
Eight saw race and social background as determinative.

The ambivalence expressed by these first-generation immigrants contrasts with African Americans' attitudes about racial group conditions.
African Americans, especially those who have high levels of racial group
consciousness, often attribute poor black group outcomes to racism and
other structural factors (Sigelman and Welch 1991). This particular view
of black group conditions – emphasizing systemic racism – is informed by
the distinctive interpretive lens associated with racial group consciousness.

The Afro-Caribbean respondents, in contrast, pointed to a mix of
structural and individual factors to account for how blacks fare in
American society. These are not diametrically opposed opinions driven
by radically different worldviews. Rather, the ambivalence evinced by
the Afro-Caribbean respondents suggests their sense of racial group
consciousness may not be as well developed or pronounced as it is among
African Americans.

Further, although almost all of the respondents declared they had
encountered racial discrimination and believed racism was still pervasive
in American life, most also claimed they were not as preoccupied with
racism as their African-American counterparts. Consider these reports
about personal encounters with racism (interview, April 10, 1997):

When I was working with the last company. I could call the name. When I
was working with [company name], we had a manager's conference in Atlanta,
Georgia. I went as the New York representative … When I reached the Atlanta
airport – you know these guys who have the little placards identifying themselves.

I saw [company name], so I went up to the guy and said, "Are you the driver for [company name]?" He said, "Yes." I said, "Well, I'm from New York." He said, "Okay, as soon as the other party comes we'll leave." I said, "But there is only one representative, and it's me." He still stand up and looking. Hmmm . . . He couldn't believe a black man coming to New York to represent [company name] in Atlanta.

This account was typical. Many of the respondents discerned racial discrimination at the workplace.

Others reported they perceived racism in the attitudes of retail personnel, following and eying them suspiciously, while they shopped in New York stores. As one Barbadian woman (interview, June 26, 1997) recalled: "I remember going into Saks one time. And the woman working in there looking at me all the time. You know, with this suspicious look on her face. She asked me if I needed help, and then kept her eyes on me all the time. I ended up just walking out. They didn't get my money." Hers was a common complaint among the respondents. Virtually all of them indicated they had felt the sting of racism at some point during their lives in the United States. The few who reported they had not encountered much discrimination nonetheless acknowledged their coethnic friends or acquaintances had (interview, November 29, 1996).

Q: Have you ever encountered discrimination in your attempts to find work or a place to live?
A: No.
Q: Do you know any other Caribbean Americans who have encountered such problems?
A: Oh yes. I have a friend who is out in Queens. When she moved out there her house was firebombed. She moved into like an Italian neighborhood there, right behind where the airport is. She was one of the first black families to move out there. Her house was firebombed. Can you believe it?

Still, most of the respondents also believed they were not as preoccupied as their African-American counterparts with these predictable racial slights. One respondent (interview, November 29, 1996) observed, "We [Afro-Caribbeans] are concerned about racism. But basically we don't walk around with a chip on our shoulders like African Americans, although, like you said, we experience a lot of racial prejudice. America owes African Americans something . . . more opportunity. We feel less owed." A Guyanese man (interview, May 19, 1997) offered a similar theory.

Q: You say that Caribbean Americans don't react to racism in the same way as African Americans? What's the difference?

A: You see, they [African Americans] believe that the white man took some-
      thing from them, which he did, and they're always thinking about how to
      beat the system to get it back.
Q: And Caribbean Americans don't have that same attitude?
A: No. We're immigrants. So we come here to uplift ourselves and go back
      home. So we keep the focus on that.

Such attitudes were prevalent among the interview subjects. Indeed,
their claim that they and their Caribbean-born coethnics are less preoccupied with racism than native-born blacks is consistent with the findings of
other research on the immigrants' attitudes about race (e.g., Waters 1999;
1994b; Kasinitz 1992). Yet it would be a mistake to read such responses as
a sign of Afro-Caribbean indifference to racial discrimination.[16] Rather,
the pattern suggests Afro-Caribbeans recognize African Americans have
a deeper sense of racial grievance than most other non-white groups in
the United States. African Americans' awareness of this history of racial
problems is almost certainly informed by their highly cultivated feelings
of group consciousness.

Differences in Collective Memory

Lower levels of racial group consciousness among Afro-Caribbean immigrants are likely the result of two factors. First, in contrast to African
Americans who have direct claim and access to a collective memory of
long-standing racial subordination in this country, Afro-Caribbeans – as
recent voluntary immigrants – do not. More than a few of the respondents
acknowledged they did not have the same historically informed view of
race relations in this country as African Americans. One man (interview,
April 2, 1997) put it this way:

I was somewhere the other day, and I heard a leading legislator talking about
what slavery and segregation had done to the psyche of blacks – but of course,
he was talking about American blacks... And I realize that our slavery in the
Caribbean passed so many years back before it did in this country... and we
didn't have segregation. I mean we didn't have much white people to speak of.
Well, in Jamaica... When I was growing up I never heard anything about slavery and segregation. Whereas for African Americans, those things seem more
immediate... more recent. And they are still living with the aftereffects.

The respondent recognizes African Americans have a historically rooted
sense of racial grievance in the United States. This grievance is a part of the
collective memory that contributes to racial group consciousness among

---

[16] I return to this point later.

African Americans. With no direct claim to the same historical memory, first-generation Afro-Caribbeans have correspondingly lower levels of racial group consciousness. Many of these immigrants also have not experienced watershed struggles, such as the civil rights movement, that were aimed at addressing this racial grievance. These struggles confirmed the value of group solidarity as a political resource and reinforced group consciousness among African Americans.

This is not to say these immigrants are oblivious to the dynamics of America's race problem. Rather, they are not as connected to its history as their native-born black counterparts. The immigrants are from island nations where the history of systematic racial domination by whites is somewhat more remote than and not nearly as extensive as in the United States (Waters 1999; Vickerman 1999; Kasinitz 1992). There was, for example, no long experience with Jim Crow segregation in the Caribbean. Hence, Afro-Caribbeans do not enter the United States with the same long-standing sense of racial grievance many of their native-born counterparts have developed.

Social and Institutional Networks

Second and perhaps more importantly, most recent Afro-Caribbean immigrants are not connected to the institutional networks that have served as sites of consciousness raising for African Americans. Insofar as they have fewer ties to these institutions, many recent Afro-Caribbean immigrants will not have the same highly cultivated form of racial group consciousness as their native-born counterparts. Although all the immigrants I interviewed reported they encounter African Americans in their neighborhoods and the workplace, few interacted regularly with their black counterparts in the networks that compose what remains of New York's "black counterpublic."

Those interview respondents who did report frequent or regular participation in black organizations dominated by African Americans, however, expressed the highest levels of racial group consciousness. For example, one respondent (interview, April 2, 1997), an active member of a mostly African-American political club, proved to be most emphatic about the linked fate of Afro-Caribbeans and African Americans and the need for collective political action to combat systemic racism.

Q: Do you feel that your fate as an Afro-Caribbean is at all linked to that of African Americans?
A: Yes. Definitely, in this country.

Q: Why?
A: Because we're all considered the same – the same, meaning minority or black. So, we're not separated or separable, in terms of discrimination. And we have to join together to fight against it.

He also expressed a much stronger sense of racial group consciousness than many of the other respondents.

Q: Why do some people make it in the United States and others don't? Is it because of their race, hard work, or a little bit of both?
A: I think it's race that prevents many of us from not having the same opportunities, and we have to make it up with hard work. It's not fair, but that's the reality. So when opportunities do become available, you have to take advantage of them.
Q: So do you think it's harder for blacks to make it in this country?
A: Yes, absolutely.
Q: If blacks don't do well in life, is it because of their race or is it because they don't work hard enough?
A: It has to be a case by case assessment. But one might not have the opportunity to work hard, because of race. Often black people don't even get the opportunity in this country.

Another respondent (interview, April 17, 1997) with similar exposure to African-American organizational networks echoed the same note of certainty about the linked racial fate of Afro-Caribbeans and African Americans. He even rejected the notion of any meaningful cultural differences between the two groups.

Q: What about African Americans, do you feel close to them?
A: Yes, because for the first seven or eight years in this country, I lived primarily among them. I came to this country and I went straight to Harlem, and that's where I stayed until I bought my own home. So my children's baby-sitter was an African American. I am sort of, fairly, familiar with the culture . . . The guy I identify as being my father away from home was an African American from South Carolina. I spent my first Thanksgiving with him and his kids, and you know, he took me in like a son.
Q: Are there any cultural differences between African Americans and Caribbean Americans, beyond food, music, and those sorts of things?
A: The differences are a figment of the media imagination . . .
Q: Do you feel that your fate as a Caribbean American is at all linked to that of African Americans?
A: Oh yes. Without a doubt.
Q: Is that because of race?
A: Yes, strictly because of race.
Q: How much of what happens to African Americans in this country affects Caribbean Americans?
A: I would say everything.

The respondents' immersion in African-American institutional networks appears to have heightened their feelings of racial group consciousness and solidarity with their native-born counterparts.

This finding is indirect evidence of the socialization thesis on racial consciousness. It suggests this form of racial identity among blacks is the result of "socializing experiences that occur within formal and informal networks" (Herring et al. 1999). But the evidence from these interviews also casts doubt on the social contact hypothesis. Recall it posits that Afro-Caribbeans living in proximity to African Americans in highly segregated neighborhoods are likely to embrace the same form of racial identity as their native-born counterparts. Despite encountering African Americans in residential and even workplace settings, however, most of my Afro-Caribbean respondents did not evince high levels of racial group consciousness.

Casual social exposure to African Americans apparently is not enough to produce high levels of group consciousness in Afro-Caribbean immigrants. Rather, consciousness appears to require a kind of inculcation in the group-based beliefs circulating within African-American institutional networks.[17] Consequently, only those respondents with a history of socialization in these networks expressed the collectivist ideologies researchers typically associate with black racial group consciousness.

Transnational Identity

Most Afro-Caribbean New Yorkers are not socialized in these traditional African-American institutional networks. Rather, they undergo much of their initial adjustment to the United States in transnational or home country immigrant networks. These networks have developed in the boroughs of Brooklyn and Queens, where the immigrants have carved out their own distinct residential enclaves within larger black neighborhoods.[18] Although the immigrants live in the same residential areas as African Americans, they have established their own neighborhood niches.

Afro-Caribbeans develop their ethnic identity in the context of these neighborhood social networks. The networks have two distinct effects on Afro-Caribbean identity. First, they put the immigrants in contact with coethnics from all over the Caribbean and thus lead them to embrace a panethnic identity. Afro-Caribbeans immigrate to the United States with their particular island-based identities, and develop a panethnic

---

[17] See the Conclusion for more on the forms of group consciousness.
[18] See Chapter 2 for more discussion of Afro-Caribbean residential enclaves.

Caribbean identity as a result of interacting with other immigrants from the region in these neighborhood-based networks.

Second, the networks also encourage the immigrants to sustain their ties to their home countries. Afro-Caribbeans in these networks typically share news and memories from back home. This ongoing attention to home country activities, acquaintances, and so on, is part of a larger socialization process that gives Afro-Caribbean ethnic identity a transnational focus. The immigrants' ethnic identity directs them toward their home countries, despite the fact that this identity is almost entirely a creation of their experiences in the United States. It divides their cognitive and emotional attachments "between two nations," the United States and the country they left behind (Jones-Correa 1998).

As Chapter 5 illustrated, home country attachments are quite pronounced among Afro-Caribbean immigrants. But they are not unique to them. Indeed, recall from Chapter 5 home country commitments have been attributed to immigrants in general, especially the most recent wave of newcomers to the United States.[19] As one researcher (Piore 1979, 65) explained, "however settled immigrants actually become, they continue to see themselves in a certain sense as belonging to some other place and retain an idea, albeit increasingly vague and ill-defined, of returning home." In short, home country or transnational identities encourage a "sojourner mentality" and fuels the "myth of return."

Afro-Caribbeans' home country identities have considerable influence on their view of life in the United States. In fact, this form of identity makes for a critical difference in how they and their African-American counterparts see themselves as blacks in this country. Although the two groups share a common racial identity and the vexing experience of discrimination, Afro-Caribbeans and African Americans map their identities on different, albeit overlapping cognitive fields. African Americans anchor their identities, especially their racial group consciousness, in the United States. As voluntary immigrants, Afro-Caribbeans, in contrast, conceive of their identities on a wider cognitive map that spans the United States and their home countries.

Consequently, the immigrants and African Americans have very different perceptual lenses for making sense of their lives in this country. Whereas African Americans often rely on racial group consciousness to evaluate their status and confront the challenges of racism,

---

[19] For a discussion of transnational or home country ties among earlier European immigrants, see Bodnar 1985.

Afro-Caribbean immigrants turn to their home country or transnational identity. As it turns out, this identity furnishes them with particular cognitive and strategic options for navigating America's racial barriers that are not available to their native-born counterparts.

Alternate Frame of Reference

First, it provides Afro-Caribbeans with an alternate frame of reference for making political evaluations and assessments about their life in the United States. Recall from earlier in the chapter many African Americans – especially those with highly developed feelings of group consciousness – measure their status in American society by comparing themselves to whites. In fact, their racial group consciousness is often reinforced by this black-white dialectic when they note the continuing racial disparities between them and their more privileged white American counterparts in resources, status, and influence.

Afro-Caribbean immigrants, in contrast, compare themselves not only to groups in the United States, but also to their former compatriots back home. "They...measure success by comparing their present condition with their lives in the [Caribbean]" (Vickerman 1994, 123). Nor are the comparisons strictly retrospective. With frequent trips to their home countries and ongoing contact with family and friends there, the immigrants easily can evaluate their status relative to that of their compatriots back home. In short, Afro-Caribbeans' home countries often serve as the yardstick by which they measure their status in the United States.

The tendency of Afro-Caribbeans to turn to their home countries as a benchmark to evaluate their condition in the United States is a rational strategy for a group relegated to a subordinate minority category. Individuals saddled with a subordinate status – as blacks are in this country – may pursue a number of different strategies to improve their standing (Chong 2000). For instance, they may seek to challenge the status quo or elevate the image of their group by emphasizing its most positive characteristics, two strategies African Americans have pursued. But they also may choose an alternative comparison group to improve their status (Hogg and Abrams 1988). Many Afro-Caribbean immigrants opt for this latter strategy.

Simply by migrating, they secure a somewhat higher status in their home countries, where they are often viewed as a highly motivated, select group. Although migration to the United States is hardly uncommon among Caribbean populations, those who immigrate still acquire a measure of prestige, or at least generate curiosity and the weight of expectations, as "locals" determined to "make good" in the United States.[20] Frequent trips and remittances to the home country allow Afro-Caribbean immigrants to signal their improved status and capitalize on the social prestige associated with migration.[21] Even if immigrants experience only modest, incremental mobility, they can compare themselves favorably to their compatriots back home.

Whether the comparisons ultimately prove favorable or not, many Afro-Caribbeans make evaluations about their status from this transnational frame of reference. Often with little or no prompting, respondents, both men and women, made comparisons between "their present condition and their lives in the Caribbean." Consider this representative pair of responses to questions about life in the United States (interview, April 3, 1997).

Q: How would you describe your standard of living?
A: Fairly good. I mean, probably better than on the island. But I'm not sure.
Q: Are you saying that you're better off now than you were on the island?
A: Well, not really. You have to consider the age difference.
Q: Sure. But even looking at your family as a whole then and now, what would you say?
A: I'd say better off. It's hard to determine what's better off. One might say we have more amenities and material things. But I'm not sure about other areas. Better off is really subjective.

A Jamaican woman (interview, July 27, 1997) used a similar transnational lens to assess the quality of her children's schooling.

Q: What local political issues do you most care about?
A: Education for sure, and quality of life issues.
Q: Are you satisfied with the quality of education at your children's schools?
A: Not really. My children are doing okay. But the teachers don't seem to care about the kids' learning like they did back in Jamaica. If I could afford it, I would send them to private school.

As these exchanges indicate, the transnational frame of reference surfaced particularly in respondents' answers to questions asking them to assess some qualitative dimension of their lives. The immigrants' political judgments, then, may often be based on assessments made from this

---

[20] On the long-standing prevalence of migration in Caribbean countries, see Kasinitz 1992; Toney 1986; Thomas-Hope 1978.
[21] Of course, many immigrants, especially men, initially suffer a decline in occupational status after immigration.

transnational frame of reference, and not necessarily on the black-white dialectic often employed by African Americans in their political decision making.

Although Afro-Caribbean immigrants are saddled with the same racial minority label as African Americans, they also derive their own sense of status, self-definition, and perspective from their attachments to their home countries. As one elite respondent (interview, May 7, 1997) explained:

Caribbean people are always looking back to the nation of their birth and upbringing. People feel that they're better respected at home and have better respectability at home than they have here. Here they're an unknown quantity, and a lot of people – even those who come from "upper crust families" – feel lost in the shuffle here. At home, they can be big fishes in a small pond.

Exit Option

Home country identities also furnish Afro-Caribbean immigrants with a strategic option for responding to racial discrimination. Several researchers have argued the transnational frame of reference leads immigrants to dismiss or minimize racial barriers as temporary inconveniences. John Ogbu (1990, 526), for instance, contends "voluntary immigrants tend to interpret the economic, political, and social barriers against them as more or less temporary problems, as problems they will overcome or can overcome with the passage of time and with hard work." He contrasts this immigrant outlook with the perspective of African Americans, who often view the same barriers as systematic or entrenched.

Although Ogbu and others correctly emphasize immigrants' alternate frame of reference, his interpretation of how it informs their view of racial barriers does not apply to Afro-Caribbean immigrants. Afro-Caribbeans do not see racial discrimination as temporary or insignificant. In fact, they are quite cognizant of the stubborn patterns of racism that often can limit their achievement and frustrate their adjustment to life in the United States. But as immigrants with ties to other countries, they recognize they have a distinct strategic option for alleviating these racial frustrations. Afro-Caribbean immigrants have an exit option for responding to American racism.

If the immigrants find their mobility blocked by insuperable racial barriers, they likely will maintain their home country attachments and keep the myth of return alive. In such instances, the myth of return becomes an option for escape or exit, which coincidentally may deflect the immigrants' attention from other potential strategic responses to discrimination such as collective mobilization or demands for systemic reform. Rather than take such costly political actions, the immigrants can simply exit the political system. When asked how they cope with American racism, many of the interview respondents spoke of this exit option. They repeatedly declared they would return to their home countries if the racial barriers proved too daunting.

One Jamaican woman (interview, April 1, 1997) explained, "If things get impossible, I can always go home to Jamaica." A middle-aged Trinidadian man (interview, April 2, 1997) reported he increasingly has begun to view his home country as a place of refuge from the rigors of American racism.

Q: Do you feel affected by the recent cases of police brutality?
A: Of course, yeah, man. It's so bad now even in my neighborhood. My teenage sons are always complaining that the police harass them. It's getting so bad that I feel like I should just take my family and move back home to Trinidad. I think about it seriously more and more these days. You know, we don't have this nonsense in Trinidad. Here you can't even feel safe with the police.

A Guyanese woman (interview, May 14, 1997) expressed a similar outlook with no prompting.

Q: Have you ever experienced racial discrimination?
A: Are you kidding?! Many times. Americans are some racist people. They look at you funny on the street. They turn up their nose at you in stores when you ask a question. It's terrible, man. Make[s] me feel like just packing my bags, selling everything, and going back to Guyana. I just thank God nothing really serious never happens, like what's going on with the police in this city. I tell you if something like what happened to Louima ever happened to me or one of my children, I'd be on the next plane out of New York back home.

An elite respondent (interview, December 14, 1996) elaborated on the cognitive utility of the exit option among her coethnic constituents.

I go back to the psychological and emotional ties to the Caribbean. People feel that "I have an option, I have an option. If things don't work out here for me, I'll work, make some money, and go back home. If I don't get respect, or I meet prejudice, I can always pack my bags and go back home, where at least people will respect me."

Vickerman (1994, 102) found this same pattern of invoking the exit option in his interviews with Caribbean immigrants. Reflecting on a past encounter with racism, one of his respondents explains his determination to return home. "This redneck guy looked around and told us that...he used to...kill people like us, meaning he used to kill black people. That only crystallized my resolve to leave here [the United States] and go home."

Even if Afro-Caribbean immigrants never resort to this exit option – and few actually ever do – it nonetheless informs their political thinking and view of themselves. Although it remains only a contemplated choice for most immigrants, it continues to factor in their outlook. The exit option was invoked even by Afro-Caribbeans who had lived in the United States for two decades or more. The choice to return to Jamaica remained a viable option for one respondent (interview, May 7, 1997), although she had been in the United States since the 1960s. Similarly, Vickerman reports the immigrants he interviewed "were 'birds of passage' in the sense that though they evinced little desire to actually return to Jamaica, they wanted to feel that the option was always there for them."

European immigrants maintained home country ties, as well. Many, in fact, resorted to the exit option, in the face of the harsh realities of immigrant life in the United States. Yet for those who remained, home country identification never took on the kind of ongoing cognitive significance it appears to have for Afro-Caribbean immigrants. Several factors account for this difference between early European immigrants and recent Afro-Caribbean newcomers to this country. First, late-twentieth-century improvements in travel and technology make it far easier for contemporary Caribbean, Latin American, and Asian immigrants to maintain home country ties than it was for their European predecessors. Second, grim conditions in their home countries also made transnational ties and the possibility of return impractical for early European immigrants from some regions, such as Russia and Italy.[22]

Even more significantly, home country ties among these European immigrants diminished under the pressure of the Americanization movement and the patriotic fervor of World War II (Gerstle 1996; 1993). Afro-Caribbeans and other recent non-white immigrants, in contrast, have not had to face comparable pressures to relinquish their home country attachments. Indeed, there have been far greater acceptance and tolerance of

[22] Nancy Foner reminds me in written correspondence, it was hardly "realistic for Jews to go back to Russia where anti-Semitism was a million times worse and many of their communities were ravaged by World War I and then of course their relatives killed during World War II. As for groups like Italians, the Depression made Italy uninviting and of course there was World War II."

immigrants' ties to their home countries since the cultural shifts of the 1960s.

Finally and perhaps most importantly, home country ethnic identification among European immigrants gradually declined as they gained entré to almost all arenas of American life after World War II, in keeping with the predictions of the pluralist model. These immigrants became the white ethnic success stories of America's melting pot mythology and soon had little need for the exit option provided by their home country ties. It is not clear, however, the racial barriers facing immigrant and native-born blacks will disappear anytime soon. Hence, Afro-Caribbean immigrants likely will continue to hold on to the exit option afforded by their home country ties as a psychological buffer against discrimination in the United States.

The continuing utility of the exit option among Afro-Caribbeans also distinguishes them from their Asian and Latino counterparts. Although Asian and Latino immigrants also encounter discriminatory obstacles, the ones they meet are not nearly as imposing or pervasive as those faced by blacks. Asian and Latino immigrants thus may have less reason than Afro-Caribbeans to maintain the exit option afforded by their own home country ties. Consider, for example, Jones-Correa's recent research (1998) on Latino immigrants in New York. Much as this study does, his findings emphasize the importance of transnational ties in the political lives of Latinos. Yet the immigrants in his account do not appear to emphasize their home country ties in response to racial discrimination quite as much as Afro-Caribbeans do.

Finally, Afro-Caribbeans' reliance on the exit option is a notable contrast to African Americans' attachments to the collectivist beliefs that constitute racial group consciousness. Recall race-conscious African Americans tend to look to collective mobilization and government intervention to eliminate racial barriers and improve their group status. Afro-Caribbeans, in contrast, see relief in the possibility of returning to their home countries. This contrast represents a serious challenge to the familiar argument that Afro-Caribbeans are more conservative than African Americans on matters of race (Sleeper 1993).

The immigrants' apparent ambivalence about government solutions to racial problems, for example, is not necessarily the result of a more conservative ideological outlook. First, it may be due simply to their lack of exposure to the collectivist beliefs associated with racial group consciousness among African Americans. Second, government solutions may seem a dubious prospect to these immigrants, insofar as they have a more viable option for responding to racial barriers: that is, they can choose to return to their home countries.

Although this exit option is a practicable strategy their native-born black counterparts do not have, it is perhaps no less radical than the familiar African-American demands for government reform. Indeed, to contemplate the exit option afforded by home country ties is to signal pessimism about the promises of American democracy. The Afro-Caribbean respondents who invoked the possibility of returning to their home countries in the face of ongoing discrimination essentially were registering their own doubts about the fundamental openness and fairness of American society. Even to consider the exit option is to hint at a latent despair over the capacity of the American political system to eradicate racial inequality.

The persisting cognitive utility of home country attachments among Afro-Caribbean immigrants is a clear contravention of pluralism's assimilationist logic. In the pluralist version of American history, immigrants have always profited from assimilation. Relinquishing their ties to their home countries and adopting the customs of this one have sped their entry into the mainstream. Afro-Caribbeans, however, may be the first group of immigrants for whom this is not the case. In fact, the racial barriers blocking their path into the mainstream make it necessary for these black immigrants to retain their home country ties and the accompanying exit option.

Linked Racial Fate

Afro-Caribbeans' concerns about racial obstacles give them obvious common ground with their native-born counterparts. In fact, respondents tended to identify most strongly with African Americans as targets of discrimination. The vulnerability to racism they share with American-born blacks casts doubt on the hypothesis that suggests the immigrants' attachment to their ethnic identity helps them avoid racial stigmatization. The Afro-Caribbeans in this study were hardly convinced their ethnicity would spare them from discrimination.

Although many of the respondents noted whites sometimes compared them favorably to African Americans, they had no illusions about their own susceptibility to the sting of racism. Many expressed feelings of linked racial fate with African Americans on this score. One respondent's sentiments (interview, November 29, 1996) typified those of many in the sample.

Q: Do you feel close to African Americans?
A: Oh, yes...Our histories are similar. It just so happens that some got dropped off here, and some in the West Indies. Yes, and how we are viewed in this country today. It's a matter of color. We basically face the same kinds of stigmas.

Expressions of linked racial fate by the respondents were qualified, how-ever. The immigrants acknowledged their shared racial predicament with African Americans but also noted historical and cultural differences between them and their native-born counterparts. Nevertheless, many also spoke admiringly of African Americans' long history of resistance to American racism and their struggles for civil rights. Not surprisingly, the most emphatic declarations of respect for African Americans and iden-tification with their antidiscrimination struggles were from respondents who had ties to traditional African-American institutional networks and those who had resided in the country for the longest periods.[23]

One woman (interview, May 3, 1997) remarked: "You have to respect black Americans. They knocked down doors to make it better for the immigrants who come today." When asked whether he felt close to African Americans, another respondent (April 2, 1997) offered: "Yes, of course. Mostly, I empathize, and sometimes I'm sorry that I wasn't here longer to help them fight the fight that they fought for all the things they have now." Consider also this Jamaican woman's reply (interview, May 15, 1997) to a similar question about linked racial fate.

Q: Do you feel that your fate is at all linked to that of African Americans in general?
A: I'm sure, because of the way I look, if nothing else. Yes. Absolutely.
Q: How much of what happens to African Americans in this country affects Caribbean Americans?
A: Well, I think a lot. A lot because, let's face it, they were here before. I mean we have a lot to be thankful [for] in terms of access that we came right into because of things that were done by them, the struggles that they won, and I'm always mindful of that. Someone had to sacrifice some-thing here, which is quite different from growing up in a place where you always saw people in power that looked like you at some point. It was never anything you had to go fight and knock down a door for, whereas they [African Americans] had to do that just to gain access and to gain recognition.

These responses reflect the affirmative dimension of Afro-Caribbeans' racial identification with African Americans. They do not suggest the immigrants' feelings of solidarity with their native-born counterparts are strictly a matter of unlucky racial default. Nor do they lend much credence

[23] Recent research also has shown Latino immigrants who have lived in the United States for long periods are more likely than recent arrivals to express views on racial discrimi-nation in line with the liberal attitudes of African Americans (Garcia et al.1996; Uhlaner 1991).

to the worry that identification with African Americans will lead to an oppositional consciousness and downward social mobility (Waters 1999; 1996; Portes and Zhou 1993).[24] Rather, they indicate Afro-Caribbean immigrants sometimes have proud feelings of racial group solidarity with African Americans, notwithstanding the differences in their histories and cultures. The immigrants recognize African Americans have a long, impressive history of turning a stigmatized racial identity into a psychological resource for solidarity and mobilization.[25]

III. CONCLUSION

One final point about Afro-Caribbean ethnic identity deserves mention. Respondents were quick to stress cultural values as part of their ethnic identity. They viewed themselves as hardworking, disciplined, and committed to education and professional achievement. Very few were willing to say African Americans were lacking in the same values, although they tended to make these attitudinal attributions only to middle-class African Americans. This is an interesting finding, but there is an even more intriguing irony implied by Afro-Caribbeans' invocation of these cultural traits.

The cultural values these black immigrants attribute to themselves are precisely the ones American society ideally is supposed to reward. The lure of the American Dream for many immigrants is the expectation their hard work and sacrifice will be compensated. If Afro-Caribbeans display these values, play by the rules, follow societal norms, and yet find their mobility hampered by racism, there is a distinct possibility those who remain in the United States may develop feelings of racial group consciousness like those evinced by African Americans. But such group consciousness is likely to take hold only if the immigrants establish or share with their native-born counterparts institutional networks in which antiracist, collectivist beliefs can be fostered and nurtured.

The same logic applies to second-generation Afro-Caribbeans. They may inherit none or very little of their parents' home country identification and attachments. Hence, they may have no cognitive or practical recourse to an exit option. If they continue to encounter racial hurdles that diminish their prospects for improving on the socioeconomic outcomes of their parents, they too might develop a form of racial group consciousness in

---

[24] To be fair, most of these studies focus on second-generation immigrants, but the caveat applies no less to this group.

[25] My thanks to Michael Hanchard for highlighting this dimension of my argument.

line with African Americans'. Such a development is even more probable for the second generation since they are more likely than their parents to share social and institutional networks with their African-American counterparts.

Of course, this newly ignited racial group consciousness among Afro-Caribbean immigrants or their children will not necessarily assume the same forms it has taken among African Americans. A whole new set of beliefs eventually may compose group consciousness among the immigrants, their children, and even their African-American counterparts. All in all, what it means to be black in America today is a highly open and contingent question, in light of the growing diversity within the black population. Not only do Afro-Caribbeans and African Americans have different ideas about what their racial identity means, the findings from these interviews suggest the immigrants and their native-born counterparts also have distinct cognitive frames of reference for making sense of the political world.

7

Black Ethnic Options

The previous chapter revealed Afro-Caribbean immigrants' ties to the home country make for notable differences in how they and their African-American counterparts understand what it means to be black in this country and respond to racial discrimination. The next logical step in the analysis is to determine whether those differences translate to political behavior. Do the differences in group identity uncovered in the previous chapter extend to political behavior and attitudes? Or do these two groups of black ethnics pursue similar options in their attempts to achieve political representation and influence? This question takes us full circle to a key empirical focus of the book: ascertaining whether Afro-Caribbeans are following the same path to political incorporation as their native-born black counterparts.

Addressing this fundamental question requires taking a closer look at the political attitudes and behavior of New York's Afro-Caribbean immigrants. Have these black ethnics developed the same political views or outlook as their African-American counterparts? Or do they subscribe to a different set of political opinions? Have Afro-Caribbeans begun to make the same demands for racial redistribution and systemic reform African Americans made in their own earlier bids for political inclusion? Or have these foreign-born blacks pursued an alternative course?

To address these questions, this chapter dissects the newly emerging Afro-Caribbean ethnic politics. First, I consider which kinds of policy interests and political claims Afro-Caribbean leaders have advanced on behalf of their immigrant constituents – to see whether they mirror or deviate from the patterns established by African Americans. Second, I turn to my interviews with Afro-Caribbean New Yorkers to explore their policy and ideological views – to see how they compare with what we know about African-American public opinion.

Exponents of the minority group perspective would expect significant political similarities between the two groups, notwithstanding the differences in how they conceive of their group identities. Minority group scholars believe Afro-Caribbean immigrants and other non-white minorities are bound to encounter some of the same racial barriers as African Americans and thus are likely to follow the same political trajectory as their native-born counterparts.[1] Following this logic, Afro-Caribbean immigrants ought to embrace many of the same policy views and political choices as African Americans. There is certainly some evidence to encourage this view. The previous chapter showed Afro-Caribbeans worry about racial discrimination and their prospects for inclusion in American society, much as their native-born counterparts do. Recall also from Chapter 4 Afro-Caribbeans and African Americans show similar levels of partisan attachment to the Democratic Party.

Yet this chapter reveals Afro-Caribbeans have not exactly followed in the footsteps of their native-born counterparts in their bid for political incorporation. The immigrants have not advanced the same kinds of demands for systemic reform and racial redistribution African Americans have made in their pursuit of incorporation. The chapter also highlights political views held by Afro-Caribbeans that set them apart from their native-born counterparts. The immigrants express far more ambivalence about government solutions to social and economic problems than African Americans typically do in public opinion surveys.

But Afro-Caribbeans' ambivalence is not a reflection of stark ideological differences between them and their native-born counterparts. Rather, it is the result of their immigrant status and cues in their home country experiences. The chapter concludes analytic attention to home country experiences is necessary not only for appreciating Afro-Caribbeans' sense of group identity; attention to those experiences is also critical for understanding their political attitudes and choices. Home country experiences

---

[1] This perspective is spelled out in Chapter 1 (e.g., Kim 2001; Browning et al. 1997; Hero 1992; Henry and Munoz 1991; Green and Wilson 1989; Takaki 1989; Barrera 1979).

and ties largely explain why these black immigrants have not reproduced the African-American model of political incorporation.

I. AFRO-CARIBBEAN ETHNIC POLITICS: ASSESSING
THE MINORITY GROUP PERSPECTIVE

This study has made it clear the majority of Afro-Caribbean immigrants in New York remain on the margins of formal political life. But what of the immigrants who have become involved in the political process? There is a politically active segment of this population whose thinking and behavior warrant consideration. Although many first-generation Afro-Caribbeans focus their civic activities on their home countries, a significant minority of these immigrants also vote in local elections, participate in campaigns, and engage in various forms of neighborhood-level politics from block associations to community board meetings. The interview respondents for this study were drawn from this politically active segment of the Afro-Caribbean population.

Also recall from Chapter 3 that Afro-Caribbean political elites have made notable inroads in the electoral arena over the two past decades. A handful of Afro-Caribbean politicians have won legislative seats in Brooklyn and Queens by making explicit appeals to the ethnic group loyalties of their immigrant constituents. Although their electoral successes fall well short of anything like full political incorporation for Afro-Caribbeans, this emerging ethnic bloc has managed to make it on to the political radar screen. In sum, Afro-Caribbean ethnic group politics has taken firm root in New York City, even if it has not yet produced a full harvest of political gains for the immigrant constituency.

Ethnic group politics is standard fare for American cities. Scholars generally agree ethnic politics is the essential starting point in the incorporation process for most groups. This is, in fact, the consensus among most observers of urban politics, whether they subscribe to the standard pluralist paradigm or the minority group view. Consider Irish Catholics in New Haven at the turn of the twentieth century, African Americans in Atlanta in the 1970s, Cuban immigrants in Miami during the 1980s.[2] All these groups began their respective bids for political inclusion by coalescing around a shared sense of group identity and lining up to support

---

[2] On the Irish in New Haven, see Dahl 1961; Wolfinger 1974. On African Americans in Atlanta, see Stone 1989. On Cubans in Miami, see Portes and Stepick 1993.

their coethnics at the ballot box. Where these groups differed, though, was in the agendas they pursued in their attempts to secure political incorporation.

Recall from Chapter 1 ethnic group politics among whites typically entailed calls for symbolic recognition through political appointments, government jobs, and neighborhood services – the standard allocational issues of bread-and-butter pluralism. Among African Americans, however, group politics tended to combine the usual calls for symbolic acknowledgment with sweeping demands for redistribution and antidiscriminatory reforms to redress racial inequalities (Reed 1988; Pinderhughes 1987). Those demands often translated into a radical-reformist policy agenda, including requests for affirmative action in city hiring and contracting, efforts to curb police brutality in African-American neighborhoods, support for welfare expenditures, and issues of community control. Moreover, African Americans did not rely exclusively on the ballot box to advance these demands. They often also turned to more unconventional political tactics, such as demonstrations and boycotts. In short, they mixed both systemic and extrasystemic forms of participation to advance their political interests.

Consider, for instance, the African-American insurgent movement within Brooklyn's Democratic Party in the 1970s described in Chapter 4. This bid for political inclusion emphasized community control and racial redistribution. Several of the movement's key leaders had their start in politics in the 1966 demonstrations for community control of the Ocean Hill–Brownsville school district. These African-American politicians routinely invoked radical-reformist and race-conscious rhetoric to mobilize their constituents in campaigns for elective office and calls for autonomy within the party. Their agenda for political incorporation thus bore little resemblance to the traditional pluralist, white ethnic model.

Now that Afro-Caribbean immigrants have launched their own bid for incorporation in New York, the question is whether they will make the same political choices as African Americans in keeping with the predictions of the minority group view. Even neopluralist scholars who decry the reformist, race-based agenda put forward by African Americans presume other minorities might be inclined to follow suit. Skerry (1993, 29), for instance, has worried non-white minorities might pursue this political strategy, not necessarily because they have a legitimate sense of racial grievance, but rather, because it has become "an obvious and accepted way to get ahead" in this country.

Symbolic Recognition and Access to Power

To date, however, Afro-Caribbean ethnic group politics has yet to put forward the kind of radical-reformist agenda that has typified African Americans' bids for political incorporation. Instead, the emerging Afro-Caribbean ethnic politics has focused primarily on issues of symbolic recognition and access to government power. The Afro-Caribbean political elites interviewed for this study repeatedly emphasized these objectives. One community organizer (interview, April 7, 1997) tersely summarized the political aims of the Afro-Caribbean ethnic constituency this way.

Q: Where is Caribbean American politics in New York headed?
A: Our goal is to get on the inside... You have to learn the system. You live here. We live here. Just learn the system. And get our own share of power.

The respondent's observations are almost more interesting for what they do not convey than for what they actually do. His vision of the Afro-Caribbean community's political goals does not include concrete demands for systemic reform. Rather, the focus is on access to political power.

Other respondents underscored the importance of symbolic recognition and group visibility. Consider these comments from the former councilwoman Clarke (interview, December 13 and 20, 1996).

Q: Do you view Caribbean Americans as a separate ethnic voting bloc with their own distinctive interests and needs?
A: Yes, of course. There's no question. It's about time that people recognize Caribbean-American voters. We deserve our own place at the table, in the halls of power. You know what I mean? People should recognize the importance of our numbers and our resources. And I think they are. That's why you see so many politicians putting in an appearance at the carnival we have on Eastern Parkway every year.

Another respondent (interview, December 14, 1996) emphasized the need for recognition in both national and local politics. "We [Caribbean Americans] don't get the acknowledgment we deserve. No, the Caribbean as such is ignored by the United States, Clinton can see fit to go to Asia, Australia; the Caribbean is next door and still it's ignored. You have in this city, where there is a major Caribbean population, how many mayors you hear have ever gone to the Caribbean. We still don't get the recognition that we're due."

The Caribbean Action Lobby (CAL) cofounder Stewart reiterated Clarke's view. He, too, insisted New York's Caribbean constituency was due separate political recognition. As he (interview, May 2, 1997) put it: "Caribbean Americans are part of the city's larger black population. But they are a distinct voting bloc that should be acknowledged separately as well. That's what our organization is all about: raising consciousness and getting politicians and power brokers to recognize the political potential of this community. We are here to help put Caribbean Americans on the political map. Now you see politicians coming to us to show their interest in the community. I guess we're doing something right (laughing)." He further added:

We need our own people to represent us and get us the recognition we deserve. That's why our organization has been so active on the reapportionment issue. At one point the issue was raised in our community about the lack of representa- tion, political representation... in terms of political jurisdiction; there were no districts, no political districts where a Caribbean could run for assembly, coun- cilperson, or senator and get elected because the majority of that district were Caribbean. OK? So, we put forth and we had a campaign during the time of reapportioning... where we actively waged a campaign to have Caribbean dis- tricts drawn in the Bronx, Queens, and Brooklyn.

In Stewart's view, the chief aim of his organization is to garner political visibility for the emerging Afro-Caribbean ethnic constituency.

To be fair, African Americans also pursued symbolic recognition and visibility in their earlier bids for political inclusion. Indeed, most researchers agree this kind of acknowledgment – whether through polit- ical appointments, sinecures, publicly sanctioned ethnic celebrations, or election to public office – is the sine qua non of group politics in American cities. Entrenched politicians, recall from Chapter 3, are often willing to accede to demands for symbolic recognition because they do not alter pre- vailing systemic arrangements. This is not to say that calls for recognition are inconsequential. Insofar as Afro-Caribbean leaders achieve represen- tation and visibility in government, they help change the face of power in New York City and signal to their immigrant constituents that the political system might be responsive to their interests.

"Ethnic groups want the legitimacy of their language, race, culture, or nationality to be affirmed by authoritative governmental action. And there are many ways in which local political leaders can give groups such recog- nition without adversely affecting the city's economic standing. [They] can... attend community celebrations... appoint [ethnic] leaders to city boards and commission . . . and above all, run ethnic candidates for high public office" (Peterson 1981, 157). African Americans pursued all these forms of group visibility but coupled them with demands for systemic reform and redistribution to redress their unique racial disadvantages. Afro-Caribbeans, in contrast, have yet to articulate a radical-reformist agenda in conjunction with their calls for group recognition.

Kasinitz (1992, 196) found the same emphasis on symbolic recognition and access to government power in his own study of Afro-Caribbean politics in New York. His conversations with community elites led him to this general conclusion: Afro-Caribbean leaders "have produced nothing like a West Indian political program, but they share a common view of their own activity, which is first and foremost intended to promote the idea of a West Indian community." Further, he (202) adds, "Caribbean identity politics is as much a strategy for gaining access to government power as an expression of distinct community needs."

Substantive Policy Issues

This conclusion begs an obvious question. Beyond the need for group recognition and access to power, what are the distinct policy needs and interests of New York's Afro-Caribbean population? Do these policy interests translate into anything like the radical-reformist agenda African Americans pursued in their own efforts to secure political incorporation? With the heavy emphasis these politicians place on symbolic group recognition and access to power, a casual observer might conclude Afro-Caribbean ethnic politics is essentially devoid of substantive policy issues. Indeed, among revisionist scholars, this has been a chief complaint about routine ethnic group politics. Most famously, Wolfinger (1974, 65 and 67) dismissed ethnic politics as largely issueless, save for the occasional interest in home country foreign policy matters one would expect from recent immigrants. "[M]ost issues that might be called 'purely ethnic' generally are substantively trivial . . . political appeals invoking ethnic consciousness tend to substitute emotional for tangible gratification."

Afro-Caribbean ethnic politics, however, is hardly issueless. My elite respondents cited several substantive policy areas of concern to their Afro-Caribbean constituents – education, crime, child care, and immigration reform. But almost none of these issues were cast in a reformist or radical framework. Consider, for instance, my conversation with Clarke (interview, December 13 and 20, 1996) about her campaign platform in her first bid for a city council seat.

Q: So what kinds of issues did you emphasize in your platform?
A: Education, one. Issues that are important to women and their development in the workplace, as well as in raising children.[3] When you look at the whole gamut of human services that were very much not forthcoming in the area. Education of our children is key. Health care is key. So I stayed on those issues . . . the aspirations of the immigrant community was the overriding factor. The very diverse immigrant community that I represent were all there, whether they were [from] Trinidad and Tobago, whether they were from Grenada, whether they were from Barbados, whether they were from Guyana. The immigrant community as a whole saw me as a symbol of their empowerment and the embodiment of our aspirations.
Q: Were there particular issues that seemed to resonate with the immigrant constituency?
A: Education. Education is always a key. You say "education," and a Caribbean American will go for it. Owning property and housing, economic development, oh yes, that's good.

Clarke couples the symbolic issue of group recognition with substantive policy concerns. But the policy issues she cites hardly typify the radical-reformist or race-conscious agenda minority group scholars might expect from these foreign-born blacks. Although she recalls her election as a symbol of group empowerment, the rhetoric of sweeping reform or radical redistribution is notably absent from her account. On the contrary, the issues she deems important to her Afro-Caribbean constituents reflect their middle-class aspirations and fall squarely within the scope of standard bread-and-butter pluralism. In short, the policy goals Clarke articulates are relatively moderate.

Other Caribbean politicians referred to the same range of policy concerns mentioned by Clarke. Consider the issues cited by a well-known political campaign organizer (interview, November 23, 1996). "Our [Afro-Caribbeans'] policy interests are pretty standard. Same as others: jobs, education. The policy issues, the needs of Caribbean Americans, of African Americans, and perhaps the needs of all people are the same. A job, education, good health, housing, it's the same basic needs. Whether you're black, white, or whatever, the needs are the same. The question is

---

[3] Clarke's attention to policy areas affecting women is hardly surprising in light of the gender composition of recent immigrant streams from the Caribbean. More women than men have immigrated to New York from the region over the last two decades. Caribbean women also outnumbered men at the community board, political club, and civic meetings I attended. Men, however, continue to dominate the leadership positions.

how you frame it, and what you put first or second, but the basic needs remain the same."

Another community leader (interview, November 23, 1996) fairly echoed former councilwoman's Clarke's observations.

Q: How would you define the major policy interests of the Caribbean American population?

A: Mostly bread and butter stuff, outside of immigration. The bread and butter is education, employment. Home ownership, to a certain extent. You find the typical West Indian or Caribbean person is miles ahead of our African-American brothers and sisters as it relates to home ownership, especially in the Northeast area here – because we come with the mentality of ownership as opposed to rental. This is not to put anybody down, but that's part of the dream. To gain that home. Very important. The other issues I think would be crime, and more or less, the situation re education. I don't think we're any different than the typical person.

One elite respondent (interview, July 5, 1997) expanded on the policy relevance of education to Afro-Caribbean New Yorkers.

Q: How important is education, as a policy concern, to Caribbean-American immigrants?

A: Oh yes, yes. Very important. That's one thing that is very crucial. Most Caribbean Americans try desperately to send their children to get a good education. As a matter of fact, among the Haitian Americans, most of the children who're doing extremely well among blacks in New York City are Haitian children.

Q: Do you think Caribbean children have any special or different kinds of needs than other children in the New York school system?

A: Yes. Again, all of those things are so broad, it depends on which instance. For example, the child who was born here and went to a private church school, when he gets into the public school system he is doing well, so there is no problem. The ones that have problems are the children who arrive in New York at twelve years old, fifteen years old. The child arrives here when they already have basic education. And because of maybe the way he speaks, his upbringing in the islands – [for example,] corporal punishment is the order of the day – he may have a hard time fitting into the new school setting. The adjustment could be difficult.

The Caribbean Action Lobby (CAL) organizer Stewart (interview, May 2, 1997) also alluded to the importance of education as a policy issue among Afro-Caribbeans:

Education is a big priority for Caribbean people here. Especially because the cultural differences sometimes create problems for Caribbean children in the schools. One is the issue of English as a second language, and programs to accommodate different accents and dialects, and so forth. We have had differences about that...We have been for years saying, yes there is Caribbean English. And we have been saying that schools need to address that, and need to address cultural differences.

Stewart frames education as a reform issue. The change he urges, however, is relatively moderate, compared to the demands for community control of schools put forward by many African-American leaders in their initial bids for political inclusion. In fact, Stewart's framing of this issue is reminiscent of the more recent symbolic political debates over multicultural education and black English vernacular. Many early African-American demands for curriculum reform in schools were part of a larger, radical community control agenda. Stewart's response hardly reflects any such designs. He uses words such as "accommodation," rather than "control." Perhaps, then, a more fitting analogy for the issue raised by Stewart is the Cuban "bilingual" agenda in Miami, which had no real radical content (Portes and Stepick 1993).

In sum, the issues cited by these Afro-Caribbean elites were fairly moderate: economic advancement through home and business ownership, education reform, and group recognition. None of these policy concerns necessarily call for significant systemic reform. Most of these issues, in fact, imply the immigrants simply want more opportunities to achieve success in American life through dint of their individual effort and initiative. These are fairly moderate aspirations in the scheme of American politics.

Race and Immigration Policy

Although the policy agenda articulated by Afro-Caribbean elites was largely devoid of radical-redistributive or acutely race-conscious issues, there were two notable exceptions: immigration reform and police brutality. Concerns over immigration reform surfaced repeatedly in my interviews. The respondents' preoccupation with the issue was not surprising, on the heels of the austere immigration reform measures enacted by Congress in 1996 and in the midst of a huge outcry from the Afro-Caribbean community. What was striking was the tendency of respondents to invoke civil rights and antidiscrimination rhetoric in their discussions of the issue. Virtually all the elites I interviewed saw racialistic overtones in the legislation. The former councilwoman Clarke (interview, December 13 and 20, 1996) bluntly summed up her view:

I don't think Caribbean Americans on a whole recognize that the whole immigration reform is geared at immigrants of color. And so whether we want to say it's a racial thing or not, it is racial. They are looking at the number of people that are coming [to this country], whether it's from Latin America or from the Caribbean, and they're saying as a country that this is a "white" nation; "We are being overrun by people of color!" And so all of this has to do with that. Whether they will admit that and say, "Yes, that's exactly what we're doing," is left to be seen.

Similarly, a prominent Afro-Caribbean businessman (interview, April 17, 1997) concluded, after some vacillation, the legislation was racially discriminatory.

Q: How do you feel about the recent legislation limiting sponsorship privileges?

A: I don't even know if that's a question that should be asked of West Indians, because it's tough to answer, because we all came [to this country] that way. But at the same time the world has changed tremendously since that. Reality tells you that the immigration law cannot continue the way it was in the past, because pretty soon we will be overrun and it will be bad for everybody. But then it's not being meted out equally. So where do you stand? You know the door has to be shut somewhere and changed that way. But it is being shut for our people, and it is being opened up wide open for others of different colors, for whites, for Chinese. If that is going to be the case, then however they could get in, let them get in. And however they could get straight, let them get straight, because they will be discriminated against anyhow you take it.

Another respondent (interview, November 22, 1996) firmly attributed the recent calls for immigration restrictions to racial fears.

Q: What about restrictions on immigration? Do you think there should be some?

A: No.

Q: Why?

A: This country is still open: the land, the opportunity, the food, everything is here, and there's room for much more [people]. And they themselves prove it; there's room for more. Because, while they are dropping from the Caribbean and other African countries, they are increasing from Ireland, and this and that. What they are afraid of is the darkening of the United States, as I put it.

Race and Police Conduct

Although the issue of discrimination was most often raised in our discussions about immigration reform, Afro-Caribbean elites also pointed to racism to explain instances of police brutality against black immigrants in New York. The case of Abner Louima, the Haitian immigrant who was brutalized while in police custody, was dominating headlines at the time of my interviews. One respondent (interview, April 7, 1997) was incisively plainspoken.

Q: What about police brutality? Is that an important issue for Caribbean Americans?
A: Yes, yes. Quite a few of our own have been brutalized by police. As they say, when the police pick on you, he doesn't care if you're from Africa, the Caribbean, India, or Harlem and there are racist cops. I don't care what they say or how much they deny it.

The respondent's declamation shows traces of a race-based or minority group perspective, inasmuch as he concludes all non-white New Yorkers are targeted for unfair police treatment.

Yet most elite respondents also agreed immigrants were particularly vulnerable to this issue because of their foreign-born status. Many linked the issue of police brutality to their constituents' anxieties about the recent immigration reforms. Recall the late 1990s legislation calls for the deportation of legal, but non-citizen immigrants convicted of serious crimes or felonies, regardless of their length of stay in the United States. As several respondents explained, non-citizen Caribbean immigrants who encounter overly aggressive police or run afoul of the law run the risk of forced return to their home countries.[4]

One community organizer (interview, April 23, 1997) elaborated: "Police brutality is a big issue. It is; it is. Now more than ever. You see, what is happening, especially from the immigration standpoint, a number of our youth have been caught up in the system. And they get a record, which makes them more liable for deportation." This observation suggests Afro-Caribbeans' anxieties about police brutality are not informed solely by their position as racial minorities. Their concerns are also influenced by their status as immigrants. This finding means when Afro-Caribbeans come to grips with discriminatory challenges, they take stock of their vulnerability not simply as racial minorities, but also as foreigners with sometimes tenuous ties to this country.

Another respondent (interview, July 3, 1997) cited police brutality as the most pressing issue for Afro-Caribbean New Yorkers.

---

[4] A number of respondents noted Afro-Caribbean men, in particular, were likely to encounter unfair or hostile treatment by New York City police and thus were more often at risk of deportation than their female counterparts.

Q: What do you think are the biggest problems facing Caribbean immigrants in New York City?
A: That is a tough one. Racism is what they will say: police brutality. But when you look at the problems, it's the same problems that all minorities face. You follow? To be frank with you, I don't think we [Afro-Caribbeans] have as many problems as other ethnic groups in New York. To me, the Hispanics, the Puerto Ricans and Dominicans especially, have much more of a problem. The Caribbean American is always hardworking, have a good background. But essentially, the problem is police brutality.

What is most interesting about this interview subject's comments is the way he qualifies the issue. Although he believes police brutality against Caribbean immigrants is often racially motivated, he stops short of placing the issue within the context of a larger race-based, radical-reform agenda for the group. In fact, he suggests reforms to address police brutality, though they would no doubt benefit Afro-Caribbean immigrants, are perhaps a more pressing policy concern for other racial minority groups in New York. He speculates Latinos suffer more from the problem of hostile police conduct than his Caribbean coethnics. His perception actually does not square with reality, inasmuch as Caribbean immigrants have been the victims of some of the city's most notorious police brutality cases.

Yet his observations are instructive, insofar as they convey his assessment of the policy needs of Afro-Caribbean immigrants relative to other minority groups in the city. Contrast this respondent's perception – that other minorities suffer more serious discrimination at the hands of police than Afro-Caribbeans – with the views of African Americans. According to public opinion data, African Americans believe with good reason they are subject to more discrimination than other non-white groups (Hochschild and Rogers 2000). Although my respondent saw police brutality as an issue affecting Afro-Caribbean immigrants, he did not view it as a more acute concern for them than for any other minority group.

Unconventional Political Tactics

Exponents of the minority group view perhaps might expect Afro-Caribbean outrage over police brutality would have ignited a radical, race-conscious movement in the immigrant community. There were, in fact, a series of black-led vigils and demonstrations in the late summer of 1997 to protest the police torture of the Haitian immigrant Abner Louima. Afro-Caribbean immigrants participated in these rallies in significant, but modest numbers. African-American political figures, such as Al Sharpton and David Dinkins, led the demonstrations. Afro-Caribbean politicians, in contrast, had a much less visible role.

The absence of Afro-Caribbean leadership in the demonstrations confirms another important insight about the group's political choices. My elite respondents reported their Afro-Caribbean constituents are generally not disposed to engaging in unconventional or extrasystemic political tactics. One community organizer (interview, November 29, 1996) explained the thinking behind this general disinclination.

Some [Caribbean] people throw out terms like pride, "I'll never be caught down there or do that . . . I'm not going to upset the apple cart . . . There must be another way to do this." Usually there are. Sometimes you have another way to make your point, probably more significant ways. Then there is another side to this, and that is, to learn the system. Get on the inside. Augment, change things from the inside. For example, you'll never catch me saying to Al Sharpton, "I agree with you that we should go picket Texaco on the street." I do my demonstration differently. I mean, I buy from Texaco. I may dump their stock, if I owned their stocks. All right? But what I'm saying is that – somebody said to me recently – is that those types of strategies in 1996 are like we on the outside throwing a pebble at bulletproof glass.

A prominent Caribbean-born magazine publisher (interview, July 3, 1997) contrasted his coethnics' apparent unwillingness to engage in demonstrations and boycotts with African Americans' ready deployment of such tactics in the aftermath of racial bias incidents in New York.

The Caribbean American isn't willing to give up a day's work to protest, even self [sic] they are hurt. That is true. And in the case of Gavin Cato, in the case of Howard Beach, all those were West Indians who were the victims. But again, the African Americans came to the rescue because they were organized . . . You have African-American leaders who are waiting for something to happen to get [in] the fray. But let's put it this way: all those major racial incidents, the Caribbean-American community only came after the African Americans took the leadership and did what is needed.

Clarke (interview, December 13 and 20, 1996) had the same view of her constituents' attitudes toward protest behavior.

Q: Do you think that Caribbean Americans are more or less inclined to participate in demonstrations, rallies, and other forms of protest activity?
A: They are definitely less inclined. It's a cultural thing. They have never had to do it before. They've never had to do it.

These elite impressions were confirmed in my interviews with Afro-Caribbeans. Of the fifty-nine respondents, only four reported they had ever participated in a demonstration.

Clarke's allusion to her constituents' home country political experiences – or lack thereof, in this instance – is an important analytical point. It suggests Afro-Caribbeans' disinclination to participate in demonstrations or other forms of political protest does not necessarily stem from ideological objections; rather, it is due to the scope of their home country political experiences.[5] It makes for a significant contrast between them and their native-born counterparts. Although African Americans often turned to demonstrations and other protest tactics to accelerate the process of political incorporation, such strategies have not been a notable part of Afro-Caribbeans' bid for political inclusion in New York.

Radical-Reformist, Race-Based Campaigns

In both policy priorities and strategy, then, the emerging Afro-Caribbean ethnic group politics has not followed the same course as the African-American model of political incorporation. Yet there have been occasional exceptions. A few Afro-Caribbean politicians have tried to fashion their campaigns for elective office in the mold of their African-American predecessors, relying on racially evocative and radical-reformist rhetoric to appeal to their immigrant constituents. Likewise, some Afro-Caribbean grassroots organizers occasionally have looked to the African-American protest tradition for inspiration. But their efforts have failed to spark significant electoral interest or garner wide support among the ranks of Afro-Caribbean leaders.

Consider, for instance, James Conolly's 1996 bid to unseat the long-time incumbent Rhoda Jacobs in the Forty-second State Assembly District race. The Caribbean-born Conolly made racial group consciousness the central motif of his campaign rhetoric. He insisted the heavily Afro-Caribbean district should be represented by a black politician and questioned whether Jacobs, the white Jewish incumbent, could ever adequately appreciate the interests of her mostly black constituents. He remarked in one interview (Sengupta 1996b), "Honestly, do you see Rhoda Jacobs, a Jewish lady, getting out on the streets, telling these young men that she understands what they're going through? Not really."

[5] See later discussion for more on this analytic point.

Conolly's racial appeals and radical rhetoric failed to ignite the district's immigrant voters, and he lost to the incumbent. Recall from Chapter 3 turnout for the race was quite low. To be fair, several of Conolly's consultants concede their candidate ran a poorly organized campaign (interview, November 22, 1996). It is thus not clear whether his radical message reached the district's Afro-Caribbean voters. Nevertheless, his campaign failed to garner solid support among Afro-Caribbean leaders. Many of the community's most prominent political figures refrained from endorsing him. In short, Conolly's radical, racially evocative rhetoric failed to resonate with the Afro-Caribbean political establishment.

More generally, campaigns like Conolly's that rely on a radical-reformist, race-conscious agenda have been the exception, rather than the rule, for Caribbean politics in New York. All in all, the emerging Afro-Caribbean ethnic group politics has yet to take on the pronounced reformist or radical cast of earlier African-American movments for political inclusion. To put it more axiomatically, the political course these foreign-born blacks have taken in their bid for incorporation confounds the predictions of the minority group perspective.

II. THE NEOPLURALIST ALTERNATIVE

Some observers might argue these findings lend support to the neopluralist view that Afro-Caribbeans and other non-white newcomers are likely to follow the traditional model of incorporation established by earlier European immigrants. One argument often put forward to support this view is that Afro-Caribbeans have more in common with the white ethnics of the mid-twentieth century than with their native-born black counterparts. That is, they are hardworking strivers, model minorities who are outperforming African Americans on most socioeconomic indicators (Sowell 1978; 1975; Glazer and Moynihan 1964).[6] According to this view, they have little or no reason to make the sweeping demands for redistribution and systemic reform advanced by their more disadvantaged native-born counterparts (Sleeper 1993). This inference, however, is not supported by the evidence. Recall both Afro-Caribbeans and African Americans suffer similar disadvantages relative to whites in certain arenas, such as the housing market and education.

Another explanation neopluralists might advance to account for why Afro-Caribbeans have not followed the path marked out by their

[6] For more on this view, see Chapter 2.

native-born counterparts is the post–civil rights era decline in racial discrimination (Thernstrom and Thernstrom 1997). According to this line of argument, the racial barriers that once impeded blacks from incorporation largely have been eliminated. Exponents of this view point to the economic and political strides African Americans have made over the last half-century. They contend the group has now secured practically full inclusion. By this light, their history of disadvantage and exclusion is today a fading memory.

These observers believe the decline in racism has obviated the minority group model of political incorporation, or at least rendered it anachronistic for Afro-Caribbeans and other non-white newcomers to American cities. In short, Afro-Caribbean immigrants have no need for the radical-reformist agenda and political strategies previously pursued by African Americans, because most of the racial barriers that necessitated this approach have been leveled (e.g., Skerry 1993; Chavez 1991).

Yet evidence of persisting racial inequalities and discrimination in housing, employment, and other arenas of American life makes this all-too-sanguine view difficult to sustain. The statistical proof of continuing black-white inequality is well known. Also important, however, is the anecdotal evidence. Recall from the previous chapter almost all of my fifty-nine Afro-Caribbean respondents reported they had encountered racial discrimination in their everyday lives – from the indignity of shopping under the racial surveillance of store security to the recognition that black home buyers are not welcomed in some neighborhoods. Afro-Caribbean elites likewise see racism in the actions of New York City police and the immigration policies of the federal government.

Some neopluralist scholars perhaps would not be troubled by such anecdotal evidence. Indeed, several have contended immigrants to the United States expect to encounter prejudice, especially because of their foreign nationality. Nevertheless, the argument goes, they maintain some abiding faith in the legitimacy of the system and their ability to extract rewards from it (e.g., Skerry 1993; Ogbu 1990). It is not uncommon, then, to hear of newcomers' hailing their new country for its openness and fairness, its liberal and egalitarian virtues, its ample opportunities.

Although this view may pertain to many immigrants, it does not apply as readily to Afro-Caribbean New Yorkers. Most of my respondents did not express great faith in the fairness of the American political system; many conveyed doubt when asked about it. Although only a few ventured opinions that matched the deep concerns about systemic inequality typically associated with African Americans, most signaled ambivalence. Consider, for instance, these responses (interview, March 27, 1997).

Q: Is the American political system fair?
A: Fair? Fair to whom?
Q: Well, from where you stand.
A: No. Not entirely. It depends. Black people don't seem to get all the same chances that other people get. It means that we have to work really hard to get a chance – probably harder than other groups.

A Jamaican woman (interview, April 1, 1997) was less equivocal. "No political system is fair. The way I see it all political systems favor some more than others. And in America, they say that whites get the lion's share of the favors." Another respondent from Trinidad (interview, April 8, 1997) soberly concluded economic and racial inequities put blacks at a disadvantage in the political arena.

Q: Is the American political system fair?
A: To me, no.
Q: Why not?
A: Because politicians believe, their yardstick to measure improvements, is how much money your neighborhood gives. Since blacks are poorer than whites, they often get ignored. I've seen that before, because when you go to a politician and ask him, well you want a street light or you want this or that, he would say, "But this neighborhood don't give any contributions." He won't tell you, "No." But you'll never get it.

Of the fifty-nine respondents in the sample, forty-three evinced misgivings about the fairness of the political system. Virtually all of them agreed racism plainly degraded the legitimacy of American democracy. The fact these Afro-Caribbeans have not embraced the radical-reformist agenda first pursued by African Americans therefore cannot be explained by the absence of racial obstacles. Although discrimination has declined, it continues to affect the lives and viewpoints of both native- and foreign-born blacks.

III. HOME COUNTRY CUES

If Afro-Caribbeans have yet to pursue a reformist political agenda in the mold established by their African-American counterparts, then, it is not because racial obstacles and antiblack prejudice have disappeared from American life. A better explanation for why these foreign-born blacks have steered a different course may lie in their home country background. Recall Chapter 1 proposed a conceptual framework on political incorporation positing that both host and home country cues influence immigrants' political attitudes and choices during the incorporation process. Home country cues, in fact, may have even greater influence on new immigrants than the frames and signals they receive from institutions and elites in this country, if only because the norms and practices of American political culture are still coming into focus for them. Sure enough, Chapters 5 and 6 demonstrated Afro-Caribbeans' home country ties and immigrant status inform their attitudes toward American citizenship, political participation, their view of themselves, and their responses to racism. These home country cues also influence their political judgments and choices.

Home Country Experiences

The exit option furnished by Afro-Caribbeans' home country ties is an obvious source of political difference between the immigrants and their native-born counterparts. Rather than follow the African-American model of voicing demands for reform to a system that may ultimately prove unresponsive, the immigrants instead can choose to exercise the exit option and return to a familiar environment with none of the racial obstacles they find in the United States. But this can hardly explain the political behavior of the many Afro-Caribbeans who remain in this country. As I noted in Chapter 5, return typically becomes an improbability, as most Afro-Caribbeans never actually make the permanent trip back home. The fact most of these immigrants stay only begs the question. If the vast majority of Afro-Caribbeans remain in New York as long-term sojourners, why have they refrained from pursuing the radical-reformist agenda predicted by the minority group perspective? The answer lies in their home country experiences.

The major analytic failing of the minority group perspective is it assumes non-white minorities such as Afro-Caribbeans inevitably will respond to the experience of racial discrimination with the same political choices as African Americans – that is, with race-based collective mobilization and demands for redistribution and systemic reform. This model of political incorporation essentially lumps all non-white groups together and uses African Americans as the "model minority" for predicting their behavior. It is certainly a reasonable first approximation to place all minorities into the general category of subordinate groups and to contrast their disadvantaged structural position and even their subjective perspective with those of whites. But buried within the common situation of minority populations are important differences of history, experience, numbers, and so on, which are bound to influence their political thinking and behavior. Those differentiating factors often have been overlooked by minority group scholars, but they make for differences in how non-white groups navigate the political incorporation process.

The political demands and strategies a group pursues are typically drawn from a limited repertoire based on their particular experiences and history, as well as their structural position. "The standard [political] forms are learned, limited in number and scope, slowly changing, and peculiarly adapted to their settings. Pressed by a grievance, interest, or aspiration and confronted with an opportunity to act, groups of people who have the capacity to act collectively choose among forms of action in their limited repertoire" (Tilly 1979, 131). Another researcher notes, "[when] mobilizing collectively, [groups] are not calculating tacticians who seize every available opportunity to act; instead they choose the form and timing of their collective action from a narrow repertoire . . . Forms of collective action are rooted in their context and history" (Jones-Correa 1998, 136).

African Americans have a long history of appealing to government authority to redress racial grievances through systemic reform and redistribution. Recent Afro-Caribbean immigrants, in contrast, are from countries without the same long-standing tradition. This is an important distinction the minority group perspective overlooks. The political claims and demands African Americans put forward in their bid for incorporation were not a reflexive, automatic response to discrimination. Rather, the radical-reformist agenda they pursued was cultivated over decades within the social institutions that constitute the African-American counterpublic.[7] Within the context of these institutions, the group learned to combine protest tactics with more routine, conventional forms of political participation. Watershed events such as the civil rights movement, in turn, confirmed the value and utility of these collective political strategies for African Americans. As a result of these experiences and their socialization within these institutions, African Americans were disposed to making calls for redistribution and antidiscriminatory reform in their earliest bids for political incorporation in cities around the country.

Political Strategies

Recent Afro-Caribbean immigrants do not enter the United States with the same set of political sensibilities and strategies for responding to racial

---

[7] See Chapter 6 for more discussion of the African-American counterpublic.

discrimination, largely because they have had little need for developing such strategies in their majority-black home countries. Recall former councilwoman Clarke speculated her constituents' relative inexperience with protest tactics in their home countries might explain why they have been slow to embrace such strategies in the United States. Her point is the immigrants' political socialization in their home countries has neither prepared nor disposed them to rely on such strategies as readily as their African-American counterparts. She (interview, December 13 and 20, 1996) expanded on this distinction.

African Americans and Caribbean Americans have different histories and traditions. I think when we come here, everybody wants you to put away that which you bring and take up something else. But it's not that simple. It took me many years of living in this country to understand some of the struggles that African Americans had been through and the choices they had to make to win their rights ... It's something to be celebrated. It's something to learn more about. But we didn't come here with the same traditions and experiences. I spent some time in the South with African Americans just trying to find out ... to learn more. You know when you think of what segregation must have done. Albeit we may come from nations where there is some racism, there wasn't the segregation. And people may not have liked you, like I said to somebody earlier today, but they had to educate their kids in the same schools ... there weren't enough of them [whites] to do exclusive schools, and even when they tried it didn't work. That difference in experiences is there.

Clarke's observations might lead casual readers to infer the islands of the Caribbean are completely without a black protest tradition. But this conclusion would not be entirely accurate. To be sure, blacks in the Caribbean do not boast the same long history of race-based demonstrations as African Americans in the United States. Yet there have been occasional instances of mass protest activity on some of the larger islands. In 1960, for example, riots in the capital city of Kingston shattered Jamaica's much vaunted reputation for racial harmony and calm. Eight years later, students mounted a series of antidiscrimination demonstrations on the island. Similarly, in 1970, black power riots broke out in Trinidad.

Still, such demonstrations have been rather infrequent over the course of the region's relatively brief postcolonial history. More importantly, race or black-white differences have neither been as central nor as deeply significant in demonstrations on these predominantly black islands as they have been in the African-American protest tradition. David Lowenthal (1972, 322) elaborates on this crucial difference in his much-cited history of the Caribbean.

West Indian black-power demonstrations and threats of violence are not racial conflicts in the American or British senses. The American civil rights movement, black power, and white backlash are racial in programme, in focus, and in purpose. British minority problems are viewed by all participants as specifically racial . . . But Caribbean conflicts are chiefly socioeconomic, and racial mainly in name. To be sure, these problems have their roots in slavery and in colonialism, both of which were racially organized. But these antecedents are not operationally significant today. Race and color are rallying points for protest, not their essential ingredients or their major determinants.

One of my respondents (interview, April 2, 1997) fairly echoed Lowenthal's insights.

Q: Is racial conflict a problem in Jamaica?
A: Only to a small degree, but in Jamaica, it's more of class discrimination.
Q: Why do you think that is?
A: Because even though the races in Jamaica are Indian, African, you have some European, Syrian – there's a large variety of people in Jamaica – but most of them, well Indians and Africans, make up the large majority, and there isn't much of a problem with race relations with those large groups.

The conflicts that have sparked mass demonstrations in the Caribbean are rarely interracial or black-white. After all, the demographic reality of these islands is that blacks dominate in virtually all spheres of life. "In a society such as the modern Caribbean, hierarchy is divorced from race, yet still tied to color. The oppressors of black people are all other black or brown people" (Waters 1999, 39). Of course, the anticolonial and nationalist political struggles on these islands historically have been pitched against white racism or a remote white imperial power and thus focused on black-white difference. But the more routine political conflicts of Caribbean life are intraracial affairs pitting blacks against other blacks or browns, and these only occasionally generate protest activity. This pattern contrasts with the interracial conflicts that typically trigger protests among African Americans in the United States.

Further, African Americans learn and maintain protest strategies in a black counterpublic removed from whites. But blacks in the Caribbean have no similar racialized institutional context for sustaining an antidiscrimination protest tradition. Of course, some Caribbean immigrants develop ties to the African-American counterpublic in New York. These immigrants are far more likely to engage in protest activity than the average Caribbean-born New Yorker. Among my Caribbean respondents, the four who reported participating in demonstrations all had a fair amount of contact with African-American institutional networks. These immigrants likely learned about such strategies in this institutional context. All in all, however, there is little in the home country experiences of Afro-Caribbean immigrants to dispose or prepare them to engage in these protest tactics as readily as their African-American counterparts.

Policy Views on Government Intervention in the Economy

The immigrants' home country experiences also make for subtle differences in the ways they and their native-born counterparts view some policy issues. Clarke and several other elite respondents believe Afro-Caribbeans are less inclined than their African-American counterparts to turn to the government for economic relief. African Americans tend to be quite supportive of redistribution and other forms of government intervention in the economy.[8] In light of the group's history, this finding should not be altogether surprising. African Americans have so often found their path to economic mobility blocked by racial barriers that they have had to turn to government for redress. Most historians, in fact, agree that government has played an important role in helping to improve African Americans' economic fortunes over the last half-century. This history undoubtedly has disposed many African Americans to look favorably on what government can do to eradicate economic inequality.[9]

Contrastingly, my elite respondents contended their Afro-Caribbean constituents were more ambivalent about turning to government for economic relief. As Chapter 2 revealed, census data bear out this claim. Afro-Caribbeans are somewhat less likely than African Americans to be on welfare.[10] But almost all of my elite respondents agreed the immigrants' views on this issue were not a matter of strong philosophical or ideological objection. Rather, they insisted, these attitudes could be traced to their

---

[8] Of course, African-American support for redistributive economic policies tails off at the upper end of the income scale. Still, a significant majority of all African Americans favor such measures (Dawson 1994a).

[9] Of course, government at times also has been a symbol of oppression for African Americans. Hence, their views on government authority are quite complex, reflecting a mix of mistrust and reliance over the course of American history. Mistrust and reliance are not necessarily contradictory attitudes, though they might appear to be. A group might recognize the need to rely on government to redress systemic inequalities and yet not be confident government can be trusted to do what is right. In that case, the group might respond not with resignation, retreat, or rejection of government solutions, but with vigilance or watchfulness. This has been the predominant pattern among African Americans. For evidence, see Gurin et al. 1989; Shingles 1981.

[10] See Chapter 2 for more discussion.

constituents' home country experiences. Clarke (interview, December 13 and 20, 1996) explains in the following exchange.

Q: You say that Caribbean Americans and African Americans are culturally different. Do those cultural distinctions translate to different public policy preferences?

A: Oh, yes. I may prefer business over social welfare, because we never came from a place where there is any social welfare. You never, ever thought that anybody could take care of you but your own self and your own family. So for me, looking at policy, economic and social policy, I'd go for economic policy before I would delve into the social policy.

Q: Surveys tell us that African Americans are generally supportive of welfare programs to aid the poor. Do Afro-Caribbeans favor such programs?

A: I don't think they do as much. It's only because it's not a tradition and not a custom. It's not something they're used to having. You know it may well be that it's government failure to take care of its poor, where we come from, but they don't have the money to take care of the poor. So the poor gotta take care of themselves.

Another elite respondent (interview, April 17, 1997) expressed the same view, albeit with less grace.

Q: Do you think African Americans and Caribbean Americans have similar policy interests?

A: To some extent, with [some of the] things that we go for. We like ownership as opposed to time-sharing. I think they too are interested in their children's education as much as we are. I think, however, that there is a lesser propensity for us to be on the welfare roll as opposed to our African-American brothers and sisters. And it's not because we don't need it sometimes. But we don't have experience with that back home on the islands. The government doesn't help that way. So if you're poor, you have to rely on yourself. So we're willing to shovel shit to survive.

Both respondents carefully avoid the standard, coarse stereotypes about hardworking Caribbean immigrants and lazy African Americans. Nor do their statements reflect knee-jerk ideological disdain for the dole. Their views are rather more subtle. Afro-Caribbeans, they contend, are often not disposed to turn to the government for economic relief because they are relatively unfamiliar with such programs in their home countries.

Clarke also noted Caribbean immigrants worry that applying for welfare benefits might jeopardize their legal privileges for sponsoring home country relatives who wish to immigrate to the United States. As she (interview, December 13 and 20, 1996) explained, "Part of it [their disinclination to apply for welfare benefits] is that people want to be able to send home for their families. And so the disinclination is probably not based so much or their need[ing] or not needing, but not setting for themselves something that can hurt them later on if they wish to bring family here and have to divulge that they ask[ed] for and received social benefits."

Clarke makes two important points here. First, Afro-Caribbeans' hesitation to turn to the government for economic relief is not necessarily an indication of their self-sufficiency or lack of need. There are probably many Afro-Caribbeans who could benefit from such economic support but reject it for fear of losing their sponsorship privileges. Second and perhaps more significantly, the immigrants rely on a transnational frame of reference – that is, their home country experiences and attachments – to make political judgments within the context of their lives here in the United States. In general, the calculations groups make about political choices and policy preferences are informed by their distinctive histories and backgrounds.

These elite impressions were largely confirmed in my interviews with Afro-Caribbean immigrants. The respondents registered considerable ambivalence when asked about government efforts to redistribute income and provide economic relief. Forty-one of the fifty-nine respondents reported they favored welfare programs, but many also claimed they themselves would be hesitant to rely on such measures. They often explained their reluctance with allusions to their home country experiences and traditions. Consider this fairly typical sampling of responses. First, a fifty-eight-year-old Jamaican woman (interview, April 1, 1997) draws an analytic distinction between her personal preferences and her view of the correct policy choice for government.

Q: Do you support government efforts to improve the economic and social position of blacks or the poor?
A: Ah, I'm not sure. I never like that sort of thing for myself. I mean, I think people who need that kind of help should get it. But it's not for me. It's just not a tradition where I come from. People just have to work for whatever they get. And then there's always that stigma when you get government help. I don't want any favors.

A fifty-two-year-old Trinidadian man (interview, April 8, 1997) made the same distinction.

Q: Do you support welfare programs? Should such programs exist?
A: Yes, to help. To help people who really need it. And then again we [Afro-Caribbeans] believe it's a disgrace to go on welfare. Just because it's not a common practice where we come from. But the programs should stay in place. And you'll find that a lot of the new Caribbean people coming

here need those programs anyway. They have no supports when they come here. I mean, like the family and people that would help them out back home.

Even those respondents who opposed such government supports pointed to their home country experiences to explain their position. One Jamaican man (interview, April 2, 1997) was emphatic.

Q: Do you support government efforts to improve the economic and social position of blacks or the poor?
A: Government efforts? I never liked it. Seems to me like people managed without them where I come from. So I'm really not in favor of too much of that sort of thing.

Another Jamaican immigrant (interview, April 3, 1997) gave a similar answer to the same question. But unlike her male counterpart, she showed a trace of vacillation in her thinking:

I don't usually support those kinds of programs. I mean, I've always thought that government should try to improve the lives of their citizenry. But those who need it the most, really need it, and those who have been prevented from getting it the longest should get the help, I think. You shouldn't just be entitled. We didn't have these programs in Jamaica really, and people just had to struggle for themselves. People can do that here too. Plus, there's a lot of abuse of the system. That's why I can't always support these programs.

A Jamaican man (interview, June 9, 1997) put it even more plainly.

Q: Do you support welfare programs? Do you think such programs should exist?
A: They're not for me. It's not part of my upbringing. Because in the Caribbean you have to work for everything. There is no welfare, there is no system, there is no Medicaid. Those kinds of help are not available. So one has to learn to work. The only problem is, the opportunities to get those things in the Caribbean are either limited or not there. So having gotten the opportunity, you jump at it.

Some readers may wonder whether the immigrants' mixed opinions about government relief stem from their desire to avoid the racial stigma associated with welfare dependency. That is, Afro-Caribbeans may be lukewarm about the idea of welfare support not so much because it is at odds with their home country experiences as because it conjures negative racial stereotypes about blacks in the United States. Eager to avoid the mark of stigma often attached to poor African Americans (Gliens 1996), Afro-Caribbean immigrants may reject welfare reliance to signal their distance from their native-born counterparts. This conjecture, however, is not supported by the views expressed by my respondents. Several did venture the opinion that African Americans rely too heavily on government. This Jamaican woman's response (interview, April 1, 1997) is typical.

Q: Do you think that African Americans depend too much on government programs?

A: I think they have become too dependent on them. Historically, there was a time when they needed to be dependent on such programs because of the shackles they had been put in. But I think that there are some who have remained too dependent, at a time when they could have used it to propel to kinda change the cycle of things. It just didn't happen for whatever reason.

Q: Why do you think it didn't happen?

A: Probably because some other kinds of supports were not readily available. Sometimes we try to help people in isolation on what the real issues are. So we're just dealing with this part of it. But I'm really having problems over here, and I may need counseling and something else. But I can only deal with this. So that this problem stays there and festers. And so then when you are expecting me to jump to one level, I can't because I still have this over here that nobody has dealt with.

Despite their belief that their native-born counterparts may rely too heavily on government, many respondents did not see dependency as an African-American problem. Rather, they deemed it a distinctively American habit that stands in contrast to their home country traditions. This Trinidadian man's comments (interview, November 23, 1996) reflect this view.

Q: Do you support welfare programs?

A: Not too much. It's kinda foreign to me.

Q: Do you feel that most Caribbean Americans share your view?

A: I have met some people ... in fact, a couple weeks ago I was talking to one young lady who is on welfare. And I said, "How could you leave Trinidad and come here to be on welfare?! You should be shamed." She said, "But, but, but ..." I said "Don't give me any buts, because you know we don't deal with that in Trinidad." And what they tell me has happened, the Caribbean-American first generation who come here young, like elementary school, they get inculcated in the welfare syndrome.

Q: You're referring to Caribbean Americans who immigrate to this country at an early age?

A: Right.

Q: Do you think the welfare system is in need of reform, then?

A: Oh yes. I think the whole system was misused, abused to be exact. Anytime you can tell me you have two, three, four generations of people on welfare, there is something radically wrong. There is no excuse for that. And don't

tell me they're all on welfare because they are poor. I see some of them
going to the store and buying the same one-hundred-and-twenty-dollar
sneakers, and this and that. And it's not just black folks, right? There are
Russians that they've brought into this country that's living high off the
hog. There's this white guy in my office who says he is so pissed, because in
his neighborhood, that's what they do. He says they [Russian immigrants]
come here and inside a week they're on welfare.

Q: So it's not a black problem, then?

A: No, no, no. Not by a long shot. Most of the people who are on welfare are
white folks. And they benefit from it, too, because of those food stamps
and what not. Who collects? Black folks don't own the stores that these
people use their stamps in. Whites own the stores and the this and the
that.

Like many of his coethnics, this Afro-Caribbean man complains of welfare
abuse but hardly views this as an African-American problem. Rather,
he considers the general problem of abuse to be endemic to American
political culture and antithetical to his home country experience.

The point here is not to suggest an ideological gulf between Afro-
Caribbeans and African Americans on questions of economic policy. After
all, the majority of my respondents favored government relief for the
disadvantaged. Their level of support was simply more tentative than
that of their African-American counterparts. What these responses make
clear, however, is Afro-Caribbeans' home country experiences inform their
political thinking. Therein lies the key for understanding why the group's
bid for incorporation has not been marked by the same radical-reformist
agenda pursued earlier by their native-born counterparts.

The influence of home country experiences on the political judgments
of these immigrants might be expected to wane as they plant roots and
commit to life in the United States. But the cognitive hold of the home
country perspective is extended and reinforced by transnational social
institutions in New York. By sustaining and solidifying the immigrants'
transnational ties, these institutions indirectly encourage Afro-Caribbeans
to use their home countries as a frame of reference for making political
judgments. Moreover, they often direct the immigrants' attention to home
country political affairs. In recent years, however, Afro-Caribbean organizations in New York have begun to shift their focus to the United States,
most notably in joining recent campaigns to encourage citizenship. But
it is impossible to predict whether this organizational network ultimately
will become a site for fashioning a radical or reformist movement for
Afro-Caribbean political incorporation, in the tradition of their African-
American counterparts.

IV. CONCLUSION

This analysis suggests there is little reason to expect Afro-Caribbeans will replicate the African-American model of political incorporation. Contrary to the predictions of the minority group perspective, shared racial status and vulnerability to discrimination do not confer ipso facto uniform agendas or strategies for political engagement. Still, some observers might question why these foreign-born blacks over time have not taken more of their political cues from the experiences of their native-born counterparts.

I asked elite and non-elite respondents whether Afro-Caribbeans should follow the example of any one group in New York City. Although many respondents averred their respect and admiration for the civil rights struggles of African Americans, very few cited them as the group Afro-Caribbeans should follow. Perhaps not surprisingly, most respondents looked to the successes of New York's Jewish immigrant population. One Jamaican woman (interview, April 1, 1997) gave what proved to be a very typical response. She offered: "I would say the Jews come to mind, because they have been successful in achieving what they want to achieve. Besides, they not only think about themselves. They pay attention to what's going on in Israel. They prepare for all the immigrants coming in to come and benefit from their years of experience here. The network is tight, so I think they would be the ones." Another respondent (interview, April 7, 1997) was more expansive.

Q: Should Caribbean Americans follow the political example of any other groups in New York City?

A: The Jews, yes.

Q: Why?

A: Because they are organized. They are very well organized. Because their leaders understand the power of politics, and the leaders can pull together, at any particular time, or any particular election, the forces to elect or defeat somebody.

Q: So they are a disciplined constituency?

A: They are a disciplined constituency. They may not be disciplined in other things, but when it comes to politics, they are disciplined.

Q: What do you think accounts for that discipline? What's the secret? Is it their institutional capacity, economic resources?

A: Yes, yes. It's all that, but it's also a question of where they come from. They understand what politics can do to you. Because it was politics that threatened to destroy them. They are sensitized to who leads them, or doesn't lead them.

Q: So are you saying that they have a strong historical memory?

A: Right.

Q: But don't African Americans have that too?
A: But we [Afro-Caribbeans] don't. We don't.

This finding certainly militates against Skerry's worry (1993) non-white newcomers to this country will be inclined to follow the radical, race-based model established by African Americans to get ahead politically.

But it prompts an even more important observation. The findings indicate Afro-Caribbeans have not pursued the same radical-reformist agenda as their African-American predecessors in their bid for political incorporation mainly because their home country experiences do not equip them with the same political traditions and sensibilities for responding to racial discrimination as their native-born counterparts. These foreign-born blacks are certainly not spared the racial obstacles that African Americans have faced. But they do not have the same long-standing "repertoire" of political strategies as their American-born counterparts for responding to discriminatory challenges.

Yet even with some exposure to these strategies, Afro-Caribbeans still might be slow to adopt a radical-reformist agenda because the odds of its success are rather dim in the current political climate. Scholars of social movements have long contended groups tend to launch mobilization strategies and agendas when the structure of political opportunities is right (e.g., McAdam 1982; Eisenger 1973). They try to gauge how responsive the political system might be to their demands and typically advance their claims only when their prospects for success seem strong. African Americans, for instance, mounted their bid for inclusion in the 1960s and 1970s, when critical realignments in national and regional politics gave them new leverage and enhanced their bargaining position (McAdam 1982).

It is not at all clear the radical-reformist agenda first pursued by African Americans in their earlier bids for incorporation would have much chance of success in New York today. First, the city's white electorate has shifted to the Right in recent decades. The white liberal reform tradition – once a critical source of support for black civil rights struggles – has declined considerably. "Since the early 1970s...the 'movement liberalism' of well-educated baby-boomers who favored civil rights and opposed the Vietnam War and the 'old liberalism' of unionized, blue collar, and lower-middle-class Jewish constituencies have both atrophied in New York" (Mollenkopf 1997, 105). In short, support for traditional liberal causes is no longer politically fashionable among whites. A radical-reform agenda pushed by blacks, whether native or foreign born, would likely meet significant resistance from these erstwhile liberal reformers.

Second, the economic shifts in New York and other cities in the last few decades make it unlikely dominant, entrenched politicians will give much support to agendas calling for significant redistributive policy measures. Several scholars of urban politics have laid out the case for this view more ably than I can here (e.g., Dreier et al. 2001; Stone 1989; Reed 1988). In brief, the combination of slower rates of economic growth, federal funding cutbacks, the exodus of wealthier residents to the suburbs and the resulting decline in the city's tax base, public opposition to tax hikes, and the increasing mobility of capital have all severely constrained the ability of elected city officials to engage in redistribution. Afro-Caribbean or African-American politicians who seek to advance a radical-reformist agenda emphasizing redistribution thus will be hard pressed to find sustained support among political insiders.

Finally, Afro-Caribbeans might not find widespread support for a radical-reform agenda even among their African-American counterparts. Although African Americans still show remarkable unanimity on a number of political questions, growing class, generational, and other divisions within the population have produced diverse opinions on certain policy issues. For instance, a considerable proportion of middle-class African Americans express the same kind of ambivalence about, weak support for, or outright opposition to welfare programs as the Afro-Caribbeans interviewed for this study (e.g., Dawson 1994a).

More generally, African Americans are hardly in agreement about the future direction or content of their political agenda (Dawson 2001; 1994b). Some African-American politicians want to resuscitate the radical group struggles of the 1960s and reignite the unfinished civil rights revolution (Jennings 1997). Others envisage the political future in more moderate, pragmatic reforms with less emphasis on race (e.g., Wilson 1999; Perry 1991). Some even believe the idea of a unified black political agenda is outmoded and undesirable (Kennedy 2003). The distinctive perspective and outlook of Afro-Caribbean immigrants only add to the political complexity. The future of black politics in New York and other cities around the country is thus unclear.

Conclusion

Reconsidering Political Incorporation and Race

Unprecedented numbers of non-white and non-European immigrants have entered the United States over the last four decades and now pose a historic challenge for the American democratic experiment. The arrival of these newcomers marks the first time this country has confronted the challenge of incorporating large numbers of non-European, non-white voluntary immigrants into the political system. To be sure, the United States has a long record of proven success in absorbing immigrants into its political, civic, economic, and social life. Indeed, this country has a long-standing global reputation for integrating newcomers from abroad. The process has not always been seamless; nor has the welcome always been warm. But immigrants to the United States historically have been able to achieve political incorporation. They have managed to adapt to the country's civic norms, participate in the political process, even influence its outcomes, and by doing so, they have reinvigorated and legitimized American democracy.

Yet the majority of the immigrants in this well-known saga of successful incorporation have immigrated from Europe. The fact that most of today's foreign-born newcomers, in contrast, are non-white, non-European racial minorities prompts questions and even doubts about whether they too will be able to achieve the standard of political incorporation attained by their European predecessors. Although this country's reputation for integrating immigrants is relatively strong, its record of incorporating non-white, non-European racial minorities has been problematic and mixed at best. The experiences of African Americans are a nagging reminder of the difficulties non-white groups have had in achieving full political incorporation in this country. Racial discrimination – in a range of historical guises from

Jim Crow segregation to gerrymandering – has made incorporation a difficult, hard-fought, and still incomplete process for African Americans.

Nevertheless, the reforms of the civil rights era helped to eliminate the most flagrant forms of discrimination from American life and to jump start African Americans' forestalled bid for incorporation. It is reasonable, then, to assume these same reforms have paved the way for today's non-white immigrants to achieve political incorporation with the relative ease of their predecessors from Europe and without the difficulties African Americans encountered. But insofar as racism and discrimination have not been eradicated entirely from American life, it is also reasonable to predict that today's non-white immigrants will encounter serious obstacles to incorporation and follow the same tortuous path as African Americans. In sum, how the United States will deal with the challenge of incorporating large numbers of non-European, non-white immigrants into the political system is very much an open question.

This question today generates fierce debate and disagreement because there is so much at stake in the answer. It is not simply a query about the long-range political incorporation prospects of recent immigrant groups from Asia, Latin America, and the Caribbean. The question also takes measure of the extent to which racism is still a significant barrier to full political inclusion for racial minorities in this country, despite the antidiscrimination reforms and measurable civil rights progress of the last half-century. What is more, the question has implications for a notable dilemma that has preoccupied Americans almost since the founding: that is, whether blacks are the lone exception to the usually egalitarian workings of this liberal democracy or whether other racial minority groups are likely to share this dubious distinction.

This book has attempted to help answer the larger question and consider these various implications by exploring the political incorporation patterns of recent Afro-Caribbean immigrants. Despite their relatively small numbers, Afro-Caribbeans provide one of the most instructive cases among the current wave of non-white, non-European newcomers to the United States. As blacks, they share obvious racial commonalities with African Americans: phenotype, vulnerability to discrimination, and a history of enslavement and domination by whites. But as foreign-born newcomers, they also share similarities with the early European immigrants of the last century: the experience of migration, ties to other countries, and their own distinct ethnic heritage apart from American culture. With their mix of racial, ethnic, and immigrant attributes, then, Afro-Caribbeans allow a straightforward test of the three questions that were at the heart of this study: how the United States is facing the challenge of incorporating non-white immigrants, whether racism is still an impediment to political integration, and whether blacks are still an exception to the liberal, inclusive tendencies of American democracy.

The study answered these questions by going back to basics. It considered whether either of the two most well-established models of incorporation in the political science literature, the pluralist and minority group perspectives, offers a reliable set of predictions and explanations for understanding the patterns in Afro-Caribbean political incorporation I find in New York City. Does the pluralist model based on the experiences of early European immigrants give a convincing account? Or does the minority group model, which takes its cues from African Americans and emphasizes the complicating role of racism, offer a more accurate theoretical and empirical picture? The study concludes neither the pluralist nor the minority group model fully anticipates the dynamics of the political incorporation process for Caribbean-born blacks. To be sure, both perspectives provide a number of valid insights, but each is mistaken in some of its fundamental assumptions and predictions about political incorporation: specifically, how the immigrants perceive and make sense of the process, its institutional workings, and the role race plays.

This concluding chapter highlights the key findings of the book. I begin by reviewing the major conceptual amendment to both the pluralist and minority group models generated by the study. I then provide a summary of the most important empirical findings, many of which are informed by this new conceptual amendment. In addition to reviewing the results of the study, I consider their larger implications. The chapter sifts through the findings on Afro-Caribbeans and distills several general conclusions about contemporary immigrant political incorporation, the American political process, racial dynamics, and black politics in the United States. Although I do a fair amount of abstracting from the Afro-Caribbean experience to draw tidy theoretical conclusions about the larger processes of American politics, I also make inferences about the messier, pragmatic issues that animate politics in the increasingly multiracial cities where most contemporary immigrants live.

I. HOME COUNTRY CUES AND THE POLITICAL INCORPORATION PROCESS

The account of political incorporation developed in this book builds on existing approaches in the literature but also has tried to broaden the standard conceptual framework. This study conceives of political incorporation as a *process*, rather than simply a set of outcomes. Although naturalization trends, voting rates, representation, and policy benefits are key variables for gauging and understanding the incorporation patterns of newcomers to the American political system, they hardly constitute the full picture. Political incorporation is also a socialization or learning process, during which these newcomers discover and adapt to the norms of American politics. They learn how to define themselves, how to frame their policy interests, where to draw their partisan and ideological allegiances, and so on.

Immigrants take time to develop these political habits and practices. Until they do, their attachments to some of the basic norms of American political life, such as party identification or ethnic and racial group labels, may be tenuous. It is no wonder, for instance, many Asian and Latino immigrant voters register ambivalence about the two major American parties (Hajnal and Lee 2003). Nor is it a surprise the Afro-Caribbean immigrants in this study did not attach the same political meanings to their racial group identity as African Americans. These newcomers are still learning the rules of the game, developing their bearings, and adjusting to the norms of American political life. Learning these rules, playing by them, or even challenging them is what it means to become a politically active American. Many studies ignore this critical aspect of political incorporation and focus solely on outcomes. But this political learning or socialization process is at the heart of the incorporation trajectory for newcomers to American politics.

Institutions and elites together are the dominant source of frames or cues to immigrants on how the American political system works and how they can influence its outcomes. Foreign-born newcomers also learn the rules of the game from their social networks, coworkers, neighbors, civic organizations, and so on. But these cues are hardly the only ones that shape the political choices and incorporation patterns of immigrants. The major empirical finding of this study is that home country experiences and ties also provide cues that influence how immigrants adapt to the American political system. Indeed, home country attachments and memories are likely to serve as the dominant cognitive lens through which these newcomers make judgments about politics in the early stages of incorporation.

During the initial phase of incorporation, the norms and routines of American politics are still coming into focus for immigrants, but their ties to their home countries are already intact and may not weaken for some time. It is no surprise, then, home country experiences and attachments can have a powerful cognitive influence on immigrants' adjustment to American political life. Their home country perspectives interact with the cues and frames they receive from American political institutions and elites to shape the choices they make in their bids for incorporation. What is more, these home country cues can influence immigrant political behavior in ways that ultimately can transform the norms and routines of American politics.

Failure to account for how home country cues influence immigrant political incorporation patterns is a major analytic and conceptual blind spot for both the pluralist and minority group models. Pluralism emphasizes the liberal or open features of American political institutions and culture to explain how newcomers attain incorporation, as in the case of early European immigrants. The minority group perspective, on the other hand, correctly faults pluralism for neglecting or minimizing how racism interferes with the liberal and egalitarian workings of these institutions and impedes the political incorporation process, as in the case of African Americans. Both perspectives, however, overlook how home country cues can influence these two fundamental dimensions of the incorporation process, especially for recent non-white, non-European newcomers to the United States.

The findings on Afro-Caribbean immigrants in this book illustrate the powerful cognitive influence home country ties have had on their adjustment to political life in this country. Many of the patterns in their political incorporation experiences not anticipated by the pluralist or minority perspectives are actually explained by the cognitive salience and utility of their home country ties, experiences, and memories.

II. RECONSIDERING THE PLURALIST MODEL

The pluralist perspective predicts the normal institutional workings of democracy encourage the integration of new groups into American political life. Dahl (1961) and other early pluralist thinkers presumed parties would function as mobilizers, routinely drawing new groups into the political process. Yet the experiences of Afro-Caribbean immigrants in New York City belie this assumption. The parties generally have ignored and sometimes excluded these foreign-born blacks and have shown little interest in mobilizing them. Still, Afro-Caribbean elites have been able to achieve some representation within the Democratic Party. But whatever inroads they have made, they have achieved mostly through dint of their own effort and initiative. In short, parties do not court passive newcomers, but they do accommodate aggressive self-starters, albeit selectively.

Self-starters are typically group members who already have political advantages to make the party take heed – elites with the time and resources to devote to political life. Contrary to the arguments of early pluralists, then, parties are no good at leveling the political playing field. They tend, in fact, to reinforce and reproduce existing patterns of inequality and stratification. Parties typically preach to the choir, confining their focus to groups who are already mobilized. For example, despite the increasing numbers of non-whites in the New York City population, whites continue to dominate the electorate. They vote more than non-whites, because they are older and more likely to be citizens. Parties have done very little to expand the electorate to reflect the city's changing demographic characteristics. They have made no concerted efforts to promote citizenship among Afro-Caribbeans and other non-white newcomers.

The fact that parties ignore newcomers such as Afro-Caribbean immigrants is not a new insight. Other scholars (e.g., Jones-Correa 1998; Mollenkopf 1992b; Erie 1988) have made this same observation about party organizations. Erie (1988) contends parties will act as mobilizers only when faced with competition. The experiences of Caribbean immigrants in New York suggest an important qualification to this argument. Even when it may be in the competitive or strategic interest of a party to court new constituencies, there will be some resistance within the party to expanding beyond the traditional core of supporters.

What is in the organizational interest of the party in the competitive political arena might clash with the self-interest of party regulars determined to retain their control of material benefits and privileges. Party regulars might resist admitting newcomers for fear of losing these advantages, even when courting them makes competitive sense. This worry helps to explain why African-American regulars within the Democratic Party have not welcomed Afro-Caribbean mobilization. But it also accounts for why the city's Republican organizations have not reached out to these foreign-born blacks. Only in the Republican case, those fears may be compounded by the prejudices of some of the party's mostly white voting base. Whatever the reason, it is clear that parties are hardly the mobilizers early pluralists portrayed them to be.

The standard pluralist perspective is also mistaken in some of its assumptions about motives and perceptions of newcomers to the United States. Dahl ascribed "assimilationalist" aspirations to immigrants. He reasoned their desire for inclusion and acceptance would lead them to participate in American political life. What he and other pluralists did not anticipate, however, are the strong lingering ties that immigrants often have to their home countries and how those attachments influence their adjustment to American political life. Home country ties make Afro-Caribbean immigrants ambivalent about remaining in the United States, and this ambivalence in turn can diminish their interest in formal political participation.

Dahl and other early pluralists overlooked this potential complication in the incorporation process for immigrants. They envisioned political incorporation as a straightforward, linear process, in which newcomers move steadily from immigrant outsider to ethnic insider status over time. But both elite and rank-and-file Afro-Caribbeans interviewed for this study conceded many of their coethnics are content to remain on the political margins. The reason, they believe, is that many Afro-Caribbeans retain ties to their home countries and expect to return. They thus see very little reason to become involved in the American political process. Scholars have noted this tendency among many contemporary immigrants and argued home country ties inevitably depress civic engagement among newcomers to the United States. Although there is some support for this view in the findings from this study, the interviews also reveal a more complicated picture. When home country ties are expressed through civic outlets, they actually tend to encourage participation in American politics.

Respondents in the sample who were involved in home country civic organizations were more likely than their counterparts to vote in city elections and engage in other forms of political behavior in this country. Scholars perhaps then need to draw an analytic distinction between home country ties reflected simply as an emotional investment in the idea of return and those expressed through civic activities. The former appear to depress political engagement in the United States; the latter actually seem to promote civic involvement. This apparent pattern has practical implications for elites eager to mobilize immigrants or frustrated by the ostensible political apathy of many newcomers to this country. If elites want to tap the potential for political mobilization in immigrant communities, they are likely to find it in home country civic organizations whose members have resources and skills that can be translated to participation in American politics. The pluralist perspective, however, tends to overlook altogether the complicated influence of home country attachments on immigrant political behavior.

To be fair, Dahl did reckon immigrants' foreign background would be politically salient in the early stages of their incorporation. He argued

their home country attachments would become a source of ethnic identification, which in turn would serve as a cue for vote choice and party
affiliation. Dahl viewed ethnic voting as the one politically significant out-
let through which immigrants would express their affective ties to their
home countries. But he and other pluralists believed the influence of these
home-country-turned-ethnic attachments would diminish as immigrants
moved up the socioeconomic ladder and into the mainstream. In short,
the pluralist perspective predicts home country attachments are mostly
ephemeral and ultimately superseded by socioeconomic interests and the
desire for inclusion in American life.

This bit of pluralist logic is wrong on two counts. First, the Afro-
Caribbean experience shows home country ties and experiences have far
more cognitive political utility and significance than pluralism anticipates.
Home country attachments do not just serve as a source of ethnic identification and a cue for ethnic vote choice. They also inform how immigrants
make sense of the political world, how they view themselves in it, and
whether they participate or not. What is more, these attachments do not
necessarily decline when immigrants attain middle-class status. Many of
the Afro-Caribbeans interviewed for this study were well off. Some were
successful professionals and homeowners with families here in the United
States. Yet they have sustained their ties to their home countries, counter
to the predictions of the pluralist model.

This last observation leads us to what remains the most serious analytic
failing of the pluralist perspective. As Chapter 6 revealed, home country
ties have cognitive value and political significance for Afro-Caribbeans,
in part because they serve the immigrants in their encounters with racial
discrimination in the United States. Home country ties give these black
immigrants a practicable exit option in the face of racism. The pluralist
model fails to anticipate how racial obstacles complicate the incorporation
process for non-white minority groups, especially blacks. To be sure, the
European immigrants, on whose experiences the pluralist perspective is
based, saw their home country attachments weaken as they moved up the
socioeconomic ladder and gained entré into the American mainstream.
The immigrants' social mobility and economic progress perhaps gradually
diminished the political significance of their home country attachments,
in keeping with the predictions of the pluralist model.

Full mainstream social acceptance and mobility for blacks in this country, however, have proved to be anything but certain. Racial barriers
impede socioeconomic progress for Caribbean- and native-born blacks
alike even today. Whites, in contrast, have been able to overcome the

prejudice faced by the immigrant generation and melt almost imperceptibly into the mainstream. This sobering black-white difference calls into
question pluralist predictions about what happens to both racial group
and home country attachments among blacks as the political incorporation process unfolds. These ties do not diminish; instead, ongoing discrimination actually leads both native- and Caribbean-born blacks to maintain
and reinforce these attachments.

A long line of scholarship has shown African Americans continue to
emphasize their racial identity and employ it to make political decisions in
part because antiblack discrimination still affects so many aspects of their
lives (e.g., Gay 2004; Dawson 1994a; Tate 1993). A similar logic seems to
hold for home country attachments among Afro-Caribbean immigrants.
On the basis of the reports of the Afro-Caribbeans interviewed for this
book, home country ties appear to have considerable cognitive utility for
these black ethnics when they encounter racism in the United States. The
respondents saw their home countries as an exit option or escape hatch
to which they could turn if racial barriers proved to be too much of a
complication in their attempts to live out the American Dream.

III. RECONSIDERING THE MINORITY GROUP MODEL

Exponents of the minority group perspective believe racism is just such
a complication. The minority group model improves on the pluralist
account of political incorporation with its emphasis on how racism complicates the process for non-white minority groups. Hero (1992), for
instance, argues the American political system is a "two-tiered" one:
whites are guaranteed full inclusion on the first tier, whereas non-whites
are relegated to the second tier and thus can expect only marginal incorporation at best. Although attention to how racism affects political incorporation patterns and prospects is a powerful corrective to the standard
pluralist approach, the minority group perspective has its own conceptual
limitations.

Many minority group accounts mistakenly assume the "view from the
bottom" tier will look the same to most non-white groups and they in
turn will have similar political responses to their condition.[1] Or these
accounts fail to spell out how and why the political strategies and reactions of these groups to their racial predicament might vary. According
to the minority group perspective, racial barriers prompt most non-white

---

[1] I borrow the phrase "view from the bottom" from Parenti 1970.

groups to demand systemic reform and redistributive policies to redress inequalities (e.g., Hero 1992; Pinderhughes 1987; Peterson 1981). This view assumes the shared experience of racial discrimination is enough to trump the differences among minority populations and lead them to pursue similar political strategies and policy priorities.

Although many racial minority groups inevitably confront discriminatory barriers, this study demonstrates that the background differences among them do matter and actually influence their responses to these obstacles as well as their other political choices. The distinctive backgrounds and experiences of these groups, in fact, often serve as the lens through which they perceive and interpret the slights and disadvantages they suffer as a result of discrimination or inequality. Consider the political differences between Caribbean- and native-born blacks uncovered in this study. Although Afro-Caribbeans and African Americans confront many of the same racial barriers, the immigrants have not exactly followed in the footsteps of their native-born counterparts in their bid for political inclusion. As Chapter 7 revealed, these foreign-born blacks have not made the same demands for redistribution and systemic reform that characterized African Americans' earlier bid for incorporation.

To be sure, racism has diminished since African Americans first began their pursuit of political inclusion in American cities, and that might explain the absence of such political demands among Afro-Caribbeans. But racial discrimination has hardly disappeared and continues to affect the lives of native- and foreign-born blacks alike. Most of the Afro-Caribbean immigrants in this study reported they had experienced discrimination and saw it as a significant challenge in their adjustment to life in the United States. Even if the racial barriers black immigrants confront today are much less imposing than those faced by African Americans in their earlier bids for incorporation, it is hard to conclude this historical shift alone necessarily would lead Afro-Caribbeans to pursue different political strategies and policy priorities. It is impossible and unreasonable, in fact, to specify just how much discriminatory harm would prompt the immigrants, or any other group, for that matter, to make the same political choices African Americans did in their bids for incorporation. What is more, political responses to racism are not shaped simply by the magnitude of the discriminatory barriers groups face.

The political choices made by racially vulnerable groups appear to be informed by the subjective meanings they attach to their experiences with discrimination and the cues or frames in their distinctive background experiences. Indeed, what groups make of their encounters with discrimination is also informed by these cues. For immigrants, this means their political choices are shaped not simply by their experiences in the United States and the frames they receive from American institutions and elites. Rather, their choices also are informed by ideas and cues they bring with them from their home countries. Home and host country cues together influence the kinds of political strategies and policy demands groups pursue in their bids for incorporation. Furthermore, recall immigrants in the early stages of incorporation are likely to rely even more on home country cues than those they receive from American institutions and elites, because they are still making sense of the political norms and practices of their new country.

Confirming this conceptual framework, this study finds the differences in how Afro-Caribbeans and African Americans have pursued political incorporation are due to factors in the respective backgrounds of the two groups. More specifically, Afro-Caribbeans' home country ties and experiences inform their political choices, view of themselves, and reactions to racial discrimination. Likewise, African Americans' long history of racial subordination in this country, and the strategic norms they have developed as a result, shape their preferences and tendencies. In sum, the respective "home country" experiences of African Americans and Afro-Caribbeans make for some of the critical differences in the ways they each make sense of the political world. The two groups have different perceptual and interpretive frames for making political evaluations.

Consider again Afro-Caribbeans' reactions to racial discrimination. As their native-born counterparts do, these foreign-born blacks worry racism may interfere with their prospects for mobility in the United States. As the minority group perspective correctly suggests, racial discrimination is a reality African Americans, Afro-Caribbeans, and other non-white groups inevitably confront during the various stages of their political incorporation and adjustment to life in the United States. The political learning process at the heart of incorporation for both Afro-Caribbeans and African Americans, then, involves coming to terms with the grim possibility racism could limit their individual achievement. Despite this shared racial predicament, however, the two groups often have different responses to discrimination. Their reactions diverge because Afro-Caribbean immigrants and African Americans see racism through different cognitive frames or lenses.

Although most of the Afro-Caribbean respondents in this study were aware of racism, they believed they were less preoccupied with racial slights than their native-born black counterparts. Many African

Americans view ongoing discrimination and each new racial impediment through the lens of their long-standing history of subordination and disadvantage in this country. This history has rendered them more alert to various forms of racial discrimination than, say, the average new immigrant to this country. Likewise, their history of collective mobilization and demands for systemic reform furnishes them with a ready repertoire of political strategies for responding to racism. These strategies and other lessons are stored in the social and civic networks that constitute the African-American counterpublic and serve as cues for their political judgments and choices (Dawson 1994b).

Afro-Caribbeans, on the other hand, often have little or no such history in their home countries to give them a similar lens for interpreting and responding to racial discrimination. Instead, the immigrants' home country ties furnish them with an exit option to which they ultimately can resort if racial barriers in the United States prove too daunting. In sum, the immigrants' home country ties and experiences shape many of the choices they make in their adjustment to life in the United States, including how they respond to racial discrimination.

The influence of home country experiences and ties on immigrants' political thinking and behavior occasionally may be subtle, but nonetheless worth exploring. Immigrants are not *tabula rasa*. They enter the United States with a host of home country experiences, memories, and ties that are likely to influence many dimensions of their political socialization and incorporation. Some of the lingering puzzles and questions in the unfolding incorporation patterns of contemporary non-white immigrants, in fact, may be explained by these home country influences. For instance, exponents of the minority group view predict racial or panethnic identification among Latino and Asian immigrants will have the same notable political effects it has had among African Americans. That is, these forms of identification are expected to be highly salient and to influence political behavior among the immigrants.

Yet researchers have yet to turn up consistent evidence of such effects among either Latinos or Asian Americans. What is more, studies have found panethnic or racial identification is more pronounced among some nationality groups than others (e.g., Lien, Conway, and Wong 2004; Jones-Correa and Leal 1996). Of course, this variation may be due to the fact that some of these groups are simply more assimilated than others to the highly group-conscious political culture and social norms of the United States. But home country experiences also may help to explain these differences in group identification. Some immigrant groups may be more likely than others to adopt the racial and panethnic labels that circulate in American life because these forms of identification resonate with their home country experiences or memories.

A similar logic may be at work in immigrants' political choices and may explain why some groups will be more likely than others to replicate the strategies African Americans employed in their bids for political incorporation. Non-white immigrants who are from countries that have similar racial regimes and histories of race-based mobilization perhaps will be most inclined to follow the African-American model, insofar as it fits with the cues or frames in their own home country experiences. Think, for instance, of Afro-Caribbean and South African newcomers to this country. These two groups of black immigrants share obvious racial commonalities with African Americans. The home country experiences of South Africans, however, more closely resemble those of African Americans. South Africans therefore might be more likely than Afro-Caribbeans to pursue strategies to combat racial discrimination akin to those historically employed by African Americans.[2] These similarities and differences make for considerable political complexity and diversity within the black population and deserve careful empirical investigation. Likewise, scholars of contemporary immigration ought to give greater analytic attention to patterns in the home country experiences of these newcomers, especially in light of their influence on their political incorporation trends.

IV. DIVERSITY WITHIN BLACK POLITICS

Observers might argue the ethnic differences among blacks uncovered by this study are ultimately meaningless in the face of persistent racial discrimination. After all, although class divisions exist within the African-American population, these cleavages have proved to be less politically significant than the unfortunate patterns of racial disadvantage that seem to unify most African Americans, or at least lead them to believe their fates are linked (Dawson 1994a; Tate 1993). Similarly, Chapter 2 found Afro-Caribbeans and African Americans, despite some economic differences, suffer many of the same racial inequalities relative to whites. The immigrants' distinctive ethnic background hardly has made them any less vulnerable to discrimination than their native-born counterparts.

---

[2] I thank Tali Mendelberg for a very useful conversation about this dimension of my argument.

Still, Afro-Caribbeans' ethnic or home country backgrounds do make for subtle differences in how they respond to racial discrimination, how they view some policy issues, and how they define themselves. Similarly, poor and middle-class African Americans, despite their shared vulnerability to discrimination, differ in some of their policy priorities and even in their emphasis on their racial identification. For instance, differences in policy preferences among African Americans pale in comparison to the black-white policy divide on a number of issues. Nevertheless, survey data suggest poor African Americans are more supportive of redistributive economic policies than their middle-class counterparts (Dawson 1994a). African Americans living in high-quality neighborhoods also appear to place less emphasis on their racial identity than their counterparts in poorer neighborhoods (Gay 2004).

Similarly, this study found that Afro-Caribbeans generally do not express the same highly developed forms of racial group consciousness as African Americans. Only a few of the immigrants interviewed for this project registered anything like the group-centered worldview associated with racial consciousness among their native-born counterparts. As it turns out, the handful of respondents who did evince such strong collectivist beliefs also interacted routinely with African Americans in civic and social networks. These immigrants likely gained exposure to African-American forms of racial group consciousness as a result of their participation in these networks. They in turn adopted black group consciousness as a source of identification. It is worth noting this form of identity appears to have had an empowering, eye-opening effect on these Afro-Caribbean respondents, with none of the demoralizing consequences typically associated with race-based oppositional consciousness among immigrants in other studies (Waters 1999; 1996; Portes and Zhou 1993). Nevertheless, most of the Caribbean immigrants interviewed for this project did not attach the same collectivist political meanings to their racial identity as African Americans. This represents a subtle, but significant source of difference between native- and Caribbean-born blacks. Although such ethnic and class differences among blacks in the United States are less substantial than the long-standing divisions between blacks and whites, they are nonetheless politically consequential and should not be dismissed.

Ethnic and class differences matter especially for questions of political agenda setting and organization within the black population. Exponents of the minority group view predict the prejudices of American society will compel African Americans, Afro-Caribbeans, and perhaps other non-white groups to make political common cause. These groups, the argument goes, are likely to join in a grand rainbow coalition in the name of combating racism. As this study shows, there are certainly grounds for this kind of race-based alliance between Afro-Caribbeans and African Americans. For example, the two groups have a shared interest in demanding policies to curb racially motivated police brutality in New York City. They also have a common interest in improving public service delivery to black neighborhoods and ending discrimination in the housing market. Yet in light of the ethnic and class differences within the black population, leaders hardly can assume political unity based solely on the shared experience of racial discrimination.

As Chapter 4 demonstrated, race-based coalitions, even between such a seemingly likely pair of partners as Afro-Caribbeans and African Americans, are far easier to imagine than to build and sustain. Ethnic differences between Afro-Caribbeans and African Americans often prove to be stumbling blocks to coalition building because they often correlate with differences in political perceptions or attitudes. When Afro-Caribbeans pursue their own ethnic political representation in New York, for example, African Americans sometimes complain the immigrants are pursuing divisive strategies and undermining the larger struggle for black empowerment. But Afro-Caribbeans are acting as immigrant ethnics, not as blacks, when they mobilize for their own share of political influence. They, therefore, do not view the election of their own ethnic leaders as antithetical to the cause of racial empowerment.

What is more, as immigrants from majority-black countries, Afro-Caribbeans are hardly unfamiliar or uncomfortable with the kind of black-on-black political competition with African Americans their attempts to win elective office sometimes engender. Such conflict is standard fare in the political life of their home countries. African Americans, in contrast, are far more accustomed to black-white political competition as a basis for mobilization and thus may be more troubled by intrablack political conflict. Differences in the "home country" experiences of these two groups appear to shape their perceptions of black-on-black political competition.

Afro-Caribbeans' desire for descriptive representation is hardly surprising for a group of newcomers to the political system. Insofar as these immigrants are at an earlier stage in the incorporation process than African Americans, seeing their coethnics in positions of political influence may have greater symbolic significance for them at the moment than for their native-born counterparts. African-American leaders might do well to recognize this subtle difference and concede a few political offices to their foreign-born counterparts, in the interest of racial coalition building. Likewise, these foreign-born blacks would be wise to join their more senior native-born counterparts, to draw on African Americans' political experience and numbers. After all, Afro-Caribbeans' policy preferences are not radically different from those of African Americans.

But if the agenda setting for such a coalition is left solely to African Americans, it very well may lead to policy choices that privilege their interests over those of their Caribbean-born counterparts. Black political agenda setting has become a far more complicated enterprise since the civil rights movement. With the increasing diversity within the black population, questions abound over which issues should dominate the agenda, which are excluded, who benefits, and who loses.[3] Recent research, in fact, has suggested there are clear patterns of bias in the mainstream black political agenda, insofar as some issues are deemed more appropriate for consideration than others (e.g., Cohen 1999).

Focusing solely on racial commonalities and ignoring intrablack differences deflects attention from the differential impact of various policies on distinct groups within the population and glosses over potential biases in the black political agenda. Only careful attention to ethnic, class, and other differences among blacks will yield the kind of quid pro quo necessary for constructing and maintaining race-based alliances. Without such attention, the varying priorities and needs of different segments of the black population might be overlooked, misunderstandings might develop, and tensions inevitably will flare.[4] Leaders who hope to organize blacks or even other minority groups for antiracist causes thus cannot afford to ignore these differences. Attention to them, in fact, can only enrich intrablack and interminority political dialogue.

Consider one more instructive example. Chapter 6 revealed Afro-Caribbeans do not ascribe to their racial identity the same political meanings African Americans do. Moreover, Afro-Caribbeans tend to cite their home country attachments as an integral part of their group identity. African Americans easily might mistake the immigrants' emphasis on their distinctive home country ties or ethnic heritage for distancing behavior; or, to put it more bluntly, they might perceive this emphasis as an attempt by Afro-Caribbeans to deny their black identity and avoid discrimination.

---

[3] There are even questions about whether a coherent black political agenda is still possible or desirable.

[4] For example, the distinctive needs and interests of the poor and working class were often overlooked in African Americans' early bids for political incorporation in some cities (Stone and Pierannunzi 1997; Bennett 1993; Reed 1988).

But Afro-Caribbeans do not see their racial and ethnic identities as mutually exclusive. The immigrants' strong identification with their home countries is actually a cognitive device for responding to racial discrimination; it is hardly a blinder for shutting out racial reality. But these subtle ethnic differences between the two groups only can be appreciated when they are addressed in an open political dialogue.

V. BLACK EXCEPTIONALISM

Despite the ethnic differences between Afro-Caribbean immigrants and African Americans, there are nonetheless troubling commonalities in their experiences that warrant consideration. African-American political incorporation is incomplete. There is not much basis for predicting Afro-Caribbeans will get much further than their native-born counterparts in their own bid for political inclusion in New York. Racism complicates the incorporation process for both groups. In fact, as blacks, Afro-Caribbeans and African Americans are likely to face far more discriminatory barriers than other groups in the United States. With their high level of racial group consciousness, African Americans have developed a keenly politicized awareness of these persisting racial inequalities in American life. Afro-Caribbeans appear to have a lower level of racial group consciousness but nevertheless see racism as an obstacle to their full integration into American society. Race eventually may assume greater political salience for the immigrants' children and future generations as they continue to encounter racial obstacles.[5]

How first-generation Afro-Caribbeans deal with the problem of race no doubt will inform the choices of later generations. But the reactions of these black ethnics to this long-standing American dilemma also have considerable implications for American politics today. Their reactions bear on the larger, ongoing political struggles and debates over the ideals of American democracy. Specifically, how much ground has this country traversed in its long, unsteady march toward racial equality, and what political agenda is required to make this ideal a reality? The standard pluralist and minority group models of political incorporation suggest starkly contrasting perspectives on these questions. Insofar as Afro-Caribbeans pose

---

[5] The political experiences of second-generation Afro-Caribbean immigrants are an important subject for future research (e.g., Kasinitz et al. 2004). By the second generation, the ethnic differences between Afro-Caribbeans and African Americans may become politically inconsequential or altogether imperceptible.

a powerful test case of the validity of these two models, their experiences have instructive implications for the debates over these weighty political questions.[6]

Pluralist and neopluralist interpretations typically begin with the premise that the United States is an egalitarian regime: that is, racial equality virtually has been achieved or, at the very least, is a secure constitutional guarantee. This perspective thus tends to reject radically reformist or transformative agendas, calling for policies such as affirmative action, to redress racial minority disadvantage. It usually finds its ideological home in right-of-center coalitions in American politics, typified most clearly by the Republican Party.

In contrast, the minority group interpretation believes racial equality has yet to be fully achieved. Exponents of this view argue inequality is still entrenched in American economic and social life and therefore routinely call for precisely the kind of transformative agenda neopluralists reject. Emphasizing civil rights protections, racial redistribution, and other types of reformist egalitarian policies, this perspective sits left-of-center on the American ideological spectrum, has a home in the Democratic Party, and often has served as a fulcrum for coalitions that include liberal whites, African Americans, and other racial minority constituencies.[7]

So what lessons or implications does the Afro-Caribbean case hold for this debate? For one, the Afro-Caribbean experiences and opinions explored in this study suggest racial equality remains an elusive goal. The immigrants report discrimination and are almost as disadvantaged relative to whites as their native-born black counterparts. These particular findings appear at first blush to discredit the pluralist view and lend support to the minority group perspective. They suggest Afro-Caribbeans will align with liberal whites, African Americans, and other racial minorities in Left-leaning coalitions emphasizing egalitarian reform.

But other findings paint a more complex picture. Recall Afro-Caribbean immigrants have made political choices that defy the predictions of the minority group model as well. For example, they have not exactly followed in the footsteps of African Americans. They have not replicated a race-based radical-reformist agenda in their bid for a share of political power in New York City. Although they have deemed issues of

---

[6] Thanks and full credit to Rogers Smith for helping me to put the findings of this study in the analytic framework that follows.

[7] Radical-reformist and transformative egalitarian perspectives have lost ground and adherents in the Democratic Party in recent decades, as the American electorate has drifted to the Right. But African Americans remain among the staunchest supporters of such views.

race important, they have focused mostly on economic interests, education, and symbolic representation. This finding suggests Afro-Caribbeans may not turn out to be the stalwart members of mostly Democratic, left-of-center coalitions their African-American counterparts have been. With their focus on economic success, for instance, they may elect to vote Republican and join conservative, right-of-center coalitions.

All in all, however, the preponderance of the findings from this study suggest Afro-Caribbeans, like African Americans, mainly will support the Democratic Party and align with coalitions pursuing a transformative egalitarian agenda. With their focus on economic prosperity and insistence on some values consistent with more conservative or Republican viewpoints, their participation in such left-of-center alliances may seem anything but a foregone conclusion. Yet as long as Afro-Caribbeans' quest for socioeconomic success in the United States is compromised by continuing racial inequality and discrimination, they likely will remain amenable to political agendas emphasizing egalitarian reform. The one caveat, however, is the egalitarian agenda in this new century may have to be refashioned to reflect some of the distinctive interests and outlook of these foreign-born blacks and other non-white immigrants who have entered the United States in recent decades.

Much as African Americans do, Afro-Caribbean immigrants worry about being relegated to a kind of second-class citizenship in this country. As blacks, these newcomers have even more cause for such concern than other non-white immigrants. Although Afro-Caribbean immigrants respond to this grim racial reality somewhat differently than African Americans, it leaves them no less conflicted about American citizenship and their prospects for full inclusion. Indeed, Afro-Caribbeans' pessimism about their chance for incorporation ultimately may prolong their attachment to their home countries and slow their political adjustment to the United States. Ironically, "living between two nations" may prove to be a far more secure position for first-generation Afro-Caribbeans than living completely in this one where they are subject to persistent racial discrimination.[8] Their children who are born and raised in the United States, however, are not likely to have this option and the strategic benefits it provides.

Whites in the United States continue to achieve incorporation and the promises of the American Dream with relatively more ease and security than blacks. In light of this continuing dilemma, Dahl's predictions

---

[8] I borrow the phrase "between two nations" from Jones-Correa 1998.

(1961) for the full incorporation of all groups into American political life forty years later still seem all too giddily sanguine. In contrast, Edmund Morgan's (1975) much more sobering view of an American liberal democracy predicated on the exclusion of a subordinate racial group has the ring of reasonable prediction. As long as racial discrimination and exclusion persist in the United States, there is a distinct possibility the promises of pluralist democracy will prove uneven, or altogether hollow, for yet another group of blacks.

Appendix A

Methodology

How are Afro-Caribbean immigrants integrated into the American political process? More precisely, how does race affect the political incorporation process for this group of foreign-born blacks? This question lies at the heart of this study. In the vernacular of the social sciences, political incorporation is the key dependent variable under scrutiny. The standard descriptive measures of political incorporation include naturalization rates, registration and voting data, party affiliation, and elective officeholding. Although this study devotes some attention to these important outcome measures, the focus is directed less on the outcomes and more on the process of political incorporation itself.

More pivotal to this study are the identities, interests, ideological agendas, and strategies that inform and animate the process for Afro-Caribbean immigrants. The aim is to provide a critical account of how Afro-Caribbean political integration has unfolded and how their experiences compare with those of African Americans and European immigrant groups. The study explores how these black immigrants relate to the political process, conceive of their political interests, view themselves, see themselves in relation to other groups, and make sense of the political world.

This last series of questions brings me to another important point about the analytic focus of this study. The project is necessarily concerned with race, ethnicity, self-definitions, and group identities. This book, as I noted at the outset, seeks to understand how race affects the political incorporation process. The project therefore treats race as an *independent variable*: that is, a variable that might explain some other phenomenon of interest – political incorporation in this case. This approach is fairly con-ventional. Political scientists long have been accustomed to factoring race and ethnicity as independent variables, first causes from which serious political consequences flow. Within political science, then, racial and eth-nic categories are often taken as brute social facts. This study parts with that more conventional approach, however, by treating race, ethnicity, and group identity as *dependent variables*, phenomena to be understood and explained, as well. The project explores Afro-Caribbean self-definitions: how the immigrants begin to view themselves as part of a particular racial or ethnic group and where they mark the boundaries of their group iden-tity. I treat group identity as a complex process, rather than as a static social fact. Accordingly, I examine the choices and constraints of this pro-cess and explore how these, in turn, inform the political incorporation trajectory of Afro-Caribbean immigrants.

To elucidate these dimensions of the political incorporation process, the study relied primarily on a single method of qualitative research: intensive interviewing. I conducted two waves of in-depth, one-on-one interviews with Afro-Caribbean immigrants between 1996 and 1997. One consisted of a series of open-ended, structured interviews with a sample of fifty- nine first-generation immigrants. The other wave of less structured interviews targeted fifteen Afro-Caribbean community and political leaders.

I decided to focus exclusively on immigrants from the English-speaking Caribbean to eliminate the potentially confounding effect of foreign lan-guage. First, interviewing blacks from the English-speaking Caribbean allows me to make a more direct comparison with African Americans than I could with French- or Spanish-speaking blacks from the region. Second, foreign language is often a barrier to political incorporation. By focusing only on English-speaking Caribbean immigrants, then, I was better able to isolate the effects of race on the political incorporation process.

I began the field research by interviewing the Afro-Caribbean leaders. My guess was they would be better prepared than rank-and-file Afro-Caribbean immigrants to address questions about political incorpora-tion. Moreover, I thought their answers might provide helpful clues for framing questions for respondents in the larger sample. For example, my interviews with elites provided insights about major issues of concern to the community at the time, such as immigration reform and police brutality.

I initially enlisted the help of community organizations in Brooklyn to identify these leaders. Personnel at the Caribbean Research Center at

Medgar Evers College were especially helpful. At my request, they prepared a list of Afro-Caribbean elected officials and other well-known
figures in the community. I also relied on Afro-Caribbean ethnic newspapers to identify the names of prominent leaders. I initially contacted
most of these elites by phone to explain the project and request their
participation. I followed the phone conversations with a formal letter.

Almost all of the elites I contacted expressed interest. Three women
and twelve men agreed to sit for interviews. Three were elected officials;
the others were political and community activists. Fourteen of them were
based in Brooklyn and one in Queens. Scheduling the meetings was a
challenge. I anticipated the interviews would run for one to two hours,
and many of the respondents did not have that much time. To accommodate their busy schedules, I conducted all the interviews at a place
of their choosing, which turned out to be their office in every case. I
explained the interviews would be recorded and transcribed on the condition of anonymity. Several of the respondents waived the requirement
of anonymity, and in fact, insisted on direct attribution. Those are the
only respondents identified by name in the text.

I used a structured questionnaire for the interviews (see Appendix B).
The questions asked about Afro-Caribbean political behavior, policy
issues, group identity, relations with other groups, politics in New York
City, and a number of other issues. In some cases, time constraints forced
me to skip or modify some questions. Moreover, some interviews deviated
from the questionnaire when the respondent took our conversation in a
different direction. All in all, these interviews proved to be less structured
than the ones with the larger sample.

The sample of fifty-nine respondents was drawn primarily from
Brooklyn. This borough was the most obvious site for finding potential respondents. It has the largest number of Afro-Caribbean immigrants
of all New York City boroughs. I used census tract data and community
board district maps to identify clusters of Afro-Caribbean neighborhoods
in Brooklyn. I initially recruited respondents for the larger sample by
canvassing community board and political club meetings. I usually intro-
duced myself to those in attendance, explained my project, and asked for
volunteers at the end of the session. Many of the immigrants appeared to
be interested, but quite a few were wary of the time commitment. Still,
a significant handful of interested immigrants gave me their name and
phone number at these meetings. I then followed up with phone calls. I
used snowball techniques to generate additional referrals from those who
agreed to interviews.

I ultimately met with thirty-five women and twenty-four men.[1] My own Caribbean background may have helped me gain the respondents' confidence and cooperation. I believe almost all were aware of my ancestry: some asked, others assumed.[2] I offered to meet respondents at a place of their choosing. Most agreed to meet me at their home after work hours or on weekends. Others met with me at their place of work. The interviews ran two to three hours. This time constraint made it impossible for me to complete the entire questionnaire with most respondents. Consequently, my strategy was to sample the most important questions from each section of the interview schedule and cover as many as the time duration allowed. The interviews were taped and transcribed on condition of anonymity. The Princeton University Institutional Review Panel for Human Subjects evaluated and approved the interview schedule.

The schedule featured a series of structured questions, both open ended and closed (see Appendix B). The questions were designed to elicit the immigrants' conceptions of group identity, political attitudes, values, behavior, and notions of citizenship and political responsibility.[3] There were also questions about their attitudes toward other racial and ethnic groups in New York City, their experiences with racial discrimination, and their views on race relations in the United States. Finally, I asked the immigrants about their past experiences in their home countries and the nature of their connections to those countries once they settled in the United States. The ultimate aim of the interviews was to examine these issues from the perspective of the immigrants and in their own words.

---

[1] See Chapter 2 for more descriptive details on the sample.

[2] Of course, the interesting question this raises is whether the immigrants' rate of cooperation and their answers might have differed if the interviewer were African American, white, or of some other racial or ethnic background. I would venture my Afro-Caribbean background helped me gain access to the respondents. It also probably served to establish trust and elicit frank answers from them. The caveat, though, is the respondents were aware of my institutional affiliation with Princeton University. I initially presumed sharing this personal detail about myself would help me gain the respondents' cooperation. In retrospect, however, I wonder whether it led them to manage some of their responses to my questions, as they might have seen me as an authority figure or expert. For example, it might have led some to emphasize the importance of education.

[3] Some of the questions on racial group identity were adapted from the National Black Election Study (NBES) for purposes of comparability. NBES is a longitudinal telephone survey of African Americans, which focuses on political attitudes and electoral behavior. Adapting questions from this survey allowed me to make more pointed and explicit comparisons between African Americans and Afro-Caribbean immigrants.

Perhaps more than any other method, interviews allow researchers to probe and illuminate respondents' self-interpretations and their views of the political world. This approach is not, however, without its problems. Qualitative methods, and intensive interviews in particular, suffer from two major methodological limitations that usually trouble social scientists. First, interviews are not as useful a predictive tool as surveys and other quantitative methods. Second, conclusions drawn from interviews with a delimited group of respondents cannot be readily or confidently generalized to a larger population. Both of these limitations stem from problems of sample size and selection bias. Interviews canvass only a small cohort of a much larger population and engage respondents who are often not very representative of the group as a whole. My own study is certainly vulnerable to these methodological problems, but I have sought to address them.

Most of my respondents obviously belonged to the same or overlapping social networks, because they were recruited through snowball referrals. I used this admittedly non-random recruitment tool for two reasons. First, snowball referrals make contacting immigrants, who are typically a "hard-to-reach" population, easier. Second, resource limitations prevented me from randomly canvassing the entire population. Of course, this non-random sampling method introduces the potential problem of selection bias. The techniques I employed yielded a sample of respondents who are probably far more politically active and economically better off than the larger immigrant population. With its emphasis on political incorporation, however, this study is concerned precisely with those Afro-Caribbean immigrants who are civically active and pursuing some form of political integration.

Level of political and civic engagement is an important selection criterion for the sample. The inherent "activist" bias of this group of respondents thus becomes an analytic strength of the study. There is also a pragmatic value in this approach. Politically active immigrants are often highly self-conscious about their experiences in this country and thus make for good interview subjects (e.g., Jones-Correa 1998; Kasinitz 1992). This bit of common sense was certainly borne out in my own interviews, which yielded some rich and insightful responses from participants.

Although the selection bias of the interviews can be viewed as an analytic virtue, the limitations of a small sample and the attending generalizibility problems are not so easily resolved. With a sample of only fifty-nine respondents, I could neither draw bold inferences nor generalize with statistical confidence from these interviews to the Afro-Caribbean population in the aggregate. To overcome this potential methodological weakness, I turned to a few other approaches.

Evidence from surveys would have been useful here; however, there are no large-scale surveys on first-generation Afro-Caribbean immigrants.[4] Nevertheless, my work does refer to findings from other small, interview-based studies (e.g., Waters 1999; Vickerman 1999; Kasinitz 1992). Second, I situate the interviews in the context of census data. Third, I supplement my interview findings with some archival material from the Afro-Caribbean press. Finally, I focus on patterns in the responses from my interviews, rather than absolute sizes. By itself, each of these methods has its own biases and limitations, but together, they give me greater leverage to draw firm conclusions and broader inferences from the interviews.

Even with their limitations, the interviews have considerable analytic value. Myriad claims have been made for intensive interviewing, and there is no need to rehearse all of them here. For my own purposes, interviews have two particular strengths that were indispensable to this project. As Jennifer Hochschild (1981) has noted, while survey researchers typically infer links between variables, interviews elicit responses from participants that illuminate the exact ways they themselves make those connections. Both approaches, Hochschild adds, may yield identical conclusions and yet issue different types of explanations for the same phenomenon.

Second, interviews can generate findings that surveys and other kinds of quantitative research cannot. Again turning to Hochschild (1981), survey data "may too often be limited by a failure of imagination or the exigencies of statistical techniques." She thus concludes interviews "may more accurately capture reality." I subscribe to the general thrust of this claim but would make the point a little differently. Interviews can capture aspects of reality other methods cannot. They can elicit more personal, descriptive, and *process-oriented* information from subjects.

Intensive interviewing is especially useful for any project seeking to describe and explain the self-interpretations and political thinking of a group of actors. During interviews, researchers induce respondents to clarify processes that cannot be easily reduced to categorical variables and the

---

[4] Waters, Mollenkopf, and Kasinitz collaborated on a major survey on second-generation immigrants in New York that included a sizable sample of Afro-Caribbeans. See Kasinitz et al. 2004.

like. Respondents can elaborate on their self-definitions and their views of the political world in ways that cannot be captured by other methods. Interviews are thus an indispensable tool for this project, which seeks to shed light on precisely those aspects of the political incorporation process for Afro-Caribbean immigrants.

Appendix B

Interview Schedules

I. Background

Where are you from originally?

How long have you lived in New York City? How long have you lived in the United States?

What was your primary reason for moving to the United States? Were there any other reasons?

What do you think of New York as a place to live? What do you think of the United States in general?

Do you consider New York to be your permanent home?

Are you a naturalized U.S. citizen or do you plan to become a naturalized citizen? If not, why?

If you are a naturalized U.S. citizen, did you retain the citizenship privileges of your home country as well? Why did you decide to become a U.S. citizen?

If you are not a naturalized citizen, do you feel pressure to become a citizen because of the new immigration and welfare reform proposals?

How often do you return to the island where you grew up?

When was the last time you visited the island and how long did you stay?

Do you maintain ties with relatives or friends on the island?

Can you tell me something about life on the island? For example, what are the economic and political conditions like?

What kind of work did your parents do?

Do most of your relatives live there? If not, where do they live?

Do you eventually plan to return to the island and live there permanently? Why or why not?

Do you maintain a bank account, business, or real estate holdings on the island?

Do you send money or material goods to relatives or friends living on the island? How often?

Do you think it is important to maintain ties to your home country? Why or why not?

Tell me about your family here in New York. Who are its members? What are their ages? Education? Occupations?

Are you married or living with a partner? Where is (s)he from?

What is your current occupation? How long have you held this job?

What is your yearly income? Under $10,000, between $10,000 and $20,000, between $20,000 and $30,000, between $30,000 and $40,000, between $40,000 and $50,000, etc.?

Have you held any other jobs here in the United States? What are they and how long did you hold each one?

What was your occupation in your home country?

What is your spouse's occupation?

Have you had any schooling here in the United States? How much?

How much of your education did you complete on the island?

How would you describe your current standard of living? Are you satisfied with it? Why or why not? How does it compare to your standard of living before you moved to the United States? Are you better off now than you were then? Do you expect your standard of living to improve steadily as you continue to live here in the United States?

Do you live in an apartment or in a house? Do you rent or own?

How would you describe your current home and neighborhood life? Is the area you are living in now the kind of neighborhood you want to continue living in? If not, what kind of neighborhood would you move to?

How would you compare life on the island with life here in the United States?

II. Group Identity

How would you describe yourself to someone who asked you about your social background?

Some people describe themselves differently according to whom they are speaking. How do you describe yourself when you are speaking to other Afro-Caribbeans? African Americans? Whites?

What is your racial identity?

Do you consider your Afro-Caribbean heritage part of a distinct ethnic or cultural identity?

Do you usually let others know that you are from the Caribbean?

Do you feel close to other English-speaking black immigrants from the Caribbean?

Do you get along with Afro-Caribbean immigrants from other islands?

Do you feel close to Spanish- or French-speaking immigrants from the Caribbean, such as Dominicans or Haitians?

Do you feel close to African Americans in this country? Why?

Do you feel that most immigrants from the Caribbean share similar values and attitudes about life in the United States? What are they? Describe them to me.

Do you feel that African Americans share the same values and outlook on life in the United States as Afro-Caribbean immigrants? If not, how are the attitudes and values of these two groups different?

Are there cultural differences between Afro-Caribbeans and African Americans? Tell me about them.

Do you feel that your fate as an Afro-Caribbean immigrant is at all linked to that of African Americans in general?

How much of what happens to African Americans in the United States has something to do with what happens to Afro-Caribbeans living in this country?

Do Afro-Caribbeans have more in common with African Americans than with other groups in the United States? Why or why not?

What is more important to you, being Afro-Caribbean, being black, being American, being from your country of origin, or none of these? Why?

Is it more important for Afro-Caribbeans generally to identify as immigrants, as Americans, or as blacks? Why?

Some people say that African Americans and Afro-Caribbeans do not get along. Is there competition or conflict between these two groups? If so, tell me about the sources of these tensions and why do you think they have developed?

Do African Americans treat you differently because you are from the Caribbean? If so, why do you think this happens?

Do African Americans discriminate against Afro-Caribbeans and other immigrants? If so, why do you think this happens?

Do you think whites make distinctions between Afro-Caribbeans and African Americans? What kinds of distinctions?

Do whites treat you differently because you are from the Caribbean? Do you think they interact with you differently than they interact with African Americans? If so, why?

Do you think that Afro-Caribbeans work harder than African Americans? If so, why?

When you look for a job do you find that being an Afro-Caribbean immigrant has an impact on your prospects of getting the job? Do you make a point of identifying yourself as an Afro-Caribbean immigrant when interviewing with prospective employers?

Do you associate mostly with other Afro-Caribbeans, with African Americans, or with whites? Are most of your friends also from the Caribbean?

Do you feel more comfortable around other immigrants from the Caribbean than you do around African Americans or whites? Why?

Do you prefer working in organizations or at the workplace with other Afro-Caribbeans, with African Americans, or with whites? Why?

Have you ever attended or participated in the West Indian Labor Day Carnival?

Who are your neighbors? Is your neighborhood composed mostly of other Afro-Caribbean immigrants, or African Americans, or whites?

What kind of people do you work with? Do you associate with them away from the job?

III. Values and Beliefs

Is the American political system fair? Why or why not?

Is success in the United States mostly a matter of hard work or is it more a matter of one's racial or socioeconomic background?

Why do some people in America make it while others don't?

Some people think it is harder for blacks in this country; what do you think?

If blacks don't do well in life, is it because they are often kept back because of their race or is it because they don't work hard enough?

Does the term "the American Dream" mean anything to you? If so, what do you think it is?

Do you make it a point to support Afro-Caribbean businesses and organizations? What about businesses and organizations run by African Americans?

Do you know any Afro-Caribbeans who own their own businesses? What about African Americans?

Should black people shop in black-owned stores?

Should black children go to schools that emphasize Afrocentric curricula?

Should the children of Afro-Caribbean immigrants go to schools with other immigrant children if they can?

Do you shop in stores that sell products from the Caribbean? Are these stores run by Afro-Caribbeans?

Are you involved in any economic cooperatives with other Afro-Caribbeans, such as "su-su" or "pardner hand"?

If so, how does it work?

Have you ever applied to a U.S. bank or other lending institution for a loan? Have you ever encountered any difficulty in securing a loan from one of these institutions? Where do you first turn when you need financial assistance?

Do you think that Afro-Caribbean professionals understand Afro-Caribbean needs better than other professionals?

Do you think that black professionals understand the needs of blacks better than other professionals?

Should blacks always vote for black political candidates? Why or why not?

Do you feel close to blacks in Africa and elsewhere around the world? Why or why not?

Do you feel close to whites? Why or why not?

Do you attend church regularly?

Is your church composed mostly of Afro-Caribbeans, African Americans, or whites?

Do you think racism and racial discrimination are big problems in the United States?

Are they problems in your home country?

How do race relations in the United States compare with race relations in your home country? Are they better or worse? Why?

Have you had any personal experiences with racism or racial discrimination here in the United States? Tell me about them.

Have you ever encountered racial discrimination in your attempts to find work or a place to live? Do you know of any Afro-Caribbeans who have encountered such problems?

Do you think Afro-Caribbean immigrants and African Americans experience the same kinds of discrimination? Please explain.

Is racial discrimination as big a problem for Afro-Caribbean immigrants as it has been for African Americans? Why or why not?

Do African Americans complain too much about racism?

Do you support government efforts to improve the economic and social position of blacks and other minorities? Why or why not?

Do you think the movement for black rights in the United States has affected you personally?

Are you in favor of affirmative action?

How do you feel about the economic position of blacks in this country relative to that of whites? Is it better, worse, or the same? What about the economic position of Afro-Caribbeans relative to that of African Americans?

Do you think that most white people want to see blacks get a better break, or do they want to keep blacks down, or don't they care one way or another?

Some people think that Afro-Caribbeans tend to do better than African Americans. What do you think? Is there any truth to this? Why or why not?

Do African Americans depend too much on government programs?

Do blacks in this country have enough political power to improve their social and economic condition?

Do whites have disproportionately too much political power?

Can voting or other kinds of political involvement make a difference for Afro-Caribbeans? For African Americans? And for blacks as a whole?

IV. Political Organization and Socialization

Do you plan to vote in the upcoming elections?

What community, civic, or political organizations are you involved in?

Are these organizations composed mostly of Afro-Caribbeans, African Americans, whites, or others?

Are you involved in any voluntary or benevolent associations with other Afro-Caribbeans? Which ones?

Are you involved in any economic cooperatives with other Afro-Caribbeans, such as a "su-su" or "pardner hand"?

If so, what kinds of services or activities do these groups provide?

Do you feel affected by local politics?

Who looks out for your interests and concerns in local New York politics?

If you needed help with a problem, which, if any, local politicians or community leaders would you turn to?

Which local political issues do you care about most?

Which politicians are most responsive to those issues?

Which politicians are least responsive to them?

Have you ever contacted a local politician or an elected official? Which ones?

What are the most important issues affecting Afro-Caribbean immigrants in New York City?

Which politicians seem to care most about those issues?

Do Afro-Caribbeans have enough power and adequate representation in local politics? Why or why not?

Do Afro-Caribbeans and African Americans have the same concerns and interests in New York City politics?

How do you feel about the amount of influence and power blacks have in New York City government and politics? What about the influence of Hispanics or other racial minorities?

What are the most important issues for blacks in New York? And in the nation as a whole?

Do African-American politicians and elected officials represent Afro-Caribbean interests?

Do African Americans seem willing to share power with Afro-Caribbeans in New York? Why or why not?

Should Afro-Caribbeans form their own political organizations or should they join organizations established by African Americans or other groups? Why?

Can Afro-Caribbeans get ahead politically in New York City without the support and cooperation of African Americans? Why or why not?

Do all blacks, Afro-Caribbeans and African Americans alike, need to form a united front to advance their position in this city and in the United States as a whole?

Do Hispanics and Asian Americans have political and economic interests in common with Afro-Caribbeans? Do these groups make for good political allies?

Should Afro-Caribbeans follow the political example of any other groups in New York, such as the Jews or the Irish? Should they follow the example of African Americans? Why or why not?

What is the best way for Afro-Caribbeans to achieve their political goals in New York City?

Should Afro-Caribbeans support white or Hispanic politicians? Can they effectively represent Afro-Caribbean interests? Can they represent the interests of black voters in general?

Have you ever voted or campaigned for a white or Hispanic politician? Which one(s)?

Have you ever voted or campaigned for an Afro-Caribbean or African-American politician? Which one(s)?

Do you think a black mayor would be better for New York? Why? What about a Hispanic mayor?

Is racial discrimination against blacks a big problem in New York City? Should this issue have an important place on the city's policy agenda?

Have you ever participated in a demonstration or rally to protest against racial discrimination or racism in New York? Do you think this is an effective strategy for addressing such problems?

How are blacks treated by the New York City police? Is police brutality an important issue for Afro-Caribbean immigrants?

How do you feel about New York City public schools? How do they compare with schools in your home country?

Do you consider yourself a liberal or a conservative on economic issues? What about on social issues such as abortion, affirmative action, and crime?

What is your party affiliation? Which party best represents your political views?

Which national leader, elected or unelected, best represents your interests and political views?

Do you consider Colin Powell a legitimate leader of the nation's black population? Are you aware of his Caribbean parentage? Does this make a difference to you? Is he representative of the Afro-Caribbean community? How?

What are your feelings about the following political figures? Al Sharpton? David Dinkins? Rudolph Guliani? Rhoda Jacobs? Edward Koch?

Who are the leaders of the Afro-Caribbean population in New York City?

Can you identify any members of the City Council, State Assembly, or State Senate who have ties to the Caribbean?

Are you familiar with any of the following elected and unelected officials? Una Clarke? Nick Perry? Lloyd Henry? Roy Hastick?

Do these officials represent the Afro-Caribbean population? Do they represent blacks in general?

Have you been following this year's elections?

Do you pay more attention to local politics or to politics in your country of origin?

Are you involved in any political activities in your home country? If so, what are they?

Do you vote in island elections?

Were you involved in any political activities on the island before you moved to the United States?

Did you vote regularly while you were living there?

Do you feel a greater responsibility to vote and participate in political and community activities here in New York than you did while you were living in the Caribbean? Why or why not?

Which newspapers do you read regularly? What kinds of news items interest you the most?

Welfare reform is in the news a lot these days. Have you been following the news on this issue?

What is your opinion on the new welfare reform legislation? Will this legislation affect you personally?

How do you think the new welfare reform legislation will affect Afro-Caribbeans in general? How do you think it will affect African Americans?

Do you think the welfare system needs reform? If so, how?

Have you ever used any of the following services? Public welfare? Food stamps? Child welfare? Or the housing authority? For how long?

Do you know any other Afro-Caribbean immigrants who have received any of these services?

Do you think most people who receive these welfare services need them? Why or why not?

Immigration reform has also been in the news a lot lately. How do you feel about the recent legislation limiting education and social services to legal immigrants? What about the provisions to limit sponsorship privileges?

Are you in favor of more restrictions on immigration to this country? Why or why not?

How would new restrictions affect Afro-Caribbean immigrants in general and you personally?

What is the biggest problem for new immigrants to this country? What is the biggest problem for Afro-Caribbean immigrants?

What do you think is the biggest problem in this country today?

What, if anything, should government do about this?

V. Becoming American

What do you think Afro-Caribbeans gain by becoming United States citizens?

What do they lose?

What is the hardest thing about adjusting to life in the United States?

What is the greatest thing about life in the United States?

Do you feel that Afro-Caribbean immigrants are as welcome in the United States as other groups of immigrants?

Do you feel that Afro-Caribbeans have access to the same opportunities as other groups of immigrants? If not, why?

Have you achieved what you planned or hoped for when you left your home country?

Would you encourage others in your home country to come to the United States? Why or why not?

VI. Self-Definition

If you had to describe yourself to someone who didn't know you, what would you say? What are your best and worst qualities?

What would you say are your most important values and beliefs? What do you think is the most important thing in life?

Are there any questions or issues I haven't raised that you would like to talk about? Tell me about them.

INTERVIEW SCHEDULE II

I. Personal Background

Where are you from originally?

How long have you lived in New York City? How long have you lived in the United States?

What was your primary reason for moving to the United States? Were there any other reasons?

Where are your parents from?

What kind of work did your parents do?

II. Political Background

Were you active in politics in your home country? Describe the extent of your political involvement while you were living there.

Are you currently involved in any political activities on the island? If so, please tell me about them.

Do you play any formal role in your home country's political affairs?

How did you become involved in New York City politics?

Tell me about the campaign that led to your election. For example, how was it organized, how was it funded, who were your challengers, etc.?

Which groups and which city leaders were most important in your election to public office?

Did any Afro-Caribbean community leaders or organizations play a role in your campaign? Which ones and what was the extent of their involvement? How important were they to your success?

Did any African-American community leaders or organizations play a role in your campaign and election to public office? Which ones and what was the extent of their involvement? How important were they to your success?

Did any white political leaders or ethnic community groups play a role in your campaign or election? Which ones and what was the extent of their involvement? How important were they to your ultimate success?

III. Identification, Interests, and Constituents

Who are your primary constituents?

Do you view Afro-Caribbeans as a distinct ethnic voting bloc or are they part of the larger African-American constituency?

Do you see yourself as a leader of New York's Afro-Caribbean population?

How would you define the major policy interests of the Afro-Caribbean immigrant population?

Do you see yourself as a leader of New York's African-American population as well? Why or why not?

Are you satisfied with the level of Afro-Caribbean representation and influence in New York City politics? Please explain.

How does their level of influence and power compare with that of African Americans and other racial minority groups in the city?

Naturalization rates among Afro-Caribbean immigrants are rather low. Are Afro-Caribbeans disinclined to become United States citizens? If so, why? If not, what other factors might help to explain the low naturalization rates?

Is this a major impediment to the group's political empowerment in New York?

Are you involved in or aware of any formal efforts to encourage naturalization among the group? How have these efforts fared? What about the citizenship drive sponsored by Caribbean Immigrants Services (CIS)?

How would you describe the level of organization and political mobilization within the Afro-Caribbean community?

Are you involved in or aware of any formal efforts to encourage political participation among Afro-Caribbean immigrants? Tell me about them. Which organizations are leading these efforts?

What are the most significant barriers to increasing Afro-Caribbean participation and representation in New York City politics?

The West Indian Labor Day Carnival has become one of the more important public celebrations in New York City. Does this event have any political significance for Afro-Caribbeans? Please explain.

Have you formally supported any other Afro-Caribbeans seeking election to public office? Which ones? What kind of role did you play?

Have you supported any African Americans seeking election to public office? Which ones? What kind of role did you play? What about Hispanic or white politicians?

Do you feel any greater obligation to support Afro-Caribbean or African American politicians? Why or why not?

Who are the major leaders or power brokers in the Afro-Caribbean community?

How would you characterize your relationship with each of these figures?

Do African Americans and Afro-Caribbeans share the same policy interests and preferences? Tell me about them. How are they different?

What are the biggest problems facing Afro-Caribbean immigrants in New York City? Are they very different from the major concerns of the African-American population? Please explain.

Do Afro-Caribbeans regularly contact your office with problems, questions, or requests? What kinds of inquiries does your office most often field from these constituents? Do the inquiries come mostly from men or women and do they come mostly from older immigrants or more recently arrived immigrants?

Can African-American politicians effectively represent the interests of Afro-Caribbean immigrants? Why or why not?

Do you find that African-American politicians reach out to the Afro-Caribbean community? How would you rate the level of outreach?

How would you rate the level of outreach from white politicians?

Do you feel that African-American elected officials recognize Afro-Caribbean immigrants as part of their constituency? Why or why not?

Do you routinely reach out to African Americans and other racial minority groups in the New York electorate? How?

Do you reach out to white voters? How?

Are you involved in any efforts to organize Afro-Caribbeans and African Americans into a single political bloc or are you aware of any such efforts? If so, tell me about them. For example, how successful have these efforts been and what are the major barriers to organizing such a political bloc? What about the Council of Black Elected Democrats?

Should this be an important goal for the city's black politicians? Why or why not?

Are you involved in any efforts to organize the city's black electorate along with other racial minority groups, such as Hispanics? Are you aware of any such efforts?

Should this be an important goal for the city's minority politicians? Why or why not?

How important are such efforts to the future of Afro-Caribbean representation and influence in New York City politics? Please explain.

Do African Americans seem willing to share power with Afro-Caribbeans in New York? Why or why not?

Should Afro-Caribbeans form their own political organizations or should they join organizations established by African Americans or other groups? Why?

There is a long tradition of island-based voluntary associations and economic cooperatives within the Afro-Caribbean immigrant population. Have any of these groups played a significant role in encouraging political participation among Afro-Caribbeans or in helping to support Afro-Caribbean candidates for elective office?

Can Afro-Caribbeans get ahead politically in New York City without the support and cooperation of African Americans? Why or why not?

Do all blacks, Afro-Caribbeans and African Americans alike, need to form a united front to advance their position in this city and in the United States as a whole?

Should Afro-Caribbeans follow the political example of any other groups in New York, such as the Jews or the Irish? Should they follow the example of African Americans? Why or why not?

Many of Brooklyn's Afro-Caribbean immigrants live within proximity of some of the borough's Jewish enclaves. How would you characterize relations between Afro-Caribbeans and Jews?

Do you have close ties to any Jewish community leaders, politicians, or groups? Tell me about them.

How do Jewish policy concerns either coincide with or differ from the concerns of Afro-Caribbean immigrants?

Should Afro-Caribbeans support white or Hispanic politicians? Can they effectively represent Afro-Caribbean interests? Can they represent the interests of black voters in general?

Who are your closest political allies in this city?

How would you characterize your own relationship with the city's African-American politicians? What about white politicians and Hispanic politicians?

What are your feelings about the following political figures? Clarence Norman? Al Sharpton? David Dinkins? Major Owens? Rudolph Giuliani? Rhoda Jacobs? Edward Koch?

Do you think a black mayor would be better for New York? Why? What about a Hispanic mayor?

What is the best way for Afro-Caribbeans to achieve their political goals in New York City?

Is racial discrimination against blacks a big problem in New York City? Should this issue have an important place on the city's policy agenda?

Is this an important issue for Afro-Caribbean immigrants? Is it as salient an issue for them as it has been for African Americans? Why or why not?

Have you ever participated in a demonstration or rally to protest against racial discrimination or racism in New York? Do you think this is an effective strategy for addressing such problems?

Is police brutality an important issue for Afro-Caribbean immigrants?

How do you feel about New York City public schools? How do they compare with schools in the Caribbean? Is education an important policy concern for Afro-Caribbean immigrants?

Which newspapers do you read regularly? What kinds of news items interest you the most?

Welfare reform is in the news a lot these days. Have you been following the news on this issue?

What is your opinion on the new welfare reform legislation? How will the legislation affect your constituency?

How do you think the new welfare reform legislation will affect Afro-Caribbeans in general? Has it encouraged more of them to become U.S. citizens? How do you think it will affect African Americans?

Do you think the welfare system needs reform? If so, how?

Immigration reform also has been in the news a lot lately. How do you feel about the recent legislative proposals to limit education and social services to legal immigrants? What about the proposals to limit sponsorship privileges?

Are you in favor of more restrictions on immigration to this country? Why or why not?

How would new restrictions affect Afro-Caribbean immigrants in general?

What is the biggest problem for new immigrants to this country?

Do you consider yourself a liberal or a conservative on economic issues? What about on social issues such as abortion, affirmative action, and crime?

Would you characterize your Afro-Caribbean constituents as mostly liberal or mostly conservative?

What do you think is the biggest problem in this country today?

What, if anything, should government do about this?

IV. Social Group Identity

How would you describe yourself to someone who asked you about your social background?

Some people describe themselves differently according to whom they are speaking. How do you describe yourself when you are speaking to other Afro-Caribbeans? African Americans? Whites?

Do you consider your Afro-Caribbean heritage part of a distinct ethnic or cultural identity?

Do you usually let others know that you are from the Caribbean?

Do you consider Colin Powell a legitimate leader of the nation's black population? Are you aware of his Caribbean parentage? Does this make a difference to you? Is he representative of the Afro-Caribbean community? How?

Do you feel close to African Americans in this country? Why?

Do you feel that most immigrants from the Caribbean share similar values and attitudes about life in the United States? What are they? Describe them to me.

Do you feel that African Americans share the same values and outlook on life in the United States as Afro-Caribbean immigrants? If not, how are the attitudes and values of these two groups different?

Are there cultural differences between Afro-Caribbeans and African Americans? Tell me about them.

Do you feel that your fate as an Afro-Caribbean immigrant is at all linked to that of African Americans in general?

How much of what happens to African Americans in the United States has something to do with what happens to Afro-Caribbeans living in this country?

Do Afro-Caribbeans have more in common with African Americans than with other groups in the United States? Why or why not?

Is it more important for Afro-Caribbeans generally to identify as immigrants, as Americans, or as blacks? Why?

Some people say that African Americans and Afro-Caribbeans do not get along. Is there competition or conflict between these two groups? If so, tell me about the sources of these tensions and why do you think they have developed?

Do African Americans treat Afro-Caribbeans differently because they are immigrants? If so, why do you think this happens?

Do African Americans discriminate against Afro-Caribbeans and other immigrants? If so, why do you think this happens?

Do you think whites make distinctions between Afro-Caribbeans and African Americans? What kinds of distinctions?

Do whites treat Afro-Caribbeans differently because they are immigrants? Do you think they interact with Afro-Caribbeans differently than they interact with African Americans? If so, why?

V. Becoming American

What do you think Afro-Caribbeans gain by becoming United States citizens?

What do they lose?

What is the hardest thing about adjusting to life in the United States?

What is the greatest thing about life in the United States?

Do you feel that Afro-Caribbean immigrants are as welcome in the United States as other groups of immigrants?

Do you feel that Afro-Caribbeans have access to the same opportunities as other groups of immigrants? If not, why?

Would you encourage others in your home country to come to the United States? Why or why not?

Bibliography

Alba, Richard D. 1990. *Ethnic Identity: The Transformation of White America*. New Haven, CT: Yale University Press.

Alba, Richard, and Victor Nee. 2003. *Remaking the American Mainstream: Assimilation and Contemporary Immigration*. Cambridge, MA: Harvard University Press.

Alonso, William. 1987. "Identity and Population." In *Population in an Interacting World*, ed. William Alonso. Cambridge, MA: Harvard University Press.

Arian, Asher, Arthur S. Goldberg, John H. Mollenkopf, and Edward T. Rogowsky. 1990. *Changing New York City Politics*. New York: Routledge.

Banfield, Edward. 1970. *The Unheavenly City*. Boston: Little, Brown.

Banfield, Edward, and James Wilson. 1963. *City Politics*. New York: Vintage.

Barrera, Mario. 1979. *Race and Class in the Southwest: A Theory of Racial Inequality*. Notre Dame, IN: University of Notre Dame Press.

Basch, Linda G. 1987. "The Politics of Caribbeanization: Vincentians and Grenadians in New York." In *Caribbean Life in New York City: Sociocultural Dimensions*, eds. Constance R. Sutton and Elsa M. Chaney. New York: Center for Migration Studies of New York.

Basch, Linda, Nina Glick Schiller, and Cristina Szanton Blanc. 1994. *Nations Unbound: Transnational Projects, Postcolonial Predicaments, and Deterritorialized States*. Amsterdam: Gordon and Breach.

Beck, Roy. 1997. "The Ordeal of Immigration in Wausau." *The Atlantic Monthly* 4: 84–97.

Bell, Derrick. 1992. *Faces at the Bottom of the Well: The Permanence of Racism*. New York: Basic Books.

Bennett, Larry. 1993. "Harold Washington and the Black Urban Regime." *Urban Affairs Quarterly* 28: 423–440.

Berger, J. 1989. "Study Ties Race and New York City Job Disparities." *The New York Times*, 26 August.

Blauner, Robert. 1972. *Racial Oppression in America*. New York: Harper & Row.

Bobo, Lawrence, and Frank Gilliam, Jr. 1990. "Race, Socio-Political Participation, and Black Empowerment." *American Political Science Review* 84: 377–393.

Bodnar, John. 1985. *The Transplanted: A History of Immigrants.* Bloomington: Indiana University Press.

Bonnett, Aubrey. 1990. "West Indians in the United States of America: Some Theoretical and Practical Considerations." In *Emerging Perspectives on the Black Diaspora*, eds. Aubrey Bonnet and Llewellyn Watson. Lanham, MD: University Press of America.

Briggs, Charles. 1986. *Learning How To Ask: A Sociolinguistic Appraisal Of the Role of the Interview in Social Science Research.* Cambridge: Cambridge University Press.

Brown, Roger. 1986. *Social Psychology*, 2nd ed. New York: Free Press.

Browning, Rufus P., Dale Rogers Marshall, and David H. Tabb, eds. 2003. *Racial Politics in American Cities*, 3rd ed. New York: Longman.

Browning, Rufus P., Dale Rogers Marshall, and David H. Tabb, eds. 1997. *Racial Politics in American Cities*, 2nd ed. New York: Longman.

Browning, Rufus P., Dale Rogers Marshall, and David H. Tabb. 1990. "Minority Mobilization in Ten Cities: Failures and Successes." In *Racial Politics in American Cities*, eds. Rufus P. Browning, Dale Rogers Marshall, and David H. Tabb. New York: Longman.

Browning, Rufus P., Dale Rogers Marshall, and David H. Tabb, eds. 1984. *Racial Politics in American Cities.* New York: Longman.

Bryce-Laporte, Roy. 1983. "Caribbean Migration to the United States: Some Tentative Conclusions." In *Caribbean Migration to the United States.* Occasional Papers No. 1. Washington, DC: Research Institute on Immigration and Ethnic Studies.

Bryce-Laporte, Roy. 1972. "Black Immigrants: The Experience of Invisibility and Inequality." *Journal of Black Studies* 3: 29–56.

Butcher, Kristin. 1994. "Black Immigrants in the United States: A Comparison with Native Blacks and Other Immigrants." *Industrial and Labor Relations Review* 47: 265–284.

Cain, Bruce, and Brendan Doherty. 2003. "The Impact of Dual Citizenship on Political Participation." Paper presented at "A Nation of Immigrants" Conference, University of California, Berkeley, California.

Carmichael, Stokely, and Charles V. Hamilton. 1967. *Black Power: The Politics of Liberation in America.* New York: Random House.

Chavez, Linda. 1991. *Out of the Barrio: Toward a New Politics of Hispanic Assimilation.* New York: Basic Books.

Chisholm, Shirley. 1975. *Unbought and Unbossed.* Boston: Houghton Mifflin.

Chiswick, Barry. 1979. "The Economic Progress of Immigrants: Some Apparently Universal Patterns." In *Contemporary Economic Problems*, ed. William Fellner. Washington, DC: American Enterprise Institute.

Chong, Dennis. 2000. *Rational Lives: Norms and Values in Politics and Society.* Chicago: University of Chicago Press.

Chong, Dennis. 1991. *Collective Action and the Civil Rights Movement.* Chicago: University of Chicago Press.

Chong, Dennis, and Dukhong Kim. 2004. "The Experiences and Effects of Status among Racial Minorities." Paper presented to the Conference on Minority Voting and Participation, Rutgers University, New Brunswick, New Jersey.

Chong, Dennis, and Reuel Rogers. 2005. "The Influence of Racial Solidarity on Political Participation." *Political Behavior* 27: 347–374.

Cohen, Cathy. 1999. *The Boundaries of Blackness: AIDS and the Breakdown of Black Politics.* Chicago: University of Chicago Press.

Cohen, Cathy J., and Michael C. Dawson. 1993. "Neighborhood Poverty and African-American Politics." *American Political Science Review* 87: 286–302.

Conover, Pamela Johnston. 1984. "The Influence of Group Identifications on Political Perceptions and Evaluations." *American Journal of Political Science* 46: 760–785.

Conway, Margaret. 2000. *Political Participation in the United States*, 3rd ed. Washington, DC: Congressional Books Quarterly.

Crowder, Kyle D., and Lucky M. Tedrow. 2001. "West Indians and the Residential Landscape of New York." In *Islands in the City: West Indian Migration to New York*, ed. Nancy Foner. Berkeley: University of California Press.

Dahl, Robert A. 1961. *Who Governs? Democracy and Power in American City.* New Haven, CT: Yale University Press.

Dao, James. 1999. "Immigrant Diversity Slows Traditional Political Climb." *New York Times*, 28 December.

Dawson, Michael. 2001. *Black Visions: The Roots of Contemporary African-American Political Ideologies.* Chicago: University of Chicago Press.

Dawson, Michael. 1995. "Structure and Ideology: The Shaping of Black Public Opinion." Paper presented at the Midwest Political Science Annual Meetings, Chicago, Illinois.

Dawson, Michael. 1994a. *Behind the Mule: Race and Class in African-American Politics.* Princeton, NJ: Princeton University Press.

Dawson, Michael. 1994b. "A Black Counterpublic? Economic Earthquakes, Racial Agenda(s), and Black Politics." *Public Culture* 7: 195–223.

Dawson, Michael, and Cathy Cohen. 2002. "Problems in the Study of the Politics of Race." In *Political Science: The State of the Discipline*, eds. Ira Katznelson and Helen Milner. New York: W. W. Norton.

Desipio, Louis. 2003. "Transnational Politics and American Citizenship: Do Home Country Political Ties Limit Latino Immigrant Interest in U.S. Citizenship?" Paper presented at "A Nation of Immigrants" Conference, University of California, Berkeley, California.

Dillingham, Gerald. 1981. "The Emerging Black Middle Class: Class Conscious or Race Conscious?" *Ethnic and Racial Studies* 4: 432–451.

Dodoo, F. Nii-Amoo. 1997. "Assimilation Differences among Africans in America." *Social Forces* 76: 527–546.

Dreier, Peter, John Mollenkopf, and Todd Swanstrom. 2001. *Place Matters: Metropolitics for the Twenty-First Century.* Lawrence: University Press of Kansas.

Dugger, Celia W. 1996. "Immigrant Voters Reshape Politics: Babel of Idealistic Citizens Charts New York's Course." *New York Times*, 10 March.

Eisinger, Peter K. 1980. *The Politics of Displacement*. New York: Academic Press.

Eisinger, Peter K. 1973. "The Conditions of Protest in American Cities." *American Political Science Review* 67: 11–28.

Erie, Steven. 1988a. "Rainbow's End: From the Old to the New Urban Ethnic Politics." In *Urban Ethnicity: A New Era*, vol. 28, eds. Joan W. Moore and Lionel A. Maldonado. Beverly Hills, CA: Sage Publications.

Erie, Steven P. 1988b. *Rainbow's End: Irish-Americans and the Dilemmas of Urban Machine Politics, 1840–1985*. Berkeley: University of California Press.

Falcon, Angelo. 1995. "Puerto Ricans and the Politics of Racial Identity." In *Racial and Ethnic Identity: Psychological Identity and Creative Expression*, eds. Herbert W. Harris, Howard C. Blue, and Ezra E. H. Griffith. New York: Routledge.

Falcon, Angelo. 1988. "Black and Latino Politics in New York City: Race and Ethnicity in a Changing Urban Context." In *Latinos and the Political System*, ed. F. Chris Garcia. Notre Dame, IN: University of Notre Dame Press.

Falcon, Angelo, F. Chris Garcia, and Rodolfo de la Garza. 1996. "Ethnicity and Politics: Evidence from the Latino National Political Survey." *Hispanic Journal of Behavioral Sciences* 18: 91–103.

Farley, Reynolds, and Walter Allen. 1987. *The Color Line and the Quality of Life: The Problem of the Twentieth Century*. New York: Russell Sage Foundation.

Fears, Daryl. 2003. "Disparity Marks Black Ethnic Groups, Report Says." *Washington Post*, 9 March.

Foner, Nancy. 1997. "What's New about Transnationalism? New York Immigrants Today and at the Turn of the Century." *Diaspora* 6: 355–375.

Foner, Nancy. 1987. "The Jamaicans: Race and Ethnicity among Migrants to New York City." In *New Immigrants in New York*, ed. Nancy Foner. New York: Columbia University Press.

Foner, Nancy. 1985. "Race and Color: Jamaican Migrants in London and New York." *International Migration Review* 19: 284–313.

Fogg-Davis, Hawley. 2005. "Black Feminism and Black Conservatism: Contested Black Civic Life." Unpublished working paper.

Fog Olwig, Karen. 1993. *Global Culture, Island Identity: Continuity and Change in the Afro-Caribbean Community of Nevis*. Chur, Switzerland: Harewood Academic.

Frymer, Paul. 1999. *Uneasy Alliances: Race and Party Competition in America*. Princeton, NJ: Princeton University Press.

Fuchs, Lawrence. 1990. "The Reactions of Black Americans to Immigration." In *Immigration Reconsidered: History, Sociology, and Politics*, ed. Virginia Yans-McLaughlin. New York: Oxford University Press.

Gans, Herbert J. 1992. "Second Generation Decline: Scenarios for the Economic and Ethnic Futures of Post-1965 American Immigrants." *Ethnic and Racial Studies* 15: 173–192.

Garcia, F. Chris, Angelo Falcon, and Rodolfo de la Garza. 1996. "Ethnicity and Politics: Evidence from the Latino National Political Survey." *Hispanic Journal of Behavioral Sciences* 18: 91–103.

Garcia, John. 1981. "Political Integration of Mexican Immigrants: Explorations into the Naturalization Process." *International Migration Review* 15: 608–625.

Gay, Claudine. 2004. "Putting Race in Context: Identifying the Environmental Determinants of Black Racial Attitudes." *American Political Science Review* 98: 547–562.

Gay, Claudine, and Katherine Tate. 1998. "Doubly Bound: The Impact of Gender and Race on the Politics of Black Women." *Political Psychology* 19: 169–184.

Gerson, Jeffrey. 1992. "Betram L. Baker, the United Action Democratic Association, and the First Black Democratic Succession in Brooklyn, 1933–1954." *Afro-Americans in New York Life and History* 16: 17–46.

Gerstle, Gary. 1996. "European Immigrants, Ethnics, and American Identity, 1880–1950." Paper presented at Social Science Research Council Conference, "America Becoming/Becoming American," Sanibel Island, Florida.

Gerstle, Gary. 1995. "Race and the Myth of Liberal Consensus." *Journal of American History* 82: 579–586.

Gerstle, Gary. 1993. "The Working Class Goes to War." *Mid-America* (October): 303–322.

Gilens, Martin. 1999. *Why Americans Hate Welfare: Race, Media, and the Politics of Antipoverty Policy*. Chicago: University of Chicago Press.

Gilroy, Paul. 1995. "Roots and Routes: Black Identity as an Outernational Project." In *Racial and Ethnic Identity: Psychological Development and Creative Expression*, eds. Herbert W. Harris, Howard C. Blue, and Ezra E. H. Griffith. London: Routledge.

Gladwell, Malcolm. 1996. "Black like Them." *The New Yorker* 10: 74–81.

Glazer, Nathan. 1988. "The New New Yorkers." In *New York Unbound: The City and the Politics of the Future*, eds. Nathan Glazer and P. D. Salins. New York: Basil Blackwell.

Glazer, Nathan. 1983. "The Politics of a Multiethnic Society." In *Ethnic Dilemmas: 1964–1982*, ed. Nathan Glazer. Cambridge, MA: Harvard University Press.

Glazer, Nathan, and Daniel Patrick Moynihan. 1963. *Beyond the Melting Pot: The Negroes, Puerto Ricans, Jews, Italians, and Irish of New York City*. Cambridge, MA: MIT Press.

Gmelch, George. 1992. *Double Passage: The Lives of Caribbean Migrants Abroad and Back Home*. Ann Arbor: University of Michigan Press.

Green, Charles, and Basil Wilson. 1989. *The Struggle for Black Empowerment in New York City: Beyond the Politics of Pigmentation*. New York: Praeger.

Green, Charles, and Basil Wilson. 1987. "The Afro-American, Caribbean Dialectic: White Incumbents, Black Constituents and the 1984 Election in New York City." *Afro-Americans in New York Life and History* 11: 49–65.

Green, Vera. 1975. "Racial versus Ethnic Factors in Afro-American and Afro-Caribbean Migration." In *Migration and Development: Implications for Ethnic Identity and Political Conflict*, eds. Helen I. Safa and Brian M. Du Toit. Paris: Mouton.

Greenhouse, Steven. 2000. "Despite Defeat on China Bill, Labor Is on Rise." *New York Times*, 28 April.

Grimshaw, William. 1992. *Bitter Fruit: Black Politics and the Chicago Machine, 1931–1991*. Chicago: University of Chicago Press.

Gurin, Patricia, Shirley Hatchett, and James S. Jackson. 1989. *Hope and Independence: Blacks' Response to Electoral and Party Politics.* New York: Russell Sage Foundation.

Guterbock, Thomas, and Bruce London. 1983. "Race, Political Orientation, and Participation: An Empirical Test of Four Competing Theories." *American Sociological Review* 48: 439–453.

Gutman, Herbert. 1977. *The Black Family in Slavery and Freedom, 1750–1925.* New York: Vintage Books.

Hacker, Andrew. 1992. *Two Nations: Separate, Hostile, Unequal.* New York: Ballantine.

Hagner, Paul, and John Pierce. 1984. "Racial Differences in Political Conceptualization." *Western Political Quarterly* 37: 212–235.

Hajnal, Zoltan, and Taeku Lee. 2003. "Beyond the Middle: Latinos and the Multiple Dimensions of Political Independents." Paper presented at "A Nation of Immigrants" Conference, University of California, Berkeley, California.

Halter, Marilyn. 1993. *Between Race and Ethnicity: Cape Verdean American Immigrants, 1860–1965.* Urbana: University of Illinois Press.

Hamilton, Charles V. 1990. "Needed, More Foxes: The Black Experience." In *Urban Politics: New York Style*, eds. Jewel Bellush and Dick Netzer. Armonk, NY: M. E. Sharpe.

Hamilton, Charles V. 1979. "The Patron-Recipient Relationship in Minority Politics in New York City." *Political Science Quarterly* 94: 211–227.

Handlin, Oscar. 1941. *Boston's Immigrants: A Study in Acculturation.* Cambridge, MA: Harvard University Press.

Hardin, Russell. 1995. *One for All: The Logic of Group Conflict.* Princeton, NJ: Princeton University Press.

Hardy-Fanta, Carol. 1993. *Latina Politics, Latino Politics: Gender, Culture, and Political Participation in Boston.* Philadelphia: Temple University Press.

Harris, Fred C. 1998. "Will the Circle Be Unbroken? The Erosion and Transformation of African-American Life." Paper presented at seminar meeting of the Center for the Study of Race, Inequality and Politics, Yale University, New Haven, Connecticut.

Harris, Melissa. 1999. "Barbershops, Bibles, and B.E.T.: A Dialogic Theory of African-American Political Thought." Ph.D. diss., Duke University.

Harris-Lacewell, Melissa. 2004. *Barbershops, Bibles, and BET: Everyday Talk and Black Political Thought.* Princeton, NJ: Princeton University Press.

Hellwig, David J. 1978. "Black Meets Black: Afro-American Reactions to West Indian Immigrants in the 1920's." *South Atlantic Quarterly* 72: 206–225.

Henry, Charles, and Carlos Munoz, Jr. 1991. "Ideological and Interest Linkages in California Rainbow Politics." In *Racial and Ethnic Politics in California*, eds. Bryan O. Jackson and Michael B. Preston. Berkeley, CA: IGS Press.

Hero, Rodney. 1998. *Faces of Inequality: Social Diversity in American Politics.* New York: Oxford University Press.

Hero, Rodney. 1992. *Latinos and the U.S. Political System: Two Tiered Pluralism.* Philadelphia: Temple University Press.

Hero, Rodney, and Christina Wolbrecht. 2004. *The Politics of Democratic Inclusion.* Philadelphia: Temple University Press.

Herring, Mary, Thomas B. Janowski, and Ronald E. Brown. 1999. "Pro-Black Doesn't Mean Anti-White: The Structure of African-American Group Identity." *The Journal of Politics* 61: 363–386.

Hicks, J. 2000a. "Term Limits Turn Old Allies into Opponents: Protege against Mentor, Backer against Incumbent." *New York Times*, 22 March.

Hicks, J. 2000b. Bitter Primary Contest Hits Ethnic Nerve among Blacks." *New York Times*, 31 August.

Higham, John. 1963. *Strangers in the Land: Patterns of American Nativism, 1860–1925*. New Brunswick, NJ: Rutgers University Press.

Hochschild, Jennifer L. 1998. "American Racial and Ethnic Politics in the 21st Century: A Cautious Look Ahead." *Brookings Review* 16: 43–46.

Hochschild, Jennifer L. 1995. *Facing Up to the American Dream: Race, Class, and the Soul of the Nation*. Princeton, NJ: Princeton University Press.

Hochschild, Jennifer L. 1984. *The New American Dilemma: Liberal Democracy and School Desegregation*. New Haven, CT: Yale University Press.

Hochschild, Jennifer L. 1981. *What's Fair? American Beliefs about Distributive Justice*. Cambridge, MA: Harvard University Press.

Hochschild, Jennifer, and Reuel Rogers. 2000. "Race Relations in a Diversifying Nation." In *African-Americans in a Diversifying Nation*, ed. James S. Jackson. New York: Russell Sage Foundation.

Hogg, Michael, and Dominic Abrams. 1988. *Social Identifications: A Social Psychology of Intergroup Relations and Group Processes*. New York: Routledge.

Holder, Calvin. 1987. "The Causes and Composition of West Indian Immigration to New York City, 1900–1952." *Afro-Americans in New York Life and History* 11: 7–27.

Holder, Calvin. 1980. "The Rise of the West Indian Politician in New York City." *Afro-Americans in New York Life and History* 4: 45–59.

Horowitz, Donald. 1985. *Ethnic Groups in Conflict*. Berkeley: University of California Press.

Horton, Peter. 1995. *The Politics of Diversity: Immigration, Resistance, and Change in Monterrey Park, California*. Philadelphia: Temple University Press.

Huntington, Samuel P. 2004. *Who Are We? The Challenges to America's National Identity*. New York: Simon & Schuster.

Ignatiev, Noel. 1997. "Treason to Whiteness is Loyalty to Humanity." In *Critical White Studies: Looking Behind the Mirror*, eds. Richard Delgado and Jean Stefancic. Philadelphia: Temple University Press.

Ignatiev, Noel. 1996. *How the Irish Became White*. London: Verso.

Irish, J. A. George, and E. W. Riviere, eds. 1990. *Political Behavior and Social Interaction among Caribbean and African-American Residents in New York*. New York: Caribbean Research Center, City University of New York.

Jackson, John L. 2001. *Harlemworld: Doing Race and Class in Contemporary Black America*. Chicago: University of Chicago Press.

Jacobson, Matthew. 1998. *Whiteness of a Different Color: European Immigrants and the Alchemy of Race*. Cambridge, MA: Harvard University Press.

James, Winston. 1998. *Holding Aloft of Ethiopia: Caribbean Radicalism in Early Twentieth Century America*. London: Verso.

James, Winston, and Clive Harris, eds. 1993. *Inside Babylon: The Caribbean Diaspora in Britain*. London: Verso.

Jennings, James. 1992. *The Politics of Black Empowerment: The Transformation of Black Activism in Urban America*. Detroit: Wayne State University Press.

Jennings, James. 1997. *Race and Politics: New Challenges and Responses for Black Activism*. London: Verso.

Jones-Correa, Michael. 2002. "Bringing Outsiders In: Questions of Immigrant Incorporation." Paper presented at Conference on Politics of Democratic Inclusion, University of Notre Dame, Indiana, 17–19 October.

Jones-Correa, Michael. 1998. *Between Two Nations: The Political Predicament of Latinos in New York City*. Ithaca, NY: Cornell University Press.

Jones-Correa, Michael, and David L. Leal. 1996. "Becoming 'Hispanic': Secondary Panethnic Identification among Latin American-Origin Populations in the United States." *Hispanic Journal of Behavioral Sciences* 18: 214–254.

Joyce, Patrick D. 2003. *No Fire Next Time: Black-Korean Conflicts and the Future of America's Cities*. Ithaca, NY: Cornell University Press.

Joyce, Patrick D. 1997. "A Reversal of Fortunes: Black Empowerment, Political Machines, and City Jobs in New York City and Chicago." *Urban Affairs Review* 32: 291–318.

Junn, Jane. 1999. "Participation in a Liberal Democracy: The Political Assimilation of Immigrants and Ethnic Minorities in the United States." *American Behavioral Scientist* 42: 1417–1439.

Kalmijn, Matthijs. 1996. "The Socioeconomic Assimilation of Caribbean American Blacks." *Social Forces* 74: 911–930.

Karpathakis, Anna. 1999. "Home Society Politics and Immigrant Political Incorporation: The Case of Greek Immigrants in New York City." *International Migration Review* 33: 55–79.

Kasinitz, Philip. 1992. *Caribbean New York: Black Immigrants and the Politics of Race*. Ithaca, NY: Cornell University Press.

Kasinitz, Philip. 1987a. "The City's New Immigrants." *Dissent* Special Issue, "In Search of New York" (Fall): 497–506.

Kasinitz, Philip. 1987b. "The Minority Within: The New Black Immigrants." *New York Affairs* 10: 44–58.

Kasinitz, Philip, John Mollenkopf, and Mary Waters, eds. 2004. *Becoming New Yorkers: Ethnographies of the New Second Generation*. New York: Russell Sage Foundation.

Katznelson, Ira. 1981. *City Trenches: Urban Politics and the Patterning of Class in the United States*. Chicago: University of Chicago Press.

Kelly, David. 2005. "Colorado Activists Push Immigration Initiative." *Los Angeles Times*, 13 March.

Kennedy, Randall. 2003. *Interracial Intimacies: Sex, Marriage, Identity, and Adoption in America*. New York: Pantheon.

Kennedy, Randall. 1997. *Race, Crime, and the Law*. New York: Pantheon Books.

Key, V. O. 1949. *Southern Politics in State and Nation*. New York: Vintage.

Kim, Claire. 2000. *Bitter Fruit: The Politics of Black-Korean Conflict in New York City*. New Haven, CT: Yale University Press.

Kim, Claire. 1999. "The Racial Triangulation of Asian Americans." *Politics and Society* 27: 105–138.

Kim, Claire, and Taeku Lee. 2001. "Interracial Politics: Asian Americans and Other Communities of Color." *PS: Political Science and Politics* 34: 631–638.

Kirkpatrick, David. 2005. "House Passes Tightening of Laws on Immigration." *New York Times*, 11 February.

Kirschenman, Joleen, and Kathryn M. Neckerman. 1991. "We'd Love to Hire Them, But . . . : The Meaning of Race for Employers." In *The Urban Underclass*, eds. Christopher Jencks and Paul E. Peterson. Washington, DC: The Brookings Institution.

Kleppner, Paul. 1985. *Chicago Divided: The Making of a Black Mayor*. Dekalb: Northern Illinois Press.

Laitn, David. 1998. *Identity Formation: The Russian-Speaking Populations in the Near Abroad*. Ithaca, NY: Cornell University Press.

Leighley, Jan E., and Arnold Vedlitz. 1999. "Race, Ethnicity, and Political Participation: Competing Models and Contrasting Explanations." *Journal of Politics* 61: 1092–1114.

Lewinson, Edwin. 1974. *Black Politics in New York City*. New York: Twayne.

Lewis Mumford Center for Comparative Urban and Regional Research. 2002. *Separate and Unequal: The Neighborhood Gap for Blacks and Hispanics in Metropolitan America*. Albany: State University of New York, Albany.

Lieberson, Stanley. 1980. *A Piece of the Pie: Black and White Immigrants Since 1880*. Berkeley: University of California Press.

Lieberson, Stanley, and Mary C. Waters. 1988. *From Many Strands: Ethnic and Racial Groups in Contemporary America*. New York: Russell Sage Foundation.

Lien, Pei-te. 2001. *The Making of Asian America through Political Participation*. Philadelphia: Temple University Press.

Lien, Pei-te, Christian Collet, Janelle Wong, and S. Karthick Ramakrishnan. 2001. "Asian Pacific American Public Opinion and Political Participation." *PS: Political Science & Politics* 34: 625–631.

Lien, Pei-te, Margaret Conway, and Janelle Wong. 2004. *The Politics of Asian Americans: Diversity and Community*. New York: Routledge.

Lin, Ann Chih. n.d. "Group Inclusion or Group Rights? Ethnic Advocacy Groups and the Political Incorporation of Immigrants." In *Framing Equality: Inclusion, Exclusion, and American Political Institutions*, eds. Kerry Haynie and Daniel Tichenor. Unpublished manuscript, under review.

Logan, John. 2003. "America's Newcomers." Albany: Lewis Mumford Center for Comparative Urban and Regional Research, State University of New York, Albany.

Logan, John, and Glenn Deane. 2003. "Black Diversity in Metropolitan America." Albany: Lewis Mumford Center for Comparative Urban and Regional Reseach, State University of New York, Albany.

Logan, John, and John Mollenkopf. 2003. *People and Politics in America's Big Cities*. NewYork: Drum Major Institute for Public Policy.

Logan, John R., and Harvey L. Molotch. 1987. *Urban Fortunes: The Political Economy of Place*. Berkeley: University of California Press.

Lollock, Lisa. 2001. "The Foreign-Born Population in the United States: March 2000. Current Population Reports, P20-534." Washington, DC: U.S. Census Bureau.

Lowenthal, David. 1972. *West Indian Societies*. London: Oxford University Press.

Macchiarola, Frank, and Joseph Diaz. 1993. "Minority Political Empowerment in New York City: Beyond the Voting Rights Act." *Political Science Quarterly* 108: 37–57.

Marable, Manning. 1995. "Beyond Racial Identity Politics: Toward a Liberation Theory for Multicultural Democracy." In *Beyond Black and White: Transforming African-American Politics*, ed. Manning Marable. London: Verso.

Marable, Manning. 1994. "Building Coalitions among Communities of Color." In *Blacks, Latinos, and Asians in Urban America*, ed. James Jennings. New York: Praeger.

Marosi, Richard. 2004. "Arizona Stirs Up Immigration Stew." *Los Angeles Times*, 6 November.

Marschall, Melissa. 2001. "Does the Shoe Fit? Testing Models of Participation for African-American and Latino Involvement in Local Politics." *Urban Affairs Review* 37: 227–248.

Massey, Douglas S. 1987. "The Ethnosurvey in Theory and Practice." *International Migration Review* 21: 1498–1522.

Massey, Douglas S., and Nancy A. Denton. 1993. *American Apartheid: Segregation and the Making of the Underclass*. Cambridge, MA: Harvard University Press.

Massey, Douglas S., and Nancy A. Denton. 1989. "Racial Identity among Caribbean Hispanics: The Effects of Double Minority Status on Residential Segregation." *American Sociological Review* 54: 790–808.

McAdam, Doug. 1982. *Political Process and the Development of Black Insurgency, 1930–1970*. Chicago: University of Chicago Press.

McNickle, Chris. 1993. *To Be Mayor of New York: Ethnic Politics in the City*. New York: Columbia University Press.

Mendelberg, Tali. 2001. *The Race Card: Campaign Strategy, Implicit Messages, and the Norm of Equality*. Princeton, NJ: Princeton University Press.

Miller, Arthur, Patricia Gurin, Gerald Gurin, and Oksana Malanchuk. 1981. "Group Consciousness and Political Participation." *American Journal of Political Science* 25: 494–511.

Mills, Charles. 1998. *Blackness Visible: Essays on Philosophy and Race*. Ithaca, NY: Cornell University Press.

Mink, Gwendolyn. 1986. *Old Labor and New Immigrants in American Political Development*. Ithaca, NY: Cornell University Press.

Mladenka, Kenneth R. 1989. "Blacks and Hispanics in Urban Politics." *American Political Science Review* 83: 165–191.

Model, Suzanne. 2001. "Where West Indians Work." In *Islands in the City: West Indian Migration to New York*, ed. Nancy Foner. Berkeley: University of California Press.

Model, Suzanne. 1995. "West Indian Prosperity: Fact or Fiction." *Social Problems* 42: 535–553.

Model, Suzanne. 1991. "Caribbean Immigrants: A Black Success Story?" *International Migration Review* 25: 248–276.

Mollenkopf, John. 2003. "New York: The Great Anomaly." In *Racial Politics in American Cities*, 3rd ed., eds. Rufus P. Browning, Dale R. Marshall, and David H. Tabb. New York: Longman.

Mollenkopf, John. 1999. "Urban Political Conflicts and Alliances: New York and Los Angeles Compared." In *The Handbook of International Migration: The American Experience*, eds. C. Hirschman, P. Kasinitz, and J. DeWind. New York: Russell Sage Foundation.

Mollenkopf, John. 1997. "New York: The Great Anomaly." In *Racial Politics in American Cities*, 2nd ed., eds. Rufus P. Browning, Dale R. Marshall, and David H. Tabb. New York: Longman.

Mollenkopf, John H. 1992a. "New York: The Great Anomaly." In *Racial Politics in American Cities*, eds. Rufus P. Browning, Dale Rogers Marshall, and David H. Tabb. New York: Longman.

Mollenkopf, John H. 1992b. *A Phoenix in the Ashes: The Rise and Fall of the Koch Coalition in New York City Politics*. Princeton, NJ: Princeton University Press.

Mollenkopf, John. 1987. "The Decay of Reform." *Dissent* Special Issue, "In Search of New York" (Fall): 492–495.

Mollenkopf, John, David Olson, and Timothy Ross. 2001. "Immigrant Political Participation in New York and Los Angeles." In *Governing Cities: Inter-Ethnic Coalitions, Compettion, and Conflict*. New York: Russell Sage Foundation.

Mollenkopf, John H., Timothy Ross, and David Olson. 1999. "Immigrant Political Participation in New York and Los Angeles." Paper prepared for the Project on Negotiating Difference, International Center for Migration, Ethnicity, and Citizenship, New School University, New York, 27 May.

Moreno, Dario. 1996. "Cuban Americans in Miami Politics." In *The Politics of Minority Coalitions: Race, Ethnicity, and Shared Uncertainties*, ed. Wibur C. Rich. Westport, CT: Praeger.

Morgan, Edmund. 1975. *American Slavery, American Freedom: The Ordeal of Colonial Virginia*. New York: W. W. Norton.

Morris, Aldon. 1984. *The Origins of the Civil Rights Movement: Black Communities Organizing for Change*. New York: Free Press.

Morris, Aldon D., Shirley J. Hatchett, and Ronald E. Brown. 1989. "The Civil Rights Movement and Black Political Socialization." In *Political Learning in Adulthood: A Sourcebook of Theory and Research*, ed. Roberta S. Sigel. Chicago: University of Chicago Press.

New York Carib News, 23 April 1996.

New York Carib News, 1 October 1996.

Ngai, Mae. 2003. *Impossible Subjects: Illegal Aliens and the Making of Modern America*. Princeton, NJ: Princeton University Press.

Nie, Norman, Sidney Verba, and John Petrocik. 1976. *The Changing American Voter*. Cambridge, MA: Harvard University Press.

Novak, Michael. 1973. *The Rise of the Unmeltable Ethnics: Politics and Culture in the Seventies*. New York: Macmillan.

Ogbu, John. 1990. "Cultural Model, Identity, and Literacy." In *Cultural Psychology: Essays on Comparative Human Development*, eds. J. W. Stigles, R. A. Shweder, and G. Herdt. London: Cambridge University Press.

Oliver, Melvin, and Thomas Shaprio. 1997. *Black Wealth, White Wealth: A New Perspective on Racial Inequality*. New York: Routledge.

Omi, Michael, and Howard Winant. 1986. *Racial Formation in the United States: From the 1960s to the 1980s*. New York: Routledge & Kegan Paul.

Parenti, Michael. 1970. "Power and Pluralism: A View from the Bottom." *The Journal of Politics* 32: 501–530.

Parenti, Michael. 1967. "Ethnic Politics and the Persistence of Ethnic Identification." *American Political Science Review* 61: 717–726.

Park, Robert. 1950. *Race and Culture*. Glencoe: Free Press.

Passell, Jeffrey S., and Barry Edmonston. 1994. "Immigration and Race: Recent Trends in Immigration to the United States." In *Immigration and Ethnicity: The Integration of America's Newest Arrivals*, eds. Passel and Edmonston. Washington, DC: The Urban Institute Press.

Patterson, Orlando. 1997. *The Ordeal of Integration: Progress and Resentment in America's Racial Crisis*. Washington, DC: Civitas Counterpoint.

Patterson, Orlando. 1987. "The Emerging West Atlantic System: Migration, Culture, and Underdevelopment in the United States and the Circum-Caribbean Region." In *Population in an Interacting World*, ed. William Alonso. Cambridge, MA: Harvard University Press.

Patterson, Orlando. 1976. "Context and Choice in Ethnic Allegiance: A Theoretical Framework and Caribbean Case Study." In *Ethnicity: Theory and Experience*, eds. Nathan Glazer and Daniel P. Moynihan. Cambridge, MA: Harvard University Press.

Patterson, Orlando. 1972. "Toward a Future that Has No Past: Reflections on the Fate of Blacks in the Americas." *The Public Interest* 27: 25–62.

Pecorella, Robert F. 1994. *Community Power in a Postreform City: Politics in New York City*. Armonk, NY: M. E. Sharpe.

Perry, Huey L., ed. 1991. "Exploring the Meaning and Implications of Deracialization in African-American Urban Politics: A Minisymposium." *Urban Affairs Quarterly* 27: 181–191.

Pessar, Patricia R. 1995. *A Visa for a Dream: Dominicans in the United States*. Boston: Allyn & Bacon.

Pessar, Patricia R. 1987. "The Dominicans: Women in the Household and the Garment Industry." In *New Immigrants in New York*, ed. Nancy Foner. New York: Columbia University Press.

Peterson, Paul E. 1981. *City Limits*. Chicago: University of Chicago Press.

Pinderhughes, Dianne. 1987. *Race and Ethnicity in Chicago Politics: A Reexamination of Pluralist Theory*. Chicago: University of Illinois Press.

Piore, Michael. 1979. *Birds of Passage*. New York: Cambridge University Press.

Portes, Alejandro, ed. 1996a. *The New Second Generation*. New York: Russell Sage Foundation.

Portes, Alejandro. 1996b. "Global Villagers: The Rise of Transnational Communities." *The American Prospect* (March–April): 74–77.

Portes, Alejandro, and Alex Stepick. 1993. *City on the Edge: The Transformation of Miami.* Berkeley: University of California Press.

Portes, Alejandro, and Doug MacLeod. 1996. "What Shall I Call Myself? Hispanic Identity Formation in the Second Generation." *Ethnic and Racial Studies* 19: 523–547.

Portes, Alejandro, and Min Zhou. 1993. "The New Second Generation: Assimilation and its Variants." *Annals of the American Academy of Political and Social Science* 530: 74–97.

Portes, Alejandro, and Ramon Grosfoguel. 1994. "Caribbean Diasporas: Migration and Ethnic Communities." *Annals of the American Academy of Political and Social Science* 536: 48–69.

Portes, Alejandro, and Ruben G. Rumbaut. 1996. *Immigrant America: A Portrait,* 2nd ed. Berkeley: University of California Press.

Portes, Alejandro, and Ruben G. Rumbaut. 1990. *Immigrant America: A Portrait.* Berkeley: University of California Press.

Ramakrishnan, Karthick. 2001. "Immigrant Incorporation and Political Participation in the United States." *International Migration Review* 35: 870–910.

Reed, Adolph, Jr. 1999. *Stirrings in the Jug: Black Politics in the Post-Segregation.* Minneapolis: University of Minnesota Press.

Reed, Adolph, Jr. 1997. *W. E. B. DuBois and American Political Thought: Fabianism and the Color Line.* New York: Oxford University Press.

Reed, Adolph, Jr. 1995. "Demobilization in the New Black Political Regime: Ideological Capitulation and Radical Failure in the Postsegregation Era." In *The Bubbling Cauldron: Race, Ethnicity, and the Urban Crisis,* eds. Michael Peter Smith and Joe R. Faegin. Minneapolis: University of Minnesota Press.

Reed, Adolph, Jr. 1988. "Black Urban Regime: Structural Origins and Constraints." *Comparative Urban and Community Research* 1: 138–189.

Reed, Adolph, Jr. 1986a. "The 'Black Revolution' and Reconstitution of Domination." In *Race, Politics, and Culture: Critical Essays on the Radicalism of the 1960s,* ed. Reed. Wesport, CT: Greenwood.

Reed, Adolph, Jr. 1986b. *The Jesse Jackson Phenomenon: The Crisis of Purpose in Afro-American Politics.* New Haven, CT: Yale University Press.

Reid, Ira. 1939. *The Negro Immigrant: His Background Characteristics and Social Adjustments, 1899–1937.* New York: AMS Press.

Rimer, Sara, and Karen Arenson. 2004. "Top Colleges Take More Blacks, but Which Ones?" *New York Times,* 24 June.

Roediger, David R. 1991. *The Wages of Whiteness: Race and the Making of the American Working Class.* London: Verso.

Rokkan, Stein. 1966. "Norway: Numerical Democracy and Corporate Pluralism." In *Political Oppositions in Western Democracies,* ed. Robert Dahl. New Haven, CT: Yale University Press.

Rumbaut, Ruben. 1999. "The Challenge of (and to) the *Pluribus*: Old Minorities, New Immigrants in the United States." Paper prepared for the National Conference on Racial and Ethnic Diversity, "What's Next? American Pluralism and Civic Culture," Northhampton, Massachusetts, 4–6 November.

Sack, Kevin, and Janet Elder. 2000. "Poll Finds Optimistic Outlook but Enduring Racial Division." *New York Times,* 11 July.

Schiller, Nina Glick, Linda Basch, and Cristina Blanc-Szanton. 1992. *Towards a Transnational Perspective on Migration: Race, Class, Ethnicity, and Nationalism Reconsidered*. New York: New York Academy of Sciences.

Schlesinger, Arthur. 1992. *The Disuniting of America: Reflections on a Multicultural Society*. New York: W. W. Norton.

Sengupta, Somini. 1996a. "A Snapshot of Caribbean Influence." *The New York Times*, 18 August.

Sengupta, Somini. 1996b. "A Candidate Cites His Race as Credential." *The New York Times*, 18 August.

Shefter, Martin. 1986. "Political Incorporation and the Extrusion of the Left: Party Politics and Social Forces in New York City." *Studies in American Political Development* 1: 50–90.

Shefter, Martin. 1985. *Political Crisis/Fiscal Crisis: The Collapse and Revival of New York City*. New York: Basic Books.

Shingles, Richard D. 1981. "Black Consciousness and Political Participation: The Missing Link." *American Political Science Review* 75: 76–91.

Shklar, Judith. 1991. *American Citizenship*. Cambridge, MA: Harvard University Press.

Sigelman, Lee, and Susan Welch. 1991. *Black Americans' Views of Racial Inequality: The Dream Deferred*. Cambridge: Cambridge University Press.

Skerry, Peter. 1993. *Mexican Americans: An Ambivalent Minority*. Cambridge, MA: Harvard University Press.

Sleeper, Jim. 1993. "The End of the Rainbow." *The New Republic* (1 November): 20–25.

Sleeper, Jim. 1990. *The Closest of Strangers: Liberalism and the Politics of Race in New York*. New York: W. W. Norton.

Smith, Anthony. 1986. *The Ethnic Origin of Nations*. Cambridge: Blackwell.

Sonenshein, Raphael. 2003a. "The Prospects for Multiracial Coalitions: Lessons from America's Three Largest Cities." In *Racial Politics in American Cities*, 3rd ed., eds. Rufus P. Browning, Dale R. Marshall, and David H. Tabb. New York: Longman.

Sonenshein, Raphael. 2003b. "Post-Incorporation Politics in Los Angeles." In *Racial Politics in American Cities*, 3rd ed., eds. Rufus P. Browning, Dale R. Marshall, and David H. Tabb. New York: Longman.

Sonenshein, Raphael. 1993. *Politics in Black and White: Race and Power in Los Angeles*. Princeton, NJ: Princeton University Press.

Sowell, Thomas. 1978. "Three Black Histories." In *Essays and Data on American Ethnic Groups*, ed. Thomas Sowell. Washington, DC: Urban Institute.

Sowell, Thomas. 1975. *Race and Economics*. New York: David Mckay.

Spradley, James P. 1979. *The Ethnographic Interview*. New York: Holt, Reinhart & Winston.

Stafford, Walter, and Edwin Dei. 1989. *Employment Segmentation in New York City Municipal Agencies*. New York: Community Service Society.

Stanfield, John H., II. 1995. "Methodological Reflections: An Introduction." In *Race and Ethnicity in Research Methods*, eds. John H. Stanfield and Rutlege M. Dennis. Newbury Park, CA: Sage.

Steinberg, Stephen. 1995. *Turning Back*. Boston: Beacon Press.

Steinberg, Stephen. 1981. *The Ethnic Myth: Race, Ethnicity, and Class in America*. Boston: Beacon Press.

Stone, Clarence N. 1989. *Regime Politics: Governing Atlanta, 1946–1988*. Lawrence: University Press of Kansas.

Stone, Clarence, and Carol Pierannunzi. 1997. "Atlanta and the Limited Reach of Electoral Control." In *Racial Politics in American Cities*, 2nd ed., eds. Rufus P. Browning, Dale R. Marshall, and David H. Tabb. New York: Longman.

Sutton, Constance, and Susan R. Makiesky. 1975. "Migration and West Indian Racial and Ethnic Consciousness." In *Migration and Development: Implications for Identity and Political Conflict*, eds. H. I. Safa and B. M. Du Toit. Paris: Mouton.

Tajfel, Henri. 1981. *Human Groups and Social Categories*. Cambridge: Cambridge University Press.

Takaki, Ronald. 1993. *A Different Mirror: A History of Multicultural America*. Boston: Little, Brown.

Takaki, Ronald. 1989. *Strangers from a Different Shore: A History of Asian-Americans*. Boston: Little, Brown.

Takaki, Ronald. 1982. "Reflections on Racial Patterns in America: A Historical Perspective." In *Ethnicity and Public Policy*, eds. Winston A. Van Horne and Thomas V. Tonnesen. Madison: University of Wisconsin System.

Tate, Katherine. 1994. *From Protest to Politics: The New Black Voters in American Elections*. Cambridge, MA: Harvard University Press.

Thernstrom, Stephan, and Abigail Thernstrom. 1997. *America in Black and White: One Nation, Indivisible*. New York: Simon & Schuster.

Thomas-Hope, Elizabeth. 1983. "Off the Island: Population Mobility among the Caribbean Middle Class." In *White Collar Migrants in the Americas and the Caribbean*, eds. Arnaud F. Marks and Hebe M. C. Vessuri. Leiden: Royal Institute of Linguistics and Anthropology.

Thomas-Hope, Elizabeth. 1978. "The Establishment of a Migration Tradition: British West-Indian Movements in the Hispanic Caribbean after Emancipation." In *Caribbean Social Relations*, ed. Colin Clarke, Monograph Series No. 8. Liverpool: Centre for Latin American Studies, The University of Liverpool.

Thompson, J. Phillip. 1996. "The Election and Governance of David Dinkins as Mayor of New York." In *Race, Politics, and Governance in the United States*, ed. Huey L. Perry. Gainesville: University Press of Florida.

Tichenor, Daniel J. 2002. *Dividing Lines: The Politics of Immigration Control in America*. Princeton, NJ: Princeton University Press.

Tilly, Charles. 1979. "Repertoires of Contention in America and Britain, 1775–1830." In *The Dynamics of Social Movements: Resource Mobilization, Social Control, and Tactics*, eds. Mayer Zald and John McCarthy. Cambridge, England: Winthrop.

Toney, Roberta Joyce. 1986. "The Development of a Culture of Migration Among Caribbean People: St. Vincent and New York, 1838–1979." Ph.D. diss., Columbia University.

Turner, John. 1999. "Some Current Issues in Research on Social Identity and Self-Categorization Theories." In *Social Identity*, eds. Naomi Elders, Russell Spears, and Bertjan Doosje. Cambridge, England: Blackwell.

Ueda, Reed. 1980. "Naturalization and Citizenship." In *Harvard Encyclopedia of American Ethnic Groups*, ed. Stephen Thernstrom. Cambridge, MA: Harvard University Press.

Uhlaner, Carol J. 1991. "Perceived Discrimination and Prejudice and the Coalition Prospects of Blacks, Latinos, and Asian Americans." In *Racial and Ethnic Politics in California*, eds. Bryan O. Jackson and Michael B. Preston. Berkeley, CA: IGS Press.

U.S. Census Bureau. 2001. "Overview of Race and Hispanic Origin." *Census 2000 Brief*. Washington, DC: U.S. Department of Commerce, Economics and Statistics Administration.

Verba, Sidney, Kay Schlozman, and Henry Brady. 1995. *Voice and Equality: Civic Voluntarism in American Politics*. Cambridge, MA: Harvard University Press.

Verba, Sidney, Kay Schlozman, and Henry Brady. 1993. "Race, Ethnicity, and Political Resources: Participation in the United States." *British Journal of Political Science* 23: 453–497.

Vickerman, Milton. 1999. *Crosscurrents: West Indian Immigrants and Race*. New York: Oxford University Press.

Vickerman, Milton. 1994. "The Response of West Indian Men towards African-Americans: Distancing and Identification." In *Research in Race and Ethnic Relations: Racial and Ethnic Politics*, ed. Rutledge M. Dennis. Greenwich, CT: JAI Press.

Waldinger, Roger. 1996. *Still the Promised City: African-Americans and New Immigrants in Post-Industrial New York*. Cambridge, MA: Harvard University Press.

Waldinger, Roger. 1989. "Race and Ethnicity." In *Setting Municipal Priorities, 1990*, eds. Charles Brecher and Raymond D. Horton. New York: New York University Press.

Waldinger, Roger. 1987. "Beyond Nostalgia: The Old Neighborhood Revisited." *New York Affairs* 10: 1–12.

Walter, John C. 1989. *The Harlem Fox: J. Raymond Jones and Tammany, 1920–1970*. Albany: State University of New York Press.

Walton, Hanes. 1985. *Invisible Politics*. New York: State University of New York Press.

Ware, Alan. 1985. *The Breakdown of the Democratic Party Organization, 1940–1980*. New York: Oxford University Press.

Warren, Christopher L., and Dario V. Moreno. 2003. "Power without a Program: Hispanic Incorporation in Miami." In *Racial Politics in American Cities*, eds. Rufus P. Browning, Dale R. Marshall, and David H. Tabb. New York: Longman.

Waters, Mary C. 1999. *Black Identities: West Indian Immigrant Dreams and American Realities*. Cambridge, MA: Harvard University Press.

Waters, Mary C. 1996. "Ethnic and Racial Groups in the USA: Conflict and Cooperation." In *Ethnicity and Power in the Contemporary World*, eds. Kumar Rupesinghe and Valery A. Tishkov. London: U.N. University Press.

Waters, Mary C. 1994a. "Ethnic and Racial Identities of Second Generation Black Immigrants in New York City." *International Migration Review* 20: 795–820.

Waters, Mary C. 1994b. "West Indian Immigrants, African-Americans and Whites in the Workplace: Different Perspectives on American Race Relations." Paper presented at the annual meeting of the American Sociological Association, Los Angeles, CA, August.

Waters, Mary C. 1990. *Ethnic Options: Choosing Identities in America*. Berkeley: University of California Press.

Waters, Mary, John Mollenkopf, and Philip Kasinitz. 1999. "The Second-Generation: A Demographic Overview." Paper presented at the Population Association of America Annual Meeting, New York, 25 March.

Watkins-Owens, Irma. 1996. *Blood Relations: Caribbean Immigrants and the Harlem Community, 1900–1930*. Bloomington: Indiana University Press, 1996.

Wilson, William J. 1999. *The Bridge over the Racial Divide: Rising Inequality and Coalition Politics*. Berkeley: University of California Press.

Wilson, William J. 1996. *When Work Disappears: The World of the New Urban Poor*. New York: Knopf.

Wilson, William J. 1987. *The Truly Disadvantaged: The Inner-City, the Under-class, and Public Policy*. Chicago: University of Chicago Press.

Wilson, William J. 1980. *The Declining Significance of Race: Blacks and Changing American Institutions*, 2nd ed. Chicago: University of Chicago Press.

Woldemikael, Tekle. 1989. *Becoming Black American: Haitians and American Institutions in Evanston, Illinois*. New York: AMS Press.

Wolfinger, Raymond, and Steven Rosenstone. 1980. *Who Votes?* New Haven, CT: Yale University Press.

Wolfinger, Raymond. 1974. *The Politics of Progress*. Englewood Cliffs, NJ: Prentice Hall.

Wolfinger, Raymond E. 1965. "The Development and Persistence of Ethnic Voting." *American Political Science Review* 59: 896–908.

Wong, Janelle. 2006. *Democracy's Promise: Immigrants and American Civic Institutions*. Ann Arbor: University of Michigan Press.

Wong, Janelle. 2000. "Institutional Context and Political Mobilization among Mexican and Chinese Immigrants." Paper presented at Immigrant Political Participation in New York City Working Conference, New York, June.

Wong, Janelle, Pei-te Lien, and Margaret Conway. 2005. "Group-Based Resources and Political Participation among Asian Americans." *American Politics Research* 33: 545–576.

Wyman, Mark. 1993. *Round-Trip America: The Immigrants Return to Europe, 1880–1930*. Ithaca, NY: Cornell University Press.

Yu, Henry. 2001. *Thninking Orientals: Migration, Contact, and Exoticism in Modern America*. New York: Oxford University Press.

Zubrinksy, Camille, and Lawrence Bobo. 1996. "Prismatic Metropolis: Race and Residential Segregation in the City of the Angels." *Social Science Research* 25: 335–374.

Index